FROM MAINTENANCE TO MISSION

FROM MAINTENANCE TO MISSION

Evangelization and the Revitalization of the Parish

Robert S. Rivers, CSP

Paulist Press
New York/Mahwah, N.J.

Cover design by Diego Linares
Book design by Lynn Else

Library of Congress Cataloging-in-Publication Data

Rivers, Robert S.
    From maintenance to mission : evangelization and the revitalization of the parish / Robert S. Rivers.
        p. cm.
    Includes bibliographical references (p.   ).
    ISBN 0-8091-4318-6 (alk. paper)
    1. Catholic Church. National Conference of Bishops. Committee on Evangelization. Go and make disciples. 2. Evangelistic work—Catholic Church. 3. Parish missions—United States. I. Title.

BX2347.4.C393R59 2005
266'.273—dc22

                                                            2005001953

Published by Paulist Press
997 Macarthur Boulevard
Mahwah, New Jersey 07430

www.paulistpress.com

Printed and bound in the
United States of America

CONTENTS

CONTENTS

Part III
The Evangelizing Parish

ACKNOWLEDGMENTS

This work would not have even been attempted if it were not for the encouragement and support of Rev. Kenneth Boyack, CSP, and Sister Susan Wolf, SND, my colleagues at the Paulist National Catholic Evangelization Association (PNCEA). These chapters began as lectures at the Seton Hall International Institute for Priests in July 2000. I proposed to turn them into a book on evangelization, and we made the commitment to go ahead with the project. Mr. Michael Scarpato, a PNCEA colleague, Ms. Paula Minaert, and I formed a writing team and began the project in the fall of 2001, with the idea that we would formulate our insights for each section of the book and each chapter. I would then write the chapters and they would provide the critique. That was our process until Michael left the PNCEA in January 2002. Paula and I brought the task to completion. Without her this book could never have been written. Many thanks to her, to Michael, and to all of the PNCEA staff members who are contributors in many different ways to this book.

I would also like to express my gratitude to my family and friends for their encouragement and support for my priestly ministry and my work as an evangelizer. Many of the experiences from the ministry that I have reported in this book derive from three parishes that will always be special: St. Paul the Apostle in Greensboro, North Carolina; St. Paul the Apostle in Los Angeles, California; and St. Rose of Lima in Gaithersburg, Maryland, where I currently work on weekends when I am at home.

Special thanks to a select group of people who gave me very helpful feedback from the original draft of the book: Rev. Robert Duggan, Dr. Susan Timoney, Dr. Susan Blum-Gerding, Rev. Thomas Rausch, SJ, Dr. Richard Gaillardetz, Sister Dominga Zapata, SH, and Rev. Robert Wister. A final word of thanks goes to the Koch Foundation and other benefactors who supported the research for the writing of this book.

In Memory of Sister Maureen O'Keefe, SSND+
1917–2002
Friend and Mentor

ABBREVIATIONS

CIC   *Code of Canon Law*

CPG   *Commentary and Planning Guide*

CSL   *Communities of Salt and Light*

EN   *Evangelii Nuntiandi (On Evangelization in the Modern World)*

GDC   *General Directory for Catechesis*

GMD   Go *and Make Disciples*

RCIA   *Rite of Christian Initiation of Adults*

RM   *Redemptoris Missio (Mission of the Redeemer)*

Latin Titles of Documents

Ad Gentes (Decree on the Church's Missionary Activity)

Apostolicam Actuositatem (Decree on the Apostolate of the Laity)

Centesimus Annus (On the Hundredth Anniversary of Rerum Novarum*)*

Christifideles Laici (The Lay Members of Christ's Faithful People)

Christus Dominus (Decree on the Pastoral Office of Bishops)

Dei Verbum (Dogmatic Constitution on Divine Revelation)

Dignitatis Humanae (Declaration on Religious Liberty)

Ecclesia in America (The Church in America)

Evangelium Vitae (Gospel of Life)

Familiaris Consortio (Apostolic Exhortation on the Family)

Gaudium et Spes (Pastoral Constitution on the Church in the Modern World)

Lumen Gentium (Dogmatic Constitution on the Church)

Nostra Aetate (Declaration on the Relation of the Church to Non-Christian Religions)

Novo Millennio Ineunte (The Apostolic Letter to the Lay Faithful at the Close of the Great Jubilee of the Year 2000)

Pastores Dabo Vobis (I Will Give You Shepherds)

Presbyterium Ordinis (Decree on the Ministry and Life of Priests)

Tertio Millennio Adveniente (On Preparation for the Jubilee of the Year 2000)

Unitatis Redintegratio (Decree on Ecumenism)

Veritatis Splendor (The Splendor of Truth)

INTRODUCTION

In 1986, the Paulist Fathers reaffirmed the centrality of evangelization as their fundamental and historic mission as a community. We had been doing evangelization since we were founded by Isaac Hecker and his friends in 1858. One of the questions that came in the aftermath of our assembly was whether the parish was a fit place for us to carry out that evangelizing mission. Actually, it was an age-old question and a source of tension right from the beginning of our community's founding.

I brought with me to the assembly the profound conviction that the parish was a wonderful setting to carry out the evangelizing work of the church. Could we create missionary parishes instead of maintenance-oriented communities to carry out that work?

This book offers an answer to that question. During the past ten years, I have worked with dioceses and parishes to help them move from a maintenance-oriented to a mission-directed parish. In creating PNCEA Parish Missions, *Disciples in Mission, ENVISION,*[1] doing workshops and training sessions here in Washington, D.C., and across the country, and creating materials to equip Catholics for evangelization, we seek to help parishes make the necessary changes to become more evangelizing.

Many Catholics have a stereotypical understanding of evangelization: it's a thing that evangelical Protestants do. On the contrary, evangelization is Catholic to the core. I write this book out of a deep love for the Catholic Church and the conviction that the reform of the Second Vatican Council, if it is to be ultimately successful, must continue to embrace the mission of evangelization because that is our true identity as Catholics.

The book is divided into three parts. In the first part, I try to make a preliminary case with the reader that evangelization holds the key to the future of the church because it was, in fact, the centerpiece of the post-Vatican Council reform. In other words, we are moving back into the future by embracing evangelization as the heart and soul of the council's reform. I propose that by becoming a community of disciples and disciple-makers, the Catholic Church can find the best model for this evangelizing church. The final chapter of this section insists that evangelization is rooted in the mission of God and is, therefore, radically trinitarian. This vision has considerable impact on the diverse modalities of evangelization, especially ecumenism and dialogue.

In 1992, the U.S. bishops promulgated a national plan and strategy for Catholic evangelization, *Go and Make Disciples (GMD)*. In the second part of this book, I take a look at planning as based on the three goals of that document, for together they constitute a comprehensive plan and strategy for authentic Catholic evangelization. An evangelizing parish is one that is implementing the three goals of *GMD*. I examine each of those three goals in turn and explore ways in which they challenge us to become Catholic evangelizers.

In the third part, I look at evangelization in the parish. How do we move from maintenance to mission-oriented parishes? After an opening reflection on the parish as an ideal venue for evangelization, I examine the importance of collaborative ministry as a foundation for successful evangelization efforts in the parish. Parish planning from an evangelizing perspective is a key strategy of collaboration. The chapter on pastoral leadership presents the best thinking and practices to organize parishes for evangelization. Finally, I offer an evangelizing spirituality based on participating in Christ's priestly, prophetic, and royal character, which all of us share by virtue of our baptism.

In a sense the entire book is a progressive argument for a comprehensive, long-term implementation strategy that corresponds to the broad and complex vision of Catholic evangelization as a way of life. Evangelization is not a program. It doesn't lend itself to quick fix strategies. Rather, it challenges us to systemic change.

Isaac Hecker founded a religious community for the conversion of America. He had a profound conviction that the Catholic Church had a great deal to offer America and that America was a great place for Catholicism to flourish. As a disciple of Isaac Hecker, I present a vision of evangelization in this book that follows in his footsteps. I am a Catholic enthusiast who believes that a reformed, evangelizing Catholic Church has a wonderful gift to offer the American culture and that America is still a great place in which Catholicism can flourish.

There are many issues the Catholic Church is facing today that seriously impede or thwart our evangelizing efforts. They cannot be allowed to keep us from carrying out our mission. I have not attempted to deal with issues that are beyond my ken or control (Psalm 131: "I do not occupy myself with things too great and too marvelous for me"), such as the vocation crisis, women's ordination, the sexual abuse crisis, and so on. They certainly need to be addressed, but they are not within the purview of this book.

My purpose, rather, is to try to place before the reader a compelling vision of Catholic evangelization and share some strategic thinking that might enable us to implement the great vision to which we have been called. I hope that Catholic leadership as well as ordinary Catholics will find themselves saying *yes* to the call to become evangelizing Catholics because it feels right, it corresponds to our deepest identity, and it truly expresses Catholicism at its best.

PART I

Vatican II and the Church's Evangelizing Mission

CHAPTER ONE

BEYOND VATICAN II

Insight: Evangelization has the power to bring new unity to the church in this period of upheaval following Vatican II.

Reflection

A co-worker—who is in his thirties—once told me the story of his family's faith journey. As I listened, I realized that it was, in essence, the experience of many Catholics in this country in the wake of the Second Vatican Council. It is a story of upheaval.

His parents were born in the first half of the 1940s and were raised in Italian-Catholic and Irish-Catholic homes. For both of them, the church was a core element of their formative years: parochial school, regular mass attendance, devotional practices, holy days of obligation, fasting, and so on. As first-generation immigrants growing up in New York City, they lived in a Catholic culture that supported and sustained this strongly Catholic worldview.

In the 1960s, they married; two children were born not long afterward. This was also the time when the effects of the Second Vatican Council were beginning to be felt. The church of their youth was slowly being displaced. Nevertheless, as dutiful Catholic parents, they "dragged" their children to weekly mass and "forced" them to attend religious education classes. For years, the father was even a lector in the new vernacular liturgy and served the local parish with enthusiasm. The parish priests were frequent guests in their home.

Over the years, the family's economic means grew substantially. They moved out of the city to the suburbs and then relocated several times after that, eventually ending up on the West Coast. Their social circle expanded and included many

Protestant and Jewish friends. Eventually, the children grew up and left home. All but one of the grandparents passed away.

At this point, their financial security was established, their obligation to raise their children Catholic was discharged, and their own parents were no longer watching them. The church of their youth was being changed by the reforms of Vatican II, and it felt foreign to them. They stopped actively practicing their faith.

The older son has fallen away, too. Oddly, the younger son—my co-worker—came into a fervent adult faith during his college years. That faith has shaped his professional life and his own family life. Now a father of two, he asks the common life-cycle question: "Will my children have faith?" Additionally, he also faces a more daunting question: "Will my parents have faith?"

The experience of my co-worker's family after Vatican II provides a good introduction to the theme of this chapter. Vatican II opened the church in the United States to a wonderful experience of reform—and also to a great deal of upheaval. Since the council, we have seen alienation from the church, declining attendance at Sunday mass, a huge reduction in religious vocations, confusion and division over the church's teachings, and, more recently, the scandal of clergy sex abuse. Let's take a closer look at this upheaval.

Disorientation in the Wake of Vatican II

In the years before 1965, the Catholic Church was a powerful institution, with strong authority structures, clear belief systems, a rather rigid ritual life, clear moral standards, and well-articulated behavioral expectations. Father was in charge, and we accepted what he said without question. We were told exactly what to believe, and it was all written down for us, in detail, in the *Baltimore Catechism*. The mass never changed, except according to the liturgical season. We knew what was right and what was wrong in every situation, because the church laid it all out for us.

This was the only church American Catholics knew. We were largely unaware that it represented only the most immediate chapter in a very long history. We didn't know that it had been different in the past, and we could not imagine that it would change in the future.

But the Second Vatican Council brought about a tremendous change in the landscape of Catholicism. Very soon after the close of the council, everything in the church seemed to be up for grabs, and this upheaval still exists. To many Catholics today, the church still seems to be in a state of crisis. This is how historian Charles Morris labels it. In his book *American Catholic,* he states: "The three-plus decades since John Kennedy's death have not been kind to institutions of all varieties. But few have suffered so wrenching a reversal as the American Catholic Church, not only in its public image, but even more corrosively, in its own self-perception."[1]

Yet we don't have to see these post–Vatican II years only as years of crisis. Instead, we can try another perspective, adapted from theologian Walter Brueggemann: as part of a cyclical process of orientation, disorientation, and reorientation.[2]

Orientation describes a place of comfort and absence of tension. *Disorientation* refers to the dislocation and distress we feel when our old paradigm—our old framework of faith—no longer enables us to deal with new experiences. *Reorientation* comes with the experience of putting our lives together again, using a new paradigm.

This way of viewing change—orientation, disorientation, and reorientation—describes well the history of the Catholic Church before, during, and after the Second Vatican Council. Before the council, we lived in what Morris calls the period of the triumph of institutional Catholicism.[3] This was a period of *orientation*. The church was a centralized, hierarchical institution that gave meaning, coherence, and satisfaction, but within a fairly narrow framework. Vatican II brought about a severe *disorientation* by dramatically changing the paradigm of Catholic life. We are still struggling through this disorientation. In this book, I propose that embracing evangelization as the essential mission of the church will lead us to a period of *reorientation* in the new millennium. Restorationism—returning to the way things were—is not the answer.[4]

Before Vatican II, during the period of orientation, Catholics lived in a powerful Catholic subculture, which existed alongside the dominant culture but was set apart from it. Catholics had their own schools and their own social organizations. They lived in Catholic neighborhoods. Some Catholics rarely ventured out of this all-encompassing subculture.

This Catholic subculture grew out of a worldview that regarded everything as evil or worthless unless it was integrated into Christianity, and specifically into Catholicism. This world-view is called integralism.[5] It held that the world outside the church had nothing to offer Catholics and was actually harmful to their faith. To be faithful, Catholics only had to accept the church's unchanging system of doctrine. They certainly were not supposed to bring their experience in the world into their faith. God's saving activity was centered within the walls and the institution of the church; there was little consideration for the idea that God's grace might be working anywhere else.

The Catholic Church in the United States had become a highly institutionalized, complex culture. The hierarchy had complete authority and enforced the system through a rigid set of doctrines, moral teachings, and legal discipline. The clergy and religious carried out the policies at the level of parish and school with the mass, sacraments, and devotions as the central religious activities. The laity were the recipients, participating in the Catholic way of life in the hope of saving their souls. The system didn't have many ambiguities.

This subculture began to change in the 1950s, when Catholics moved to the suburbs in large numbers and reached higher levels of education and income. It changed even more in the early 1960s, when they participated in, and were touched by, the social changes taking place in the United States. The civil rights movement, the sexual revolution, changes in the role of women, growth in the consumer culture, and increased divorce rates are notable examples. These trends form a backdrop to the ecumenical council that Pope John XXIII called in 1959 for the entire Catholic Church.

The Second Vatican Council, and its aftermath, brought about a paradigm shift in Catholic life. It opened the doors of the Catholic Church to the world. The one, holy, Catholic, and apostolic church opened itself to the messy reality of the many, the secular, and the diverse. It interacted with other Christian denominations, other religions, and other ways of life found in the world. Latin gave way to the vernacular; immutable truths had to make room for the concrete and the particular; unity had to coexist with pluralism.

William V. D'Antonio and his colleagues, in their book *American Catholics,* highlight some of these changes.[6] The church went from being an institution to being the people of God. Catholics went from unquestioning compliance to relying on their conscience. Even the vision of God changed, from a punitive to a loving one.

There was a profound, rapid change of landscape, and we were ill-prepared to deal with it. Is it any wonder that the post–Vatican II era brought about such disorientation in the church?

Theological Controversy

Much of the disorientation took the form of theological controversy. We are all familiar with the issues that have disrupted the church since the council: women's ordination, religious pluralism, liturgical inculturation, and moral relativism, to name just a few. Though they take different forms, they all arose from that original decision of John XXIII and the bishops to open the Catholic Church to the world. In effect, they opted for a more open church and, in retrospect, for all the problems that go along with it.

Being open to the world means being open to history. At Vatican II, the church embraced the hazardous task of finding the path of truth in love *amid* the ambiguities of history, rather than *apart* from history. It turned away from the notion that it was possible to build a system of truths free from history. Instead, it moved to a theology based on looking at faith experience in the light of history. In theological terms, the church rejected the theological fundamentalism that gives either a document (the Bible) or a doctrine absolute, ahistorical, self-interpreting authority.

This theological shift has had a profound impact on the everyday life of Catholics. It means that everything around us—our non-Catholic neighbors, local politics, decisions we make at work—is the stuff of faith and affects our faith. It means that our faith must take into account all these things in the world, because God works in the world and is not separate from it.

Liberal Versus Conservative

The church today is sharply divided between liberal and conservative forces.[7] This division is intensified by the fact that compromises were made in the texts of the Vatican Council documents to satisfy opposing positions, thus leaving the council open to varying interpretations. The documents are often ambiguous and can offer, as Morris says, "quotable pearls to support the position of almost any dedicated partisan."[8] Liberals express discontent with the resurgence of the power of the curia, the appointment of conservative bishops, and retrenching on implementing Vatican II. Conservatives accuse liberals of ignoring the literal text of some council documents in favor of interpretations in the "spirit of the council" that take them beyond the council itself.

As a pastoral council, Vatican II was not called to counter heresy and made no new doctrinal pronouncements. With the exception of the Lefebvre movement,[9] no heresy or break-off resulted from it. There has been no formal schism. Yet it is obvious that the split between liberal and conservative is very real; it undermines the unity of the church and causes much suffering.

I once went to a midwestern diocese where this split was very pronounced. A conservative bishop had staked out a clear ideological path. Diocesan policies and practices reflected this hard-line approach, and most of the leadership positions were in the hands of very conservative priests. This caused a whole segment of the clergy to feel alienated, angry, and betrayed, because their vision of the church and the hard work they had done to bring it about were neither appreciated nor supported. They felt like exiles in their own diocese.

The liberal-conservative split also shows itself in the ease with which some liberals dismiss conservative individuals, parishes, or dioceses out of hand. What good can possibly come out of Lincoln? Or St. Agnes? There is little effort to get beyond the stereotype. It strikes me that many liberals are so paralyzed by their own vision of what they think should have come out of

Vatican II that they are increasingly incapable of relating to the church that we have.[10]

Authority Versus Conscience

Since the council, we have experienced growing conflict about the roles of authority and conscience. Vatican II placed a renewed emphasis on the role of conscience in the life of Catholics, and this teaching has certainly taken hold in the church.[11] This emphasis contrasts sharply with the minimal role given to conscience before the council. Pre–Vatican II Catholics were taught to accept the magisterium's determination of what was right and what was wrong. The role of their conscience was to decide whether they had sinned in any given instance, within this framework. Typically, the ordinary Catholic with a well-formed conscience was able to determine in a particular situation whether he or she had sinned (*subjective* guilt), but they would often ask their pastor about whether something was regarded as right or wrong according to church teaching (*objective* right or wrong).

Some observers, in describing the change since the council, speak of the movement from compliance to conscience.[12] We can see an example of this in the early days after *Humanae Vitae (On the Regulation of Birth)*, when many Catholic couples decided for themselves that they could not accept, or follow, the document's teaching on birth control. In doing this, they were giving conscience a role that it had not had before in the life of the ordinary Catholic—a role of dissenting against the official teaching of the magisterium.

Ever since this weakening of church authority in the wake of *Humanae Vitae*, the willingness of Catholics to follow their own consciences in determining objective right and wrong (even when the determination is contrary to the magisterium) has grown. Father Charles Curran challenged the objective teaching of the church on sexual matters;[13] other theologians debate the existence of moral absolutes.[14] Most Catholics have long since created their own personal list of serious sins, rather than accepting the official one. (Missing mass on Sunday is notably absent from many people's lists, to give one example.)

Studies show that since 1987 larger numbers of Catholics tend to make up their own minds about sexual morality, and specifically about birth control, premarital sex, divorce and remarriage, homosexuality, and the morality and the politics of abortion. D'Antonio and his colleagues show that attitudes and beliefs over a fifteen-year period continue to move "away from conformity toward personal autonomy."[15]

The study *American Catholics* also reveals declining levels of attachment to the beliefs of the Catholic Church. In 1999, significant percentages of the respondents said that a person could be a good Catholic without going to church every Sunday, without their marriage being approved by the church, and without donating time or money to help the poor or the parish—and these figures had risen since 1987. Some respondents even said that to be a good Catholic it was not necessary to believe that Jesus physically rose from the dead or that the bread and wine become the body and blood of Jesus.

Simply put, many Catholics no longer look to the church for answers when they have questions. They do not ascribe to the church the authority they formerly did to shape their beliefs. This erosion of authority came about in part because the church lost credibility over the birth control issue. It was a logical step from rejecting its authority on this one issue to questioning its authority in other areas of morality. Catholics who were taught for years that certain actions were mortal sins (eating meat on Friday, not attending mass on Sunday, many sexual matters) have now dismissed those teachings as exaggerated assertions of authority. Some of them perceive the practice of confession as the church's attempt to control moral behavior. The result has been a rebellion against all of it. Recently, I heard someone wonder how it would feel to be the last Catholic on earth who went to hell for eating meat on Friday!

Policy Versus Practice

We have official policies from Rome or from the diocese, and we have the world of pastoral practice—and there is often a vast divide between them. Interestingly, this divide reaches back to the very beginning of the church. One of the most ingenious aspects of Catholicism is its way of affirming both moral principles and pastoral practice, abstract law and concrete application, official policy and lived reality.

The Italians are rather notorious for their disregard for the rules. They have a wonderful expression that captures their sense of this discrepancy between the rules and the travails of ordinary life: *si arrangia*. One somehow makes do; one finds a way to get by. One can have both rules and pastoral practice, structure and flexibility. This attitude infuses the ordinary Italian's views on the church. And curia members—Italians—are often surprised at the seriousness and literalness with which Americans regard church law. The Anglo-Saxon tradition of rule of law doesn't always apply in church matters.

This is exactly what Rosemary Haughton is describing in *The Catholic Thing* when she states that the genius of Catholicism is both/and. It is both institution and imagination, both Mother Church and Sophia-Wisdom. They are twins, and we need them both. When the creative equilibrium between them is destroyed, this Catholic thing is lost. When the discrepancy between official policies and pastoral practice becomes too widespread, then the balance between law and practice, rules and reality, is destroyed. There is a breakdown.[16]

We saw this increasingly after Vatican II. For example, in the 1970s, some priests simply stopped doing the paperwork required for marriages. Without seeking annulments or dispensations of any kind, they witnessed marriages and recorded them in the book. It seems that they did not agree with all the legal prescriptions surrounding marriage. They dismissed the Catholic tradition that sees law as a powerful way of supporting gospel values—but in ignoring the law, they upset the balance between official policies and pastoral practice. The result was disorientation.

This disorientation throws off the subtle balances that make Catholicism work. Catholicism works best when the balance between official policies and pastoral practice is reverenced, respected, and scrupulously observed in practice. And it is not only a balance; it is a tension, something that requires constant attention and effort. Practically speaking, a pastoral practitioner must think, pray, and attend to the situation at hand, while still respecting the letter and spirit of the law. This is hard work. Many people become legalists because they don't want to go through the agony of thinking things through and figuring out how the law must be applied in different circumstances.

In the disorientation of the post–Vatican II era, we have lost that balance. Spirituality is valued, but religion is disdained. The way of love is divorced from the path of truth. Conscience is exalted over authority. Authorities ascribe bad faith to dissent. Law and institution (in the minds of some) cannot embody gospel values. All too often, we forget that Catholicism is a religion of both/and, not either/or.

Fewer Priests and Religious

One of the most obvious signs of the disorientation that followed the Second Vatican Council is the dramatic decline in the number of active priests and religious. In 1950, there was one priest for every sixty-six laypeople; in 1999, there was one priest for every 1,330 people. The story is similar for women religious; their numbers dropped from 170,000 in 1960 to 84,034 in 1999. All across the country, Catholics face the closing of churches, parishes without priests, and schools with few or no religious.

This picture is not likely to improve anytime soon, because there has also been a sharp drop in the number of candidates for the priesthood and religious life. We have fewer priests and religious—and those we have are rapidly aging—and they are not being replaced. The seminary where I live was built for ninety students; it now has only a handful—literally—of seminarians in residence today.

Moreover, the attempts that have been made to solve this problem are probably not viable. The most common reaction is to bring in priests from other countries to do pastoral work. But usually they have not been educated in the United States, and they are unfamiliar with our culture. It is an uncomfortable fit for everyone involved.

The church is also not really addressing certain nagging problems that affect the clergy that we do have, particularly the secular clergy. The most insidious problem is the lack of community. I lived the first six years of my priesthood as a secular priest, and I can say that the celibate lifestyle of secular clergy puts them at great risk. These men are largely without effective support, accountability, or adequate companionship. They live in rectories, often by themselves, and their role seems to demand that they work in a sort of holy isolation. They will, inevitably, have bad times, times when they need emotional nourishment or a challenge to their actions. But many of them don't have anyone who can do this for them. This usually spells trouble.

Can we foresee any dramatic changes in this picture? It seems unlikely without some change in our ordination policies, and at this time these discussions are not allowed to take place.

The vocation story is a complex one. We cannot simply contrast our current vocation shortage with the vocation boom of the 1950s, because the context has changed. The world at that time was very different. For one thing, people believed then that if you wanted to serve God, the best—if not the only—way was to become a priest or a religious. The notion that laypeople could also serve God, and that the lay vocation was valuable, was an alien one. Additionally, the large Catholic families that produced so many religious vocations are a thing of the past. Another critical difference between that time and our own is that the rapid upward mobility of Catholics in the late 1950s had not yet happened. There were few avenues of advancement for Catholics, so becoming a priest had genuine prestige, especially in large, blue-collar families—and this was the source of most of the vocations. In short, pursuing a religious vocation received a great deal more support then than it does now. In fact, recent studies show that 68 percent of Catholic families today would *not* encourage their sons to enter the priesthood.[17]

Apart from these objective differences, there are also subjective differences. We see some pain and tension surrounding religious vocations that were not evident before. In the past, the priesthood enjoyed a kind of unalloyed attraction and reputation, both within the church and outside it. After the council, many men left the active ministry while the oils of ordination were still drying. The pure, unfettered enthusiasm for the priesthood dimmed. In addition, the issue of women's ordination has, for some men, complicated any unconditional embrace of the priesthood. Some priests feel reluctant to invite young men into a priesthood that excludes women. Also, the large number of gay men in seminaries and in the priesthood has become more of a concern. And, whether or not the number of priests involved in sexual abuse has grown, whether or not it is proportionately higher than in other professions, sexual scandals in the priesthood tend to get more than their share of publicity and have had a damaging effect.

How does all this affect priests? A recent study by Donald Cozzens, *The Changing Face of the Priesthood,* concludes that even though numbers are down, the morale of priests is quite high. There is, however, a great deal of resentment and anger among them, caused by the church's unwillingness to face the vocation crisis with more honesty and openness.[18] How these factors will impact the church in the future is unknown.

More Inactive Catholics

Inactive Catholics are people who were born into Catholic families, and probably raised as Catholics, who no longer participate in the institutional church. Overall, Catholics today participate less in, and are not as attached to, the church as an institution[19] than in the past.

Why do Catholics become inactive? *Another Look,* a PNCEA publication based on Gallup studies of the time, offers reasons ranging from marriage to a non-Catholic or nonpracticing Catholic, to boredom with worship, to the impersonal nature of large Catholic parishes.[20]

Chapter Seven will explore this issue more deeply, and offer a definition of inactive Catholics, in the context of Goal II of *Go and Make Disciples.*

Skeptical Young Adult Catholics

Some years ago, my niece and her fiancé asked me to celebrate their wedding, which they wanted to hold in a park. I explained that most dioceses don't allow two Catholics to get married outside church premises, and especially not in a park. My niece told me that she was a professional with the Girl Scouts and had a strong love of nature. Much of her spirituality, and much of the couple's relationship, was linked to the outdoors. I said that I would try to help them, but I was not confident of the outcome.

In fact, their midwestern diocese had a very strong policy against outdoor weddings, and the pastor of my niece's parish was not willing to be much of an advocate. I wrote a letter to the bishop on their behalf, but their appeal was turned down. So they were married by a nondenominational minister, who had no objection to holding the ceremony in a park.

Before this experience, my niece and her husband had a relatively strong connection to the church, and attended mass regularly. However, they had little appreciation for the rules that prevented them from celebrating their wedding in a park. In many ways, they are typical of the young adult population of the church: they consider themselves Catholic, but have a less than satisfying relationship with the institutional church, for many reasons. Today, as a result of a request to be godparents for their nephew, they went to their pastor and had their marriage blessed. So the story had a good ending, but this is not always the case with young adults. This failure to appreciate the rules is another aspect of the disorientation we are experiencing in the wake of Vatican II.

Young adult Catholics—the future of the church—are a real concern. The good news is that many of them do still see themselves as Catholic. The not-so-good news is that many of these same young people who claim to be Catholic do not actually practice their faith. Moreover, being Catholic does not mean the same thing to them as it did to previous generations of Catholics. Their Catholic identity is what some would call a watered-down version. They don't take part as much in church activities, and they feel much less adherence and loyalty to the church. Inevitably, the questions arise: will they pass on their faith to the next generation? And what kind of Catholic identity will they pass on?

In trying to answer these questions, it is helpful to turn to generational studies, which are based on the premise that each generation (a generation is identified by a specific range of birth years) is shaped by what was happening in the world around them in their adolescent years. So we can learn a great deal about any generation by examining the historical events and peer influences that affected them when they were between the ages of fifteen and twenty-five. The idea is that the experiences of these formative years are not outgrown, but strongly impact people throughout their lives. For example, think of the Great Depression: it impacted a whole generation's way of looking at the world and shaped its coping habits as well.[21]

When we look at generational studies of the post–Vatican II generations, the news is not reassuring.[22] Pre–Vatican II Catholics—those born before World War II—have a high degree of Catholic identity and loyalty to the institutional church. Vatican II Catholics, born between 1941 and 1960, tend to have a weaker attachment to the church, and post–Vatican II Catholics are even less attached. The same trend applies in other areas as well, with the two younger generations being more selective in their Catholic beliefs and and weaker in Catholic practices.

To sum up, the two younger generations are more similar to each other than they are different, and both differ from the pre–Vatican II group.[23]

We have, then, some typical characteristics of the post–Vatican II generation. Obviously, these characteristics will not be found in every individual in this group, but they do offer a helpful portrait of the generation as a whole. This is valuable information, particularly since it involves 46 percent of the Catholic population in this country today.[24]

The post–Vatican II generation is skeptical of institutions of all kinds, including the church. This means that these Catholics are reluctant to accept teaching and direction from the church—and this has always been one of the church's primary roles. Instead, they tend to construct their own worldview, with little input from the church, and they make decisions without deferring to its teachings.

The subtitle of a recent study of young adults highlights this contemporary trait. In *Young Adult Catholics: Religion in the Culture of Choice*, Hoge, Dinges, Johnson, and Gonzales put their finger on the major characteristic of the assimilated Catholic of the postmodern era: a belief in the right to choose. America has enshrined freedom of choice and the autonomy of the individual as the pillars of democracy. Not surprisingly, post–Vatican II Catholics have been profoundly affected by these values of our culture. They were born between 1961 and 1982, and thus grew up during a time when Catholic families had been largely assimilated into the culture. So young Catholics tend to be more strongly influenced by the culture than their parents and grandparents were and they have a correspondingly weaker attachment to the church.[25]

Much has been made of what some call the "pick and choose" character of the post–Vatican II generation's approach to doctrines and morals. Its members do not look to the church for guidance in areas of sexual morality. There is significant agreement on major doctrines, but there is also significant dissent in areas like women's ordination, married priesthood, and many aspects of religious practice (Sunday mass attendance, the practice of confession, and the support of the church). In fact, only one in five young adult Catholics actually practices the faith actively. Many observers have noted that this generation, while admiring the Holy Father immensely, feels no great need to obey him. They often speak of themselves as spiritual and define their religion as being a "good person."

It is too early to give a reliable description of the so-called millennial generation. There are some indications that they differ considerably in their religious attitudes and practices from the preceding generation, being more open to the church as an institution and more traditional in some of their religious behaviors. This generation could bring about a significant shift in the overall picture of Catholics who have come to maturity since Vatican II; we will have to wait and see.

Other characteristics of post–Vatican II Catholics contribute to the disorientation we are experiencing, particularly because they raise major questions about what is the essence of Catholicism and what, if anything, is unessential. Their value system is not significantly different from that of the main culture, especially in areas of sexual mores and consumerism. They lack a solid knowledge of the Catholic faith and its teachings. They disagree in some important ways with these teachings and are willing to follow their consciences. They emphasize personal spirituality without making a real commitment to the institution. All this leads to concern about the future of the church.

This is the picture of the disorientation we are experiencing in the Catholic Church in the wake of Vatican II. We have reform, but also upheaval. We have much-welcomed change, but also conflict and losses.

Evangelization Can Make a Difference

Evangelization has the power to bring new unity to the church in this period of upheaval. It can give us a new perspective, help us find our way through the disorientation, and lead us to a reorientation in the church.

The Essence of Evangelization

What is Catholic evangelization? It is at the same time a very simple and a very complex reality, but at its core it is a way of being church. Pope Paul VI says: "[E]vangelizing all peoples constitutes the essential mission of the Church...it is in fact the grace and vocation proper to the Church, her deepest identity" (*Evangelii Nuntiandi [EN, On Evangelization in the Modern World]*, no. 14). The church, he said, exists in order to evangelize. How do we know when we are evangelizing? Paul VI tells us:

> The Church evangelizes when she seeks to convert, solely through the divine power of the message she proclaims, both the personal and collective consciences of people, the activities in which they engage, and the lives and concrete milieu which are theirs. (*EN*, no. 18)

So evangelization touches deeply and profoundly our inner selves, our activities, and our world: in other words, everything. Put another way, evangelization challenges all baptized persons to a conversion to Christ, by living their faith fully, inviting others to faith, and living these gospel values in the world. It gives us a new lens through which we can view our Catholic faith.

That lens is threefold: spiritual renewal, missionary activity, and action for justice in the world.[26]

Evangelization is, first of all, spiritual renewal in Christ. Spiritual renewal has always been a constant in Catholic life, though its shape was different in every age. In the past, Catholics defined spirituality as their fundamental obligation to save their souls. This obligation was part of a Catholic culture that was very clerical and authoritarian. These conditions powerfully impacted the way Catholics pursued their spiritual lives. Bishops and priests were seen as truly holy people, followed closely by religious sisters and brothers. Laypeople came a distant third, because marriage and family life were not seen as paths to holiness in an era when the preferred (in fact the only) spirituality was monastic spirituality. Ordinary Catholics probably wondered if they were called to holiness at all or if they could even achieve it.

Vatican II changed all that. It affirmed that *all* people are called to holiness, laypeople as well as clergy and religious, by virtue of their baptism. It emphasized that baptism was the foundation of the spiritual life for everyone; no one is exempt from the task of seeking holiness. And this holiness was not a monastic holiness either, but a genuinely lay secular holiness, based on laypeople's specific vocation in the world. Their path in life was no longer seen as second best, but as the normal path for most people. This renewed emphasis on baptism and the laity's call to holiness continued after the council, and has resulted in the wide acceptance of the challenge of spiritual renewal among the laity. The vision and place of holiness in the ordinary life of Catholics are captured beautifully in the tapestries of the saints that dominate the nave of the recently completed Cathedral of Our Lady of the Angels in Los Angeles.

The missionary consciousness of Catholics in the pre–Vatican II church assumed the following form. The missions were Africa, the Fiji Islands, China, and India; the missionaries were the Jesuits, the Franciscans, the Maryknolls, and the Missionaries of Africa. The laity were certainly not thought of as missionaries. Vatican II, however, asserted that the entire church was by its very nature missionary: the mission is wherever we are, and we are the missionaries. It is the normal activity of the church.[27] Interestingly, Catholics after Vatican II have been very quick to embrace the call to holiness, but not as quick to respond to the call to become more missionary. For one thing, we need to overcome some of the stereotypes associated with evangelization and mission. It will take time, but we are slowly beginning to own mission as something truly Catholic.

Just as Vatican II expanded our understanding of the universal call to holiness and missionary awareness, it also expanded our understanding of social justice. Prior to the Second Vatican Council, we had no real consciousness of social justice as an integral element of Christian life. Moral formation often concentrated on the role of the individual and had a fairly narrow view of authentic discipleship. Furthermore, the integralist viewpoint that prevailed at the time saw spirituality as keeping the world out of the church, rather than the church transforming the world. Vatican II changed this. In the years after the council, we grew in our awareness of the need to address the structures of society, as well as to rectify individual instances of injustice. Throughout these post–Vatican II years, Catholics have come to accept the fact that action on behalf of justice is a constitutive dimension of the gospel, and this vision has become part of parish life.[28]

So we see that a great deal of what we have been doing in these last forty years of renewal—focusing more deeply on scripture, enriching the liturgy, working for justice for all—is evangelization. This broad scope is one of the strengths of Catholic evangelization: it cannot be reduced to one-on-one conversion efforts, door-to-door visitation, or televangelism. As Paul VI states, we distort the authentic vision of evangelization when we identify it with one or more of its elements at the expense of the entire vision. In its broadest and most comprehensive sense, evangelization is how we are church. It defines what it means to be Catholic (*EN*, no. 17).

Evangelization Can Move Catholics...

...From Fragmentation to Unity

Since, as Paul VI said, evangelizing all peoples is the essential mission of the church, then evangelization is not just one program among many. It is, rather, the umbrella under which all ministries are carried out. Everything we do must be seen as evangelization.

We did not really understand this when we first began to carry out the council's renewal agenda. We expended a lot of energy implementing separate aspects of the renewal independently of each other, instead of looking at the whole picture. Often, we began with the liturgical renewal. We also concentrated heavily on equipping the baptized to carry out their rightful ministry, so social justice became a central concern. Catechesis, originally limited to schools and religious education programs, grew to include the family, youth, and young adults. The RCIA has become the ordinary way of initiating new members into the church. The result of all this is that parishes have become very busy places; they sometimes seem to follow a philosophy that "more is better." The end result is fragmentation.

This multiplication of ministries often leads to compartmentalization and harmful "turfism." We see ministers focusing on one area of ministry, at the expense of the whole picture. Repeatedly, one encounters situations where "the left hand doesn't know (or always care) what the right hand is doing." Up until recently, many people in the Catholic Church could be heard saying: "I don't do evangelization; I am into social justice." Or "Adult education is my thing." "I am into liturgy, not catechesis." We all recognize the syndrome.

Evangelization, once it is understood as the essential mission of the church, has a unifying power that can break down both turfism and excessive compartmentalization in ministry. For example, evangelization can have a salutary effect on the role of catechesis in the church, which currently is being undermined by a growing divide between Catholic schools and parishes. Many parishes find themselves sponsoring and supporting schools with an increasingly large population of families of inactive Catholics or people with no church family. And some of those school families direct their primary loyalty to the school, rather than to the parish. Mutual distrust and lack of support often result.

However, the *General Directory for Catechesis (GDC)* makes it very clear that catechesis is an essential part of evangelization.[29] Catechesis does not exist in isolation, but is fixed firmly within the context of evangelization. We catechize in order to evangelize. The *Directory* says: "The ministry of catechesis appears, then, as a fundamental ecclesial service for the realization of the missionary mandate of Jesus."[30] So we can establish a new unity between school and parish, under the overall ministry of evangelization, because the purpose of the parish and the purpose of the school are the same: evangelization.

...*From Maintenance to Mission*

One Sunday, an elderly couple came up to me after mass and said, "Father, all this talk about evangelization is fine. But while you are out taking care of *them*, who is going to take care of *us*?"

This is an example of being maintenance-oriented: looking inward, focusing on keeping oneself in order. According to evangelizer Patrick Brennan, many parishes are maintenance-oriented, and it is because their parishioners have a consumer consciousness.[31] Influenced by our consumer culture, they come to church to *get* something, and they expect the leadership to provide it. These good people have little missionary awareness. Parishes end up spending a lot of time and energy serving them, the people who are present, rather than reaching out to those who are absent.

The people we need to reach out to are not around to tell us what their needs are. The people who don't feel welcome aren't present to tell us why. The poor who don't feel at home in our church simply remain on the margins. As a result, we all too often think that everything is wonderful because the people who are present are contented. They tell us so—and they tell us when they aren't. But we don't hear from the voiceless.

This is not what we find in scripture. Jesus said to his listeners: "Those who are well have no need of a physician, but those who are sick; I have come to call not the righteous but sinners" (Mark 2:17). At the end of all the gospels, when Jesus appears to his followers after he has risen, he gives them a missionary mandate. The most dramatic is in Matthew: "Go therefore and make disciples of all nations..." (28:16–20).

In keeping with this mandate, canon law emphasizes that the pastor is responsible for everyone within the parish boundaries, not just the people who regularly come to church. Canon law states [can. 528]: "The pastor...is to make every effort with the aid of the Christian faithful, to bring the gospel message also to those who have ceased practicing their religion or who do not profess the true faith."[32]

But the need to reach out beyond our boundaries is more than a mandate; it is a practical necessity for the parish. In his monumental work, *Transforming Mission,* David Bosch comments that movements, in order to survive, have to institutionalize themselves. But institutions, in order to stay vital, have to stay in touch with the original inspiring character of their founding as a movement.[33] For the church, this means we have to reawaken ourselves constantly to the boundary-breaking, all-inclusive character of Jesus' original mission of salvation for all. John Paul II makes the same point in *Redemptoris Missio (RM, Mission of the Redeemer)* when he says: "For in the Church's history, missionary drive has always been a sign of vitality, just as its lessening is a sign of a crisis of faith" (no. 2). The church needs mission to stay vigorous and alive.

All organizations need mission if they are to stay healthy. Organizational development theory tells us that healthy organizations are ones that have a clear sense of mission. Low morale often results from the aimlessness and malaise that come from the lack of mission.[34] When we have a clear outward focus, some of our internal problems tend to fall into perspective. When we are not absorbed by the mission, these internal problems are magnified. When we do have an outward missionary focus, our problems diminish in importance because we identify with, and seek to do something about, suffering in the world. In adopting a missionary rather than a maintenance approach, parishes are not only being faithful to the mandate of Christ, but they also find a remedy for the malaise that comes from excessive focus on their internal dissensions.

We have certainly found this to be true in the Paulist Community. Since the formation of a strong Mission Direction Statement in 1986, the community has experienced a measure of well-being that comes from clarity about our mission and firm commitment to carry it out. The Paulists, of course, are a missionary society, but then so is the church!

...*From Blindness to Conversion*

We human beings are like fish living in the ocean. We are largely oblivious to the culture that surrounds us and how it affects us. Ronald Rolheiser, in *The Shattered Lantern: Rediscovering a Felt Presence of God,* writes about how many of us are impacted in ways we don't perceive by the culture's narcissism, pragmatism, and unbridled restlessness.[35] The validity of Rolheiser's analysis can be seen in how families get caught up in the rat race, with too many activities and too little time. They lose the ability to evaluate critically what is important and necessary for their well-being.

One of the principal tasks of contemporary spirituality is to allow the gospel to smash these cultural idols so we can truly come to see God in our ordinary life experience. This seeing God is called *contemplatio* and is the true meaning of the word *contemplation.*

The blind beggar, Bartimaeus, symbolizes this struggle to see things rightly (Mark 10:46–52). He is often regarded as a foil for the disciples. They too are blind; only they don't realize it. Bartimaeus, though, knows it. He is ready to throw off the cloak of fear and come to Jesus so he might see—and thus we may view him as a model disciple.

I believe that God has made us with a powerful desire for truth, but also with a considerable capacity for self-delusion. We need to have our eyes opened constantly, so we can see things as they really are; it is an ongoing process. This is the struggle to conversion, and we are all called to it. Conversion to the gospel of Jesus Christ is the heart of evangelization; it is the core of the message we bring to the world.

When we proclaim the gospel to all people—including ourselves—in every time and every place, we actively open ourselves to the power of the gospel. We are allowing it to function as a two-edged sword that cuts through to the bone of the human situation, and we will indeed be changed. We will be converted. And the call to conversion falls upon all of us, the faithful as well as people outside the faith. God wants all people to be converted. God wants all of us to open our hearts so the gospel might take root in us, whatever our circumstances, and touch us in the depths of our being.

So much of the disorientation in the wake of Vatican II is ideologically-based finger pointing and blaming. Opening ourselves to the transforming power of the gospel and asking the questions—How do we need to change? How do I need to change?—will inevitably have a healing effect. Conversion brings about healing. And the heart of evangelization is a call to all of us to convert to a gospel way of life.

...From Rugged Individualism to Solidarity

A dear friend of mine once told me a story about her cousin, who had a family of nine boys and three girls. When her husband got sick with cancer and began undergoing chemotherapy, he lost all his hair. One day, all nine sons showed up at the hospital with their heads shaved. That's solidarity. We are willing to walk in the other's shoes.

When the Pharisee in Luke's gospel stands up and defines himself apart from and against humanity, we see a lack of solidarity. When Lazarus is invisible to the rich man, this is an offense against human solidarity. When Paul reminds Christians that the body is one, and if one part suffers, all the parts suffer with it; if one part is honored, all the parts share its joy (1 Cor 12:26)—he is describing solidarity.

Solidarity is the conviction that humanity is rooted in a common origin as a family and bonded together in an obligation of mutual charity. It is a virtue, however, often unappreciated by Americans, many of whom identify more with the rugged individualism that forms part of our national myth. We admire the self-made man; we feel that people should be able to pull themselves up by their bootstraps. These attitudes spring from the assumption that we really are on our own. And many people equate this rugged individualism with freedom: we are free to make our own way, unhindered by any obligations to anyone else.

But both scripture and Catholic tradition give us a different perspective. *The Catechism of the Catholic Church* speaks of solidarity as a social charity that is a direct demand of human and Christian brotherhood.[36] Paul says, "We do not live to our-selves, and we do not die to ourselves" (Rom 14:7). We live in a common bond and are required to live not just for ourselves, but in service of the common good. This is solidarity: the conviction that human existence is coexistence. This is not a solo trip.

Solidarity lies behind Goal III of *Go and Make Disciples:* "To foster gospel values in our society, promoting the dignity of the human person, the importance of the family, and the com-mon good of our society, so that our nation may continue to be transformed by the saving power of Jesus Christ" (no. 117). In effect, this goal focuses on the social justice aspect of evange-lization; it is, in some ways, the hallmark of Catholic evange-lization. The document also states: "The fruit of evangelization is changed lives and a changed world—holiness and justice, spir-ituality and peace" (no. 18). We are not simply content to change individuals; we want to change the world.

So this goal calls for a powerful sense of solidarity with the world, a groaning together with the world as we try to bring God's creation to its fulfillment. This solidarity must be with the world's poor and those without recourse. The Latin American community, over the years, has helped us to see the importance of a "preferential option for the poor." John Paul II states in *Redemptoris Missio:* "It follows that the poor are those to whom the mission is first addressed, and their evangelization is *par excellence* the sign and proof of the mission of Jesus" (no. 60).

The concept of solidarity, rooted deep in our tradition, honed in the Latin American experience of the struggle for lib-eration, given new and rich articulation by John Paul II, expresses best what social justice is all about. If the church in the United States, in its struggle to become an evangelizing church, embraces the virtue of solidarity as its way of carrying out the social justice element of evangelization, this will bring great healing to the Catholic culture in the new millennium.

Evangelization: The Catholic Thing

It remains to be seen, of course, if evangelization can in fact bring new unity in the midst of the current fragmentation, or if it can move the church from a maintenance to a more missionary posture. Will the focus on conversion that is essential to evangelization bring about the kind of ongoing renewal of the entire church that is needed? Will a serious implementation of the goals of *Go and Make Disciples* turn Catholics from rugged individualism to an embracing of solidarity?

Catholics have something special to offer the world. That was a deep and profound conviction of Paulist founder Isaac Hecker. As a follower of Hecker, I share that conviction. I am an unabashed enthusiast of what Rosemary Haughton calls "the Catholic Thing" or what Greeley terms "the sacramental imagination." I can relate to the notion that Catholics remain Catholic because they love being Catholic. That's me. The Catholic Church is the place where I want to be. I am, however, a "reforming" Catholic in the sense that I am committed to a Catholic Church that is *semper reformanda,* that continues to occupy itself with carrying out the reform agenda of the Second Vatican Council, which, to my mind, is clearly unfinished.[37] We are only beginning to undertake what I see as its principal unifying agenda: evangelization as the essential mission of the church, not different from the rest of the reform agenda of the Vatican Council, but embracing it and giving it unity and missionary purpose.

Evangelization has the power to bring new unity to the church in this period of upheaval, and can lead to an experience of reorientation within the church and a renewed impact on the society in which we live in this new millennium.

CHAPTER TWO

EVANGELIZATION— THE CHURCH'S ESSENTIAL MISSION

Insight: The church has yet to embrace evangelization as its essential mission, even though it was the very purpose of Vatican II.

Reflection

Sometimes we think we know why we do something, and then discover later that we had other, more meaningful motives for our action, motives that we hadn't realized at the time. I had been a diocesan priest in Winona, Minnesota, for six years when I sought, and received, permission to join the Missionary Society of St. Paul the Apostle—more commonly known as the Paulist Fathers. I did this because I was looking for a greater level of community life and collaboration with my brother priests than I was able to find in the diocesan setting.

A year later, in 1976, I read Pope Paul VI's apostolic exhortation *Evangelii Nuntiandi*, which had recently been promulgated, and I realized why I had become a Paulist. I felt called to carry out the work of evangelization, which had always been the work of the community (although we didn't call it that). The document gave new life to the historic Paulist mission, and when I read it I understood why I had been drawn to this particular community.

The church has had a similar experience with its discovery of evangelization as the deeper purpose of the Second Vatican Council. Originally, John XXIII used the word *aggiornamento*— Italian for *updating* or *renewal*—to explain why he called the council.[1] Later, Paul VI stated that the single most important objective of the council was to "make the Church of the twentieth century ever better fitted for proclaiming the Gospel to the people of the twentieth century" (*EN*, no. 2). Essentially, he was giving us a new interpretation of the council.

John Paul II, in *Redemptoris Missio,* echoes this thought:

> The Second Vatican Council sought to renew the Church's life and activity in the light of the needs of the contemporary world. The Council emphasized the Church's "missionary nature," basing it in a dynamic way on the Trinitarian mission itself. The missionary thrust therefore belongs to the very nature of the Christian life.... (no. 1)

John Paul II continues to emphasize evangelization as the theme of his pontificate. In fact, ever since the promulgation of *Evangelii Nuntiandi* in 1975, the entire church has been growing more open to evangelization as its essential mission. Put together, all these things point to the Spirit at work, revealing that evangelization was the purpose of the Vatican Council. However, the church has yet to accept evangelization as its essential mission. This chapter will elaborate on this theme. It will also trace the history of contemporary Catholic evangelization from its beginnings in Vatican II to the Jubilee Year 2000.

Evangelization—The Very Purpose of Vatican II

Evangelization is as old as the church itself. It has its roots in the ministry of Jesus, who was the first and greatest evangelizer, and in the New Testament. Yet in many ways evangelization is new for Catholics. The word was not part of our Catholic vocabulary prior to the Second Vatican Council.

Previous reform councils of the church, such as Nicea, Chalcedon, Trent, or Vatican I, were all summoned to combat heresy. Vatican II is unique; its purpose was essentially pastoral, rather than doctrinal. John XXIII very openly called the council to update the church. In September 1962, a month before the council began, the Holy Father spoke of the need for renewed vitality in the church, both internally and in its relations with the world. He listed the challenges the world was facing—indifference, denial of God, exaggerated individualism—and the need for humanity to come together in peace and love. He referred to Jesus' command to go and teach all nations and then, at the end of his speech, simply stated that the purpose of the council was, therefore, evangelization.[2]

The Holy Father never did outline a formal agenda for the council, but he set its theme: renewing the church for the sake of its mission in the world. He emphasized that the church has something to offer the world, if it can express age-old truths in new and meaningful ways. Thus did John XXIII conceive the evangelizing purpose of the Second Vatican Council.

The word *evangelization* in its different forms occurs forty-nine times in the Vatican documents.[3] There is actually no one document specifically on evangelization, but all of them, taken together, lay a solid foundation for contemporary Catholic evangelization.

What came out of Vatican II was a clear pastoral vision of a renewed church—a vision that forms the core of Paul VI's perspective on evangelization. Before the council, the church saw evangelization as the initial proclamation of the gospel to the nonbeliever. It was separate from catechesis and sacramental initiation into the church; these came later. However, in *Evangelii Nuntiandi,* Paul VI presents evangelization as something much more comprehensive: the essential mission of the church. As such, it touches all phases of Christian life.[4] It is the widest possible vision of evangelization.

Paul VI's comprehensive view of evangelization has important implications. In effect, he is saying that evangelization is the pastoral strategy of the renewed church that came out of Vatican II. That pastoral strategy, as he stresses, is one of renewing the church so the church can in turn bring the good news to the world.

Evangelizing Themes of the Council

The Church and the Kingdom

In the past, the church saw itself as a perfect society, complete unto itself. The concept of the kingdom of God was not in most people's consciousness, but if they thought about it at all, they tended to see the church as the kingdom. Vatican II articulated a new vision: the church as the mystery of God's presence in the world as sacrament, sign, and instrument of salvation.[5] The church's purpose in the world was to work for the coming of the kingdom. The church is not the kingdom; rather, it serves the kingdom. This new perspective laid the foundation for a kingdom-centered, rather than a church-centered, approach to evangelization. Evangelization would focus not on bringing people into a perfect society—the church—but rather would convert them and transform the world, to make way for the coming of God's kingdom.

The Nature of the Church

Lumen Gentium (Dogmatic Constitution on the Church), one of the major council documents, revolutionized the way Catholics experienced themselves as church. This document gave us a new vision of church: not as clerical and hierarchical, but as a much more participatory experience, rooted in baptism. The second chapter, on the people of God, emphasizes the equality of all members of the church by virtue of their baptism and the universal call to share fully in the mission and ministry of the church. This changed the perspective of the laity, and they changed from passive recipients to active participants. This document laid the groundwork for the vision of an evangelizing church, in which all the baptized are active disciples carrying out the mission of evangelization.

The Church and the World

Gaudium et Spes (Pastoral Constitution on the Church in the Modern World) made clear that evangelization is not a triumphal enterprise, an attempt to conquer a world that is essentially an adversary. Evangelization is, rather, a journey in and with the world. The Holy Spirit is at work in the church and the world. Evangelization serves the kingdom and witnesses to God's work of redemption in the church and in the world. This led logically to the realization that the world then is to be valued, not condemned. This marked a significant change from the church's previous anti-Modernist attitude toward the world. It now looks at the events of the world and sees what John Paul II, echoing *Gaudium et Spes,* calls the *signs of the times:* indications that the values of the gospel are taking root in human society.[6] The church can see, for example, that when all the people of a country have a voice in their government, this is a sign of God at work, because the dignity of the individual is a gospel value. This was a new perception, and it opened the church to the profound challenge of defining itself in relation to the world in a more positive fashion.

Inculturation

Another contribution—perhaps the most enduring—of *Gaudium et Spes* is that it paved the way for a postconciliar reflection on inculturation. Paul VI called this issue of inculturation the biggest drama of every age (*EN,* no. 20). How do we incarnate the gospel in the culture? How does the gospel penetrate the culture, and how does the culture shape our way of experiencing the gospel? This post–Vatican II reflection was especially significant, and especially urgent, because it took place in a church that had turned away from the old Western European model and had become a truly global church. The question of inculturation, raised in a systematic way during the council, continues to be a preeminent question for evangelization. After a good measure of struggle over this question, a very happy formulation of inculturation was promulgated in the U.S. bishops' document *Our Hearts Were Burning Within Us,* where inculturation is defined as a "process of mutual enrichment between the gospel and culture."[7]

The Missionary Church

An important insight of Vatican II was its affirmation that the church is, at its core, missionary. "The whole Church is missionary and the work of evangelization is the fundamental task of the people of God...."[8] The church is like an ellipse with two focuses: its internal life and its external mission. They cannot be separated. "Without mission the Church cannot be called Catholic."[9] Vatican II also came to the critical insight that Christ is identified with, and acts through, the local church, as well as the universal church. When we say that the church is essentially missionary, this means that each diocese, each parish, is essentially missionary. This realization cleared the way for renewing the role of the local church as the primary agent of mission, which is not just something the universal church does. It is not far away, carried on by elite orders of missionaries. Mission is wherever we are and the missionaries are the baptized faithful.

Ecumenical Reconciliation and Interreligious Dialogue

The Second Vatican Council recognized that in order for renewal to happen, there first must be an honest confession of the misdeeds of the past. There must be reconciliation, which thus became a major thread of the council. The bishops initiated a new era of reconciliation by acknowledging past wrongs, calling for new mutual understanding and a change in our way of relating to each other. This marked a major shift for the church, and this spirit of openness and reconciliation came to a certain climax in the Jubilee Year 2000, when Pope John Paul II spoke more explicitly of the church's need for repentance of past errors and instances of infidelity, especially those actions that have offended against the unity of the people of God (*Tertio Millennio Adveniente [On Preparation for the Jubilee of the Year 2000]*, nos. 33–34). The council also laid down principles to create better relationships with Christian churches in the future. These actions had profound implications for the path Catholic evangelization would take. They separated it firmly from proselytism, basing it instead on a respect for and appreciation of other Christian traditions, a regard for freedom of conscience, and the recognition of the need for authentic dialogue and collaboration among religions.[10]

With regard to other world religions, the council's *Nostra Aetate (Declaration on the Relation of the Church to Non-Christian Religions)* states that the church "rejects nothing of what is true and holy in these religions,"[11] even as it proclaims Christ as the way, the truth, and the life for all people. It rejects the notion that the Jews are repudiated or accursed by God, and it recognizes God's enduring covenant with the Jewish people. It calls for an end to every form of discrimination. In many ways, this decree marked the beginning of a new journey in the church's relationships with other faiths, a journey that has had a tremendous impact on our understanding of Catholic evangelization. We live in a global village, and Catholics are constantly interacting with people of different religions. How does our proclamation of salvation in Jesus Christ relate to the role of these other religions? The council established an important foundation of respect and dialogue as the church wrestles with these questions—a struggle that continues to this day.

Renewal of Scripture

Another council teaching that proved very significant for evangelization was the reaffirmation of the centrality of the scriptures in the life of the church. In the years leading up to the council, the church did not focus on scripture as a major part of the spiritual lives of Catholics. Scripture was proclaimed during the liturgy, but Catholics were not encouraged to study it for themselves. *Dei Verbum (Dogmatic Constitution on Divine Revelation)* did a great deal to place scripture once again at the center of church life. It identified one single divine wellspring from which both scripture and tradition flow. The church is not above the scriptures, nor can the scriptures stand alone. Basically, the council redressed the balance of word and sacrament in Catholic life. Since so much of evangelization is the proclamation of the word of God, this laid an invaluable foundation for future evangelizing work.

New Perspectives in Theology

Another important contribution of the council that had a direct impact on evangelization is what has been called *new perspectives in theology*. Chapter One described the theology that prevailed before the council: it was dominated by the curia and set the church firmly against the world and apart from history. With the Second Vatican Council, the church rejected this anti-Modernist theology. The council laid the foundation for a new way of looking at theology, one with biblical, patristic, and liturgical sources and a strong historical and experiential character.

This development has made it possible for Catholics to speak of their experience of God as a true way of understanding God. This break with the anti-Modernist nature of the pre–Vatican II church is one of the council's greatest contributions. Yet it is also one of its most problematic, because it highlights the problem of just how the Holy Spirit works in the church, how it works in the world, and the Spirit's role in other churches and religions. These questions lie at the heart of Catholic evangelization, but they have no easy answers.

These are some of the principal themes of the Vatican II documents that relate directly to evangelization. They provide a foundation for the later thematic formulation of evangelization, which Paul VI presented in *Evangelii Nuntiandi.*

Postconciliar Developments

It was nine years after Vatican II—in 1974—that a worldwide synod of bishops convened around the theme of evangelization. Paul VI's groundbreaking document on evangelization, *Evangelii Nuntiandi,* came out of that synod.

Until *Evangelii Nuntiandi,* the theme of evangelization was at best implicit in the council documents. Paul VI made it explicit in this apostolic exhortation. Avery Dulles, SJ, later stated that, with this document, Paul VI gave a new interpretation to Vatican II. In effect, Paul declared, harking back to the words of John XXIII, that evangelization was the purpose of the council.[12] In fact, in his perspective, evangelization is synonymous with the council's renewal agenda. The bishops of the world sought to lead the church to an ever-more faithful embrace of the gospel through the process of *aggiornamento* or renewal, both *ad intra* and *ad extra,* both within its walls and out in the world.

The documents of Vatican II laid the foundation for an evangelizing church. It is precisely because we are implementing the vision of the council that we are in a place today to undertake the mission of evangelization. Catholics who have never heard of the word *evangelization* often have been participating in its mission simply because they have been active participants in the renewal called for by the council.

Evangelization—The Essential Mission of the Church

John Paul II has given continual emphasis to evangelization from the beginning of his papacy. He expressed the conviction that God had called him to lead the church into the new millennium and that his main theme would be the new evangelization.[13]

This new evangelization should not be seen as a contrast to the vision in *Evangelii Nuntiandi*.[14] They are basically one and the same. However, John Paul II has added his own nuances to Paul VI's vision. He focuses on the new millennium and the need for a new zeal, new expression, and new methods to carry out evangelization in our time. He stresses as well the importance of reinvigorating the mission to the nations, and facing the challenge of reevangelizing whole countries.

John Paul also has emphasized the importance of interreligious dialogue as a form of evangelization and gives a greater focus on the reign of God as a central feature of the evangelizing mission of the church. Ultimately, this has facilitated a less church-centered approach to evangelization.

With the publication of *Redemptoris Missio*, John Paul II continued to reiterate his conviction that the whole church has evangelization as its essential mission. He reemphasized this message on the eve of the Jubilee Year 2000, when, in *Ecclesia in America (The Church in America),* he challenged the church to get on with the task of creating a *missionary* church. He said:

> I urgently desire to encourage all the members of God's People, particularly those living in America—where I first appealed for a commitment "new in its ardor, methods and expression"—to take up this project and to cooperate in carrying it out.[15]

In effect, it seems that the thrust of the document is an exhortation in the new millennium to get on with the task. We have a great vision; there is a tremendous need. Let's do it!

The Great River

From 1975 to the Jubilee Year 2000, then, there has been a consistent theme in papal leadership: evangelization is the essential mission of the church. We picture a great, flowing river of evangelization that had its origins in the Second Vatican Council and then received a tremendous impetus with Paul VI's meditation on evangelization. John Paul II has reasserted the message of Paul VI and has given it his own particular emphasis, particularly on the importance of inculturation.

This great river has had many tributaries flowing into it over the past thirty-five years. The Latin American bishops have given us the gift of small Christian communities and the preferential option for the poor. From the African American and Hispanic communities come the experience of grass-roots planning and multiculturalism. The U.S. bishops and the Vatican have given us documents on social justice, and the lived experience of parishes has added to the river in many ways.

Evangelization received a great boost in 1992, when the bishops of the United States promulgated *Go and Make Disciples: A National Plan and Strategy for Catholic Evangelization in the United States.* The document synthesizes the vision of evangelization from the writings of Paul VI and John Paul II. It also presents three goals for evangelization, with a generous number of objectives and many concrete strategies for each goal. We now possess both a vision of evangelization and a road map to implement it as the essential mission of the church.

The great river of evangelization is growing in depth and breadth. Its current is quickening as many tributaries feed into it. What is needed now is more explicit teaching about evangelization as the essential mission of the church and for Catholics to be aware more explicitly of their call to proclaim actively their faith.

Evangelization Still Not Rooted

Evangelization is rising on the priority list of every parish and diocese across the country; however, it has not yet fully taken root as the essential mission of the church. A number of indicators point to this.

Many Priorities, Not One

As explained in Chapter One, evangelization is often only one priority among many at the ministerial table. In many parishes and dioceses, it becomes a committee or department, along with finance, catechesis, and liturgy. It is rarely seen as the mission of the entire church, nor is it accepted as the responsibility of the entire parish.

Maintenance, Not Missionary

Most parishes today are maintenance-oriented. They focus their attention, resources, and energy primarily on the people who are already there. Little attention is directed outward, toward mission. As Frank DeSiano, CSP, points out in his book *Sowing New Seed*, "We see the people we are conditioned to see."[16] Many of the people we should be ministering to are invisible to us.

This tendency is strengthened by what DeSiano calls the "parochial-centrism" of the modern-day parish.[17] The parish has become the center of Catholics' lives, because it places many demands on them to participate in organizations and activities that are part of this maintenance orientation. Many active parishioners spend an additional evening or two at the parish every week meeting the demands of the ministries or organizations in which they participate. There is little focus on our mission to the world, which is the heart of evangelization.

Many years ago, I remember Archbishop Rembert Weakland warning of an excessively inward emphasis in ministries. He commented that too much of our energy is being spent on the maintenance of the parish, rather than on our mission to the world. How many ministries are needed to take care of the important needs of the parish community? How many ministries can we direct to carry out the missionary activity of the church?

Consumers, Not Disciples

Patrick Brennan, cited in Chapter One, in his book *Re-Imagining the Parish* refers to the ordinary believer as a consumer—a receiver of ministerial services.[18] This consumer attitude can be fueled by a pre–Vatican II mentality, where the goal of every good Catholic is getting to heaven. The main way of achieving this goal is by being in church every Sunday, going to confession at least once a year, and avoiding mortal sin. There is little sense of the baptismal call to share actively in the mission and ministry of Jesus as our way into the kingdom.

This consumer attitude, according to Brennan, can also be fueled by our contemporary society. Much of life today is a shopping mall, where we spend our time looking for what we need to live the good life. Churches can become part of the consumer society when they simply meet the consumer needs of their customers and do not ask anything of them in return. Brennan says that traditionalistic ecclesiology has created a consumer church, in which God's people are being catered to as customers rather than formed as active disciples.[19] In some wealthy parishes, the staff is viewed as an extension of the service network with which people surround themselves in order to live this good life. As long as Catholics view baptism as an entitlement[20] rather than a call to active discipleship, our parishes will continue to be fundamentally maintenance-oriented service stations that only take care of the needs of their own.

The Reasons Why

A number of reasons lie behind the failure of evangelization to be received fully as the essential mission of the church.

Newness

It has been only twenty years since *Evangelii Nuntiandi* was promulgated. In the years immediately after that, Alvin Illig, CSP, the Johnny Appleseed of evangelization, visited virtually every diocese in the country. He proclaimed the good news of the rebirth of evangelization in Catholic life. Upon his return, the staff would ask him how things went. He often said, with a wan smile on his face: "The response was underwhelming."

We have had years of strong leadership from John Paul II and the U.S. Catholic bishops. Little by little, evangelization is becoming more of a priority in the nation's parishes and dioceses. But it is simply too soon to ask Catholics to have an adequate understanding of the vision of evangelization as the essential mission of the church. It will take more time before this vision is grasped.

Lack of Understanding

In the minds of many ordinary Catholics, evangelization is still associated with street-corner preaching, door-to-door Bible-toting Jehovah's Witnesses, and televangelists. We need to overcome these stereotypes. Those elements are definitely part of evangelization for the people who are called to such approaches, but they are not the whole of it. We need education to help us know what Catholic evangelization is and formation to foster commitment to carry it out. We are not there yet.

Pluralism

The postmodern phenomenon of pluralism holds that there is no one right way to do anything. Everything has its claims; no belief is truer than any other belief. We are so accustomed to a plurality of choices that we are reluctant to consider that any one of them might claim to be the truth. Such a claim seems pretentious. Pluralism also tends to make us wary of making commitments to any clear and unambiguous view of reality—although this is exactly what evangelization asks of us. Yet to do so flies in the face of the dominant thinking today.

Pluralism tends to create a kind of "live and let live" atmosphere—and this is unfavorable to any kind of missionary activity. As Cardinal Francis George states: "Evangelization challenges us to 'propose,' not 'impose,' our faith in Jesus Christ and the Catholic Church."[21] While respecting other people's beliefs and religious practices, we should not hesitate to make truth claims about our Catholic tradition. Until we work this issue through, evangelization will continue to experience difficulty in assuming its claim to be the essential mission of the church.

New Perspectives in Theology

Pre–Vatican II theology, with its emphasis on the fear of hell, provided a strong motivation for people to engage in certain pious activities. Faithful Catholics usually baptized their children within two weeks of their birth to save them from original sin and to open the gates of heaven in case they died. They hastened to confession whenever they committed a mortal sin, lest they die outside the state of grace. For the same reason, they would call a priest to administer extreme unction to anyone in danger of dying.

The new perspectives in theology present a different lens through which we view the individual's journey to God. Grace and the experience of salvation are not limited to the sacraments. It is not always simply a matter of some people being "in" and some being "out," some saved and others damned. Our theology is not so quick to judge the state of someone's soul simply by whether or not that person has ordered his or her life according to the right standards of a good Catholic life.

This new way of theologizing poses a distinct challenge when we evangelize people with no active practice of the faith or no church affiliation whatever. Do we presume that they will go to hell if they don't come back to an active practice of the faith? Or that unless nonbelievers are baptized, they will go to hell? We are being asked to find a new motivation for evangelization. Rather than the fear of hell, Catholics are being called to work with all peoples so that God's kingdom of peace, justice, and love will reign on earth. The best answer is, as Francis Sullivan, SJ, states, we evangelize "out of love: love of Jesus Christ and of the people who will be graced by what his reign of love, peace, and justice will bring into their lives."[22]

In the past, things seemed so much clearer. We knew all the answers. We knew what you had to do to get to heaven and what took you to hell. Now we are not so sure, and this lack of clarity affects the way we carry out the work of evangelization.

Resistance to Change

One of the reasons parishes tend to favor maintenance over mission is that being mission-oriented is difficult. It is easier to take care of our own than to reach out to the stranger, the inactive Catholic, or the person with no church family. Making evangelization the essential mission of the church demands a change on many levels, especially in our vision of the church (ecclesiology), our understanding of the sacraments, particularly baptism (the call to become active disciples), and our spirituality (missionary). It is not surprising that people hesitate to take on the work of evangelization.

Challenge to the Clergy

There is no question that we are experiencing a crisis in priestly vocations today. The increase in the number of priestless parishes, the aging of the clergy, and the increasing demands being made on active clergy all attest to a serious problem. In the face of this crisis, many Catholic priests are reluctant to embrace the missionary calling of evangelization. "Why do we want to bring more people into the church? We can't take care of the ones we have" is a frequent response heard from the clergy. Does it ever occur to them that embracing the missionary vocation of the church anew might be the very thing that is needed to change the vocation picture?

CHAPTER THREE

Disciples and Disciple-Makers

Insight: Individual Catholics must recover disciple-making as a part of discipleship for the church to own evangelization as its essential mission.

Reflection

After Jesus returned to heaven, he and the archangel Gabriel were talking. Jesus still bore the marks of his crucifixion.

Gabriel said, "Master, you must have suffered horribly! Does everyone know and appreciate how much you loved them and what you did for them?"

Jesus replied, "Oh, no, not yet. Right now only a few people know."

Gabriel was perplexed. "Then what have you done to let everyone know about your love?"

Jesus answered, "I have asked Peter, James, Mary, and John, and a few other friends to tell people about me. Those who are told will tell others and still others, until the last man and the last woman in the farthest corners of the earth will have heard my story. They will know about my life, death, and resurrection. They will know of my love for them."

Gabriel frowned and looked rather skeptical. "Yes, but what if Peter and the others grow weary? What if the people who come after them forget? Surely you have made other plans?"

Jesus said: "Gabriel, I have no other plans. I am counting on them."[1]

Jesus trusts his friends to tell the story. He is counting on them to be disciple-makers. His trust was not misplaced; with the help of the Holy Spirit, the first disciples brought the good news of Jesus Christ to the known world. A good case can be made that disciple-making is a core feature of the early understanding of discipleship. How else can one account for the remarkable growth of the church in its first three centuries?

We need disciple-makers in our day as well. In this chapter, I will examine disciple-making from a Catholic perspective. I will show how it is an integral part of being a disciple today, just as much as in the early church. Finally, I will explore what happens when Catholics embrace disciple-making: the church is able to own evangelization as its essential mission.

The Meaning of *Disciple*

When we examine the use of the word *disciple* in the New Testament, we see that in essence it functions as a synonym for baptized Christian. If you were a baptized Christian, you were a disciple. The disciples of the gospels, then—not just the twelve apostles but all the people who followed Jesus and those who were part of the early church—model for us what it means to be a Christian today.

Discipleship has been a part of Catholic spirituality since the beginning. Thomas Rausch, SJ, in the *New Dictionary of Catholic Spirituality,* tells us that the classic medieval expression of discipleship was the *Imitation of Christ.* This devotional book, along with the *Spiritual Exercises* of Saint Ignatius of Loyola, best represents a Catholic spirituality of discipleship, one that gives preeminence to following Jesus and living according to gospel values.[2]

Vatican II referred to church members as disciples more than twenty times, yet the actual concept of discipleship does not play a major role in the council documents. Since the council, few theological works have discipleship as a central theme. Several theologians do acknowledge its central importance, but no one has developed a Catholic theology based on it.[3]

Despite this lack of theological emphasis, the concept of the baptized person as a disciple seems to enjoy some measure of favor in this post–Vatican II era. No doubt the biblical renewal has a great deal to do with it. Homilists talk about the need for

Catholics to see themselves as disciples, pointing to the first disciples as examples for us. Adult religious education and RCIA programs sometimes explore what it means for us to be disciples today. It is my thesis that discipleship actually plays a significant role in our Catholic life. Discipleship and disciple-making are important elements in a post–Vatican II vision of church.

What Is a Catholic Disciple-Maker?

Catholics are never going to see themselves as disciple-makers as long as they link the disciple-maker with the evangelist—whose picture in their minds is shaped by a long-held stereotype. This stereotype has been fed by their experience of televangelists, street-corner preachers, Bible-toting door-to-door missionaries, and campus evangelists. It is a negative stereotype reinforced by many critical portrayals of evangelists. Sinclair Lewis's book *Elmer Gantry,* Robert Duval's movie *The Apostle,* and reports of scandals in the media all contribute to it.

What is this stereotype? Usually, Catholics see the stereotypical evangelist as someone with a fundamentalist[4] view of the Bible—a view that is not part of our Catholic tradition. Catholics perceive the evangelist's message as overly simplistic and lacking nuance, a one-size-fits-all message with the premise that anyone who doesn't accept this view of things is in need of conversion. These evangelists believe that Catholics don't know the Bible and, by implication, are not really Christians because they haven't "turned their lives over to Jesus." What's more, the invitation to do this is usually couched in highly individualistic terms. It is a transaction that takes place between Christ and the believer, with little appreciation of Catholic sacraments and little regard for faith as a communal reality.

Many Catholics see this kind of religion as tinged with fanaticism. The true demands of religion, such as love of neighbor, are being replaced by a false construct, an artificial scale to measure authentic Christian life. On this scale, the word of God means strictly the Bible. Discipleship to Christ means abiding by arbitrary behaviors, such as not drinking alcohol or caffeine, not smoking or dancing, or not celebrating birthdays and holy days. When people view a religion's demands as unreasonable and unfounded, they tend to label that religion fanatical. This is the stereotype of the evangelist, and it inhibits Catholics from becoming disciple-makers because these two roles are linked in their minds.

This stereotype also tends to blind Catholics to several important realizations. First, fundamentalism and evangelism are not the same thing. Fundamentalism interprets the Bible literally and makes it the absolute standard of faith, placing it outside history and culture. Fundamentalists often focus on faith in Jesus Christ without explicitly linking it to any particular church or understanding of the Bible; hence the frequent "nondenominational" designation. Fundamentalism is a narrow and incomplete understanding of scripture, and is a blight on all forms of authentic religion. Evangelism, on the other hand, is a real and vital element of the Christian faith. Second, fundamentalism exists in our Catholic tradition as well, and is a serious problem for us. We Catholics are in no position to throw stones.

Last, there is much good in Protestant evangelism and we Catholics could learn some things from it. Some Protestants come from a covenanting tradition, where baptism follows some kind of personal conversion to Christ. They can teach a lot about the importance of personal decision as a foundation of discipleship to those churches that baptize people and then hope that they will become disciples! This emphasis on a strong personal relationship with Christ as the foundation of authentic Christian life is the core heritage of evangelical Protestantism and one that we can well imitate. With the loss over the last several decades of a strong Catholic family culture and parish affiliation, this growing up into discipleship may not happen for many Catholics.

Another feature of many Protestant churches is the small congregation, where it is difficult to be anonymous. This, of course, can be a curse as well as a blessing! However, in the best of circumstances such small church communities can foster a more active participation on the part of all members. This active participation in the missionary activities of the community is an expectation that comes with membership. Baptism is not seen so much as a sacrament of entitlement as a commission for ministry as a disciple of Christ.

Finally, we can learn much from the Protestant community about the centrality of scripture in the life of the Christian. Many former Catholics speak of joining Protestant evangelical congregations and discovering the power of the word in their lives in ways they never experienced as Catholics—long after Vatican renewal has been in place. We have a long way to go in making all baptized Christians hearers and doers of the word, and we can learn much from our Protestant brothers and sisters.

With this in mind, I would like to offer a picture of the Catholic disciple-maker. Some elements of this picture contrast sharply with those of the evangelist, but some elements are common to both.

Believes in a Triune God

Catholics have a different view of God than the one held by the fundamentalist evangelizer. That image tends to cast God as a stern judge, ready to cast into hell all who don't confess their belief in Jesus.[5] This does not reflect our Catholic experience of God as a loving Father.

Some years ago, Kenneth Woodward, writing about the Holy Spirit in *Newsweek* magazine, spoke of how many Christians practice serial monotheism; that is, they emphasize either the Father or the Son or the Holy Spirit, but not all three at once.[6] Catholics, however, emphasize all three. Although we may not be able to articulate adequately our trinitarian faith, Catholic life is trinitarian. When we make the sign of the cross, invoking the name of the Father, and the Son, and the Holy Spirit, we are expressing this trinitarian foundation of the faith.

A Catholic disciple-maker's life begins with baptism and is rooted firmly in a trinitarian experience of God, which is reinforced in worship, doctrine, spirituality, and the moral life. It has for guidance Matthew 28:16–20, which explicitly links discipleship with the Trinity. This passage defines discipleship as disciple-making, and it includes baptizing people in the name of the Trinity and teaching them to follow Jesus' way of life.

Catholic evangelizers start with the premise that this triune God is at work in the world and in all people.[7] The disciple-maker tries to help people become aware of God's presence in their lives and commit to becoming active disciples of Jesus Christ, because he is the way, the truth, and the life. Beginning with this assumption means that the first task of the disciple-maker is to listen rather than speak, to discern how God is already at work, rather than give a canned speech. Jesus promised that he would be with us throughout our mission (Matt 28:20) and said that, even in hostile circumstances, we are not to worry about what we are to say. It will be given to us. "For it will not be you who speak, but the spirit of your Father speaking through you" (Matt 10:19–20).

Perhaps the most critical difference between the Catholic and some Protestants' understanding of God is in the meaning of the incarnation. Catholics believe that the incarnation of the Son of God has hallowed our humanity. God is present in all creation and is at work in history. The Redeemer God and the Creator God are one and the same. The upshot of this is that we are not comfortable with the extremely narrow definition of salvation that is offered to us by the stereotypical fundamentalist evangelist. We have an instinctive sense that things are more complicated than that. Creation and redemption cannot be reduced to a rigid formula of turning one's life over to Jesus.

Andrew Greeley, as we mentioned in Chapter One, calls this broad understanding of the presence of grace in the world the *Catholic imagination.* Mary Catherine Hilkert, in *Naming Grace,* describes the elements of this Catholic or sacramental imagination: the goodness and redemption of creation, an incarnational Christology, the presence and action of the Holy Spirit in the community of the church, the transformation of humanity by grace, the role of human cooperation in the process of salvation, and the relationship between word and sacrament.[8]

Baroque art in many ways represents this incarnational perspective. It was fashioned in part as a conscious response to the more dialectical vision of the Reformation, where God was seen as more transcendent than immanent, as a God totally different from us, totally other. In contrast, baroque art is chock-full of people, beautiful scenes of nature, and stunning buildings. These are the paintings where we see cherubs everywhere, peeking out from behind trees and people's robes. In baroque art, God is right next to us. The world, and everything that is human, becomes a playground where God joins us and celebrates his vision for the world.

However we name this sacramental imagination, we know that fundamentalist evangelism utterly lacks it, and that is why we are so put off by it. For Catholics, God is love. And we come to experience this God who is love and enter into relationship with this God by the way we love one another. Thus, the mutual love of a husband and wife is a sacrament of God's love. The Christ we proclaim is the Christ we continue to meet in each other. The Holy Spirit working in us does not so much give us messages or extraordinary revelations, but transforms our natural powers so we can come to the truth in love, and generally does this in community. We used to say, "Grace builds on nature." A better way of putting this, however, is, "Grace does not destroy nature but rather brings it to its perfection." It is not a question of grace sitting on top of an inherently negative or evil nature; instead, grace enters nature and moves it toward its supernatural destiny.[9] Nothing truly human is foreign to a Catholic way of life. A Catholic disciple-maker is an ambassador of a different vision of redemption than the one the fundamentalist represents. A Catholic disciple-maker represents a triune God who works in history in manifold ways through Jesus and the Holy Spirit.

Devoted to Prayer

Both the Protestant evangelist and the Catholic disciple-maker are devoted to prayer. The prayer tends to take different forms, but each has its strengths. The Protestant evangelist tends to pray informally and from the heart, using his or her own words to speak to God. There is no hesitation in praying spontaneously, something we Catholics often are not comfortable doing. This is an area where we can learn from Protestant evangelists.

Because Catholics root evangelization in the Trinity, prayer takes on added importance. Disciple-making is God's work; therefore we need to pray in order to do our part. Luke, more than any other gospel writer, emphasizes the importance of prayer in disciple-making, not only in the life of Jesus but especially in the life of the Christian community. Only in Luke's gospel do the disciples ask Jesus to teach them to pray (11:1). Throughout Acts, the community is depicted at prayer, especially at crucial moments relating to the mission (1:14; 10:9–30; 11:5; 13:3) and their community life (1:24; 2:42; 6:4). In John's gospel, Jesus explicitly prays for those who will believe in him through the word of the disciples (John 17:20). Paul urges Christians to pray unceasingly (1 Thess 5:17), making their requests known to God "by prayer and petition, with thanksgiving" (Phil 4:6).

It stands to reason, then, that the specific action of disciple-making would be undertaken in a spirit of prayer, as we recognize that it is the Holy Spirit who changes hearts. Pope Paul VI, in defining evangelization, makes the point that it is by the power of the gospel that the world is changed (*EN*, no.18). Prayer recognizes that the Holy Spirit is the principal agent of evangelization and that we are servants of God in this work. Prayer gives courage, focus, and confidence to the disciple-maker in preparing for and carrying out this work.

The key question for a disciple-maker is not whether I will succeed (that's God's business) but whether I am called to take this outreaching action. A popular saying, attributed to Mother Teresa, captures this point: God asks us not to be successful but to be faithful. Prayer enables us to discern God's will in these circumstances and gives us the courage to do it.

Personally Committed

Like the Protestant evangelist, the Catholic disciple-maker is personally committed to faith. Catholicism is profoundly personal in its practice. It does not allow vicarious discipleship. One of my favorite scriptures that expresses this reality comes from 1 John 4:16: we have come to know and believe in the love God has for us [as we have experienced it in our life in Christ Jesus]. No one can be a disciple for me; it depends on my own personal commitment. Becoming a disciple-maker also depends upon personal commitment.

In the Catholic Church, we baptize most people when they are infants and trust that they will become disciples through the experience of being brought up in the community of the church.

However, as we well know, this may or may not happen. Many people who are baptized when they are infants are never catechized, because their families do not actively practice the faith or belong to the community of the church. Thus, baptism has not been followed by the kind of *kerygmatic* commitment essential to the Christian life—that is, a life through which we come to believe in Jesus as our Lord and Savior.

Whether raised in the community of the church or not, each person still needs to make a conscious decision to be a follower of Jesus Christ. For people who grow up in an active Catholic family, an authentic domestic church as we have come to know it in the post–Vatican II perspective,[10] that decision may not be a dramatic one, made at a specific moment. Rather, it is often a dynamic, cumulative process, made over time. The sacrament of confirmation may be part of that process. It is usually presented to young people as an opportunity for them to ratify the baptismal commitment made for them by their parents and godparents.

Where there has been no active practice of the faith after baptism, the decision to live as a disciple of Christ is often dramatic, coming about as part of an adult faith conversion. But however that decision is made, it is a highly personal one that each of us must make at some point in our lives.

We see this personal aspect of disciple-making in the New Testament; Jesus constantly called people to make a decision to follow him. Not everyone did. The author of John's gospel gives personal encounters with Jesus a definite ultimacy: the person must choose between light or darkness, life or death. At one point, some people decide to abandon Jesus, who turns to Peter and asks: "Do you also wish to go away?" Peter answers: "Lord, to whom can we go? You have the words of eternal life" (John 6:67–68).

Lives in Community

Yet the personal decision to live as a disciple of Jesus is also a communal affair. John D. Zizioulas says the "person cannot exist without communion."[11] One person is no person. Richard McBrien echoes that sentiment when he says, "Human existence is co-existence."[12] Catholic disciple-makers come out of a communal experience of faith, and they invite other people to that same experience. Here the Catholic disciple-maker differs from fundamentalist evangelists, especially media types, who tend to focus less on this communal element. The Rite of Christian Initiation of Adults makes this aspect of Catholicism very clear: the process of becoming a Catholic Christian is a thoroughly communal experience.

An authentic community is perhaps the most powerful evangelizing tool the church has today. More and more in our society, we are seeing that extreme individualism is killing individuals. People are disconnected from the bonds that protect and support them when faced with life-threatening conditions: loneliness, addiction, and violence. People are looking for community. The church offers a way of life in which people care about one another and are bonded to one another in a common commitment of faith. God is present, people are connected, and there is a powerful experience of hope. This is very attractive to people when it is real—and it is real in the church. This notion of community is not simply a conceptual assertion of Vatican II, but also a lived experience of the faithful. Ordinary Catholics experience their parishes as faith communities. Although Catholicism has institutional aspects, and parishes are part of the diocesan and universal church, to be a Catholic is not only to be part of an institution, it also is to share in the life of a community.

The faith community is united in worship, common belief, and common practice. These bonds give a shared identity and meaning to the word *Catholic*. Today, as we know, there is much tension around these common bonds in both the universal church and in the parish. It is difficult to hold the church together. But Catholics continue to claim membership in the faith community of the parish because the parish signifies what it means to be Catholic. It unites Catholics with all others of the same name, under the leadership of the pope and the bishops. We are not Congregationalists. Like it or not, Catholicism embraces all these elements under the name of community.

This communal dimension is inherent in the New Testament picture of the disciples. The disciples are the people who are in relationship with Jesus and who follow him. Some of them, as

Gerhard Lohfink points out in *Jesus and Community,* leave behind family, friends, and work to follow literally behind him; together, they constitute a new family.[13] Others bear the name *disciple* but do not share that itinerant lifestyle. *Disciple* is not limited to the Twelve and it includes both women and men.

The gospels all assert, in different ways, that the disciples' relationship with Jesus brings them into a relationship with the Father and the Spirit. Thus, the community of the disciples pictured in the New Testament anticipates a later understanding of the church as a communion in the life of the triune God. The gospels also assert that the disciples' relationship with Jesus commits them to a life in which they seek to love God above all things and their neighbor as themselves. Matthew and Luke extend this love to include enemies. In John's gospel, the disciples' love for each other becomes a major theme: the world will know you are my disciples by the love you have for each other.

In the New Testament letters, this theme becomes a major focus. Paul asks how the Corinthian community can come together to celebrate the Eucharist when their behavior toward one another undercuts the very meaning of the sacrament. The hymn on love in 1 Corinthians is more than a paean to be read at Christian weddings. It is a biting critique of a community big on knowledge but weak in the practice of the community's most fundamental virtue: love (1 Cor 11:17–12:13). In the first letter of John (4:20–21), the writer asks: How can you claim to love God, whom you cannot see, when you do not love the brother you do see?

The entire New Testament confirms that creating authentic, loving community is the major challenge of Christian living. It is the pearl of great price that so many people seek and do not find. If its evangelizing potential is great, it is precisely because the challenge is so real. A Catholic disciple-maker is formed by and lives in this experience of community and invites others to share it.

Ongoing Conversion

Someone I know had the following experience. On the twenty-ninth anniversary of their marriage, her husband informed her that he wanted his freedom: no discussion, no explanation, no counseling—just a quick exit. The wife was left defenseless. The divorce went through. Shortly afterward, the husband married his secretary. The whole thing was probably a midlife crisis.

I had known the husband since he was in high school. Raised as a Catholic, he had been in church every Sunday of his life, from his infancy to the breakup. How can someone be in church every Sunday, hear what we hear, do what we do—and engage in behavior that contradicts it all? But the truth is that it could happen to any one of us if we fail to maintain a vital connection with Jesus Christ in our lives. A one-time conversion does not cut it. Discipleship is a life of ongoing conversion. This is something emphasized more in the Catholic tradition than in the Protestant.

The New Testament image of discipleship is that of a journey, with good times and bad, ups and downs, successes and failures, betrayals and reconciliations. Today, as I write this, the Catholic Church in the United States is undergoing a severe trial over the issue of clergy sex abuse. Unfortunately, this is a train that is going to make many stops before it comes to a halt. The experience reinforces an important point of post–Vatican II theology: we have a common unity in baptism, which precedes any later distinctions that arise from holy orders. As the document *Decree on the Ministry and Life of Priests* states: "[T]hey [priests] are disciples of the Lord along with all the faithful . . . [they are] brothers among brothers and sisters as members of the same body of Christ which all are commanded to build."[14] As disciples of Jesus Christ, all of us—clerical leadership and laity— are in need of ongoing conversion. All too often, clerical exemption and arrogance have prevented us from taking our common journey of conversion with the whole church. Augustine once said: "For you I am a bishop; with you I am a Christian." Our hope lies in our common unity as disciples, not in an emphasis on our separate orders, true though the distinction may be.

In the New Testament, discipleship is synonymous with ongoing conversion. Disciples are works in progress, men and women who are continually being remade through their relationship with Jesus. It is a picture of the not-quite-perfect followers of Jesus, and this is what makes it such a compelling image of the disciple-maker. Far from being fanatics, far from inviting people into an unrealistic way of life, disciple-makers call people to be truly human by living in the presence of a love that allows us to keep growing. The operative words of New Testament discipleship are *learning, struggle,* and *growth.* As one writer stated, "Unwavering faith is to be seen more as a goal of discipleship than as a prerequisite."[15]

The call to ongoing conversion as a disciple begins with baptism. It involves the experience of a graced relationship to God in Christ, in which our sins are forgiven and we are given new life. We become members of the community of disciples called the church. We are charged with living a new life, based on the values of the gospel. And, because the community of the church has its origins in the resurrection, the disciple's journey follows Jesus on his journey to the cross.

From Matthew, we learn that a disciple has to struggle to be faithful to Jesus' teachings and way of life. The Beatitudes are not only a shorthand synopsis of who Jesus is, but also a portrait of the faithful disciple as well. For Matthew, what is core is putting the teaching into action. Crying out "Lord, Lord," won't do it. Ongoing conversion means we are always working to transform our lives into a work of love. Sometimes the disciples falter and fail badly as they try to do this.[16] Sometimes they are open and learn their lesson; sometimes they have to learn the hard way—as when they abandon Jesus. The disciples' experience reveals that repentance and reconciliation form an ongoing part of the life of the disciple.

Luke's vision of discipleship is unique because his narrative extends beyond Jesus' ministry into the life of the early church. Mary is presented as an ideal disciple, who listens to God's word and does it (Luke 1:38, 45; 8:21; 10:38–42; 11:27–28; Acts 1:13–14). Luke emphasizes the role of the Holy Spirit in Jesus' life and in the lives of the early disciples. Like Matthew, he presents a challenging portrait of the disciple in his Beatitudes, focusing especially on their need to minister to the poor, as Jesus did. Disciples are to take up their cross daily and follow Jesus. In the gospel, Luke paints a clear picture of the cost of discipleship by describing the specific conditions for following Jesus (14:25–33). In Acts 5, would-be disciples are treated harshly when they deliberately turn away from the ideal of discipleship set before them, but for those who ask, forgiveness is always given.

According to John's gospel, a disciple is someone who believes in Jesus. *Believing* is a comprehensive term; it includes action as well as thought. It is the core of what it means to be a disciple of Christ, and it separates the disciple from the world. The Gospel of John is the story of the disciples' encounters and journeys with Jesus as their path to becoming authentic believers, where *believer* is synonymous with *disciple*.[17] They go through various trials: misunderstandings, lack of awareness, failure to grasp even the most basic facts of Jesus' mission and ministry, failure to understand the call to serve rather than be served, and failure to understand "the hour" of ultimate revelation in his death.[18]

In what is perhaps the most profound commentary on discipleship in John's gospel, Jesus tells the disciples: "Very truly, I tell you, unless a grain of wheat falls into the earth and dies, it remains just a single grain; but if it dies, it bears much fruit. Those who love their life lose it, and those who hate their life in this world will keep it for eternal life. Whoever serves me must follow me, and where I am, there will my servant be also" (12:24–26). Discipleship is a conversion road and disciple-makers are keenly aware of its ongoing character.

Committed to Dialogue[19]

While proclaiming the message of God in Jesus Christ, the evangelizing Church must always remember that her task is not exercised in a complete void. For the Holy Spirit, the Spirit of Christ, is present and active among the hearers of the Good News even before the Church's missionary action comes into operation. They may in many cases have already responded implicitly to God's offer of salvation...they may have already been touched by the Spirit....[20]

In many ways, listening is the first virtue of the evangelizer. How is God already at work in the hearts of those whom we evangelize? Before we speak, we must listen. Thus, there is always room for dialogue in the process of sharing the good news. Evangelization doesn't mean that we have all the answers. A listening posture also opens us to mutuality. We are changed by our encounter. The principle that dialogue is an essential part of evangelization is not merely operative in ecumenical and interreligious encounters. It ought to be present in all forms of evangelization; this openness to dialogue is a particular strength of the Catholic disciple-maker.

One form that this dialogical dimension of evangelization takes is ordinary conversation with people, which sometimes yields extraordinary results when it touches upon spiritual matters. Saint Philip Neri was a master of this type of "evangelizing conversation." During those difficult times right after the Reformation had begun, Philip went out onto the streets of Rome and engaged people in conversation in the hopes of calling them to renewal. He was eminently successful in his efforts. His methods were simple, ingenious, and quite prophetic. It is noteworthy that Philip did a good deal of this ministry on his own, as a layman. He came to Rome in 1534 and was not ordained until 1551, and then only reluctantly. He spent a good deal of time with the people—on the streets of Rome, using his natural, attractive gifts of personality to engage people in spiritual conversation. He had a great sense of humor and was something of a clown, not averse to outlandish means to accomplish his ends. As Cardinal Newman said about Philip: "Nothing was too high for him, nothing too low."[21] What is probably most significant about Philip's evangelizing conversations is that they arose out of a powerful experience of God's love. He was especially effective with young people, but he embraced rich and poor alike, seeking to open them to the love of Christ.

Importance of Witness and Proclamation

Saint Francis of Assisi is supposed to have said: "Proclaim the Gospel at all times and, if necessary, use words." Paul VI points out: "The first means of evangelization is the witness of an authentically Christian life" (*EN*, no. 41). He goes on to point out that people believe witnesses more readily than teachers, because witnesses evidence in their conduct a compelling proclamation of the word. One of our contemporary sayings expresses this: "You can't talk the talk unless you walk the walk." There is no substitute for a life authentically lived. A disciple-maker is, first of all, a witness.

Yet the witness of life must often be accompanied by proclamation. People want to hear the reason for our hope (1 Pet 3:15). We must be ready to tell them how our belief in Jesus Christ and our life in the Catholic Church explain the way we live. One of the most effective tools of a disciple-maker is the ability to share his or her faith story. Everyone loves a good story. A disciple-maker must fashion a convincing narrative and be ready to share it when appropriate. At the heart of a disciple-maker's story must be the testimony of the experience of coming to know and believe in the Lord Jesus and experiencing the gift of new life in him. To paraphrase John 20:20, we tell these witness stories so others may come to believe that Jesus is the Messiah, the Son of God, and that through their belief people may come to have life in his name. This is an area where we Catholics could learn much from Protestant evangelists, who have a long history of proclamation.

Disciple-makers invite people to become followers of Jesus Christ. Prior to the Second Vatican Council, the Catholic Church badly needed renewal. In many ways, institutional Catholicism was failing to bring people into relationship with Jesus Christ. Many aspects needed reformation: laws, rituals, authority structures, doctrines, and morals. Since the council, we have been struggling to make such badly needed changes, and we are not finished with that renewal agenda. Fixing our eyes on Christ and faithfully continuing the renewal are part of the ongoing conversion of a church that is a community of disciples. Disciple-makers are inviting people to become part of a church of disciples in need of renewal. Yet, the Catholic community of believers is still a place where all who seek Christ will find him.

A disciple-maker is not primarily an apologist, important as that task may be. A disciple-maker doesn't have to have all the answers. Many of those answers are available, and we may have to find someone who has them, but we do not have to know everything about the Catholic way of life. It is too complex a story, so we need to keep the simple things simple.

The Holy Spirit, the principal agent of evangelization, is the one who changes hearts. Therefore, the disciple-maker needs to root his or her efforts in prayer and must rely on the Holy Spirit. Disciple-makers pray about how and when we should approach people, trusting in the Lord to give us wisdom about what to say and putting the entire process in his hands. Our concern is not success but fidelity to the task.

A disciple-maker always invites and is always willing to be a companion on the journey. The operative words are the words of Jesus: "Come and see." Come and you will see for yourself. So much will become clear after a person begins to walk the journey of discipleship himself or herself. There is no need to settle all things in advance. This is the beauty of the RCIA: it is a journey with many points along the way where people can stop and decide if they really want to continue. The task of the disciple-maker is to bring people to the point where they are willing to start the journey.

What does a Catholic disciple-maker look like? Here are some examples of Catholic disciple-makers in action.

- When a Catholic, trying to share his or her faith with someone else, struggles to put into words the reason for hoping in Jesus Christ, that person is a disciple-maker.

- When a preacher struggles to proclaim the faith to help people live their lives as modern-day disciples, and connects the word with life, he or she is a disciple-maker.

- When parents give themselves to the unending task of witnessing to and proclaiming their faith in Jesus Christ by their words and example, they are disciple-makers.

- When a parishioner visits prisoners and tries to help them discover the meaning of their lives in the light of the Christ who loves them, that person is a disciple-maker.

- When a person who works with the RCIA helps people come to faith in Jesus Christ through the rites and stages of their faith journey, that person is a disciple-maker.

- When a frequent flier takes every opportunity to meet people and converse with them in ways that open them to conversations that allow them to talk about their commitment to Christ, that person is a disciple-maker.

- When a Catholic reaches out to invite another person to join us in some activity or event for the purpose of sharing our Catholic way of life, that person is a disciple-maker.

Conclusion

Discipleship is a form of spirituality that impacts our way of thinking, feeling, and behaving; it transforms our lives.[22] Because discipleship is intensely personal, it can help change evangelization from a faraway, corporate issue that doesn't affect us to something we can claim and appropriate as our own. Therefore, evangelization, when we look at it "up front and personal," translates into making a commitment to be a disciple-maker as an integral part of our personal spirituality.

This chapter began with a simple parable. God has no other plan; therefore we must do it.

CHAPTER FOUR

EVANGELIZATION IS OUR DEEPEST IDENTITY

Insight: Evangelization is the church's deepest identity because our God is a missionary God.

Reflection

Our images of God emerge from our different experiences. One of my images of God comes from the free, uninhibited love shown by Down's syndrome children. I had a cousin, Danny Lila, who had this condition. He was born suffering, but probably never knew it. He died when he was seventeen, and in his short life brought a lot of love into the world. Danny was affectionate, innocent, simple, and happy. And he made other people happy. He loved everyone, and he never rationed his love. He didn't measure it out to people like a scarce commodity. Love flowed out of him like a river, completely unself-consciously. It came naturally to him. Danny didn't have to be born again; he came as a ready-made gift to us.

In his unselfish and unself-conscious love for people, Danny reminds me of the kind of overflowing love that God has for us—the love that is the root and source of all our evangelization efforts.

Identity

When Catholics are asked to share their faith with others, they tend to become uncomfortable. Their immediate reaction is, "This is not who I am." These feelings must be respected, but I question the notion that this is not who Catholics are (and, by implication, what Catholics do). This is who we are. We are evangelizers. Paul VI said that evangelization is the church's deepest identity—and the deepest identity of individual Catholics as well.

What are the implications of this? First of all, it means that we were made to evangelize—all of us. It is God's purpose for all Catholics, not just for the saints. It is simply part of being Catholic, part of how we are faithful to God. Moreover, it is not an obligation imposed on us from outside; rather, it is a calling that arises from within, because it is woven into our very being. It is how we are most true to ourselves.

More than this, however, is the fact that evangelization is not our work; it is God's work. When we evangelize, we participate in the missionary activity of God. And this is why evangelization is the church's deepest identity: it is because our God is a missionary God. John Paul II states this truth with great force in *Redemptoris Missio*: "This definitive self-revelation of God is the fundamental reason why the church is missionary by her very nature. She cannot do other than proclaim the gospel, that is, the fullness of the truth which God has enabled us to know about himself" (no. 5). And *Decree on the Church's Missionary Activity* states: "The Church on earth is by its very nature missionary since, according to the plan of the Father, it has its origin in the mission of the Son and the Holy Spirit. This plan flows from 'fountain-like love,' the love of God the Father."[1]

Our God Is a Missionary God

Seeing our evangelizing activity as a participation in the very missionary activity of God is taking us back to our roots. As John Paul II points out in *Redemptoris Missio*, the Second Vatican Council made the same kind of connection when it stated that the church was missionary in nature and based that missionary character in a "dynamic way on the Trinitarian mission itself" (no. 1). Evangelization is God's work, because it is a participation in the original missionary activity of God, who sends the Son and the Spirit for our salvation.

A cursory glance at the principal documents of contemporary Catholic evangelization *(Evangelii Nuntiandi, Redemptoris*

Missio, and *Go and Make Disciples),* including those of Vatican II, shows how evangelization is anchored in the life of the triune God. Everything begins with the passionate, overflowing, and outreaching love of the Father, who sends the Son to share in the fullness of our human life and the Holy Spirit to carry out the transformation of the world into the image of Christ. Traditional theology speaks of these "sendings" as missions. God is outreaching love, coming to us from the Father through the Son and the Spirit.

In the New Testament, Jesus and the Holy Spirit carry out God's missionary intentions. The Synoptic Gospels portray Jesus as the agent of the Father, coming to inaugurate the reign of God. The early Christian community, as depicted in Acts, understood Jesus as the Son who came to carry out the Father's plan. John has the strongest missionary language of all the gospels: Jesus is the one who has been sent. As the Father has sent Jesus, so Jesus breathes the Holy Spirit upon the disciples and sends them out to proclaim the gospel to all who would believe and have eternal life.[2]

A parallel picture is drawn of the Holy Spirit. The Synoptics describe the Spirit in much the same way the Old Testament does—as the embodiment of God's life-giving power. All the gospels present Jesus as a man upon whom the Spirit descends from the Father at his baptism. Luke in particular emphasizes the role of the Spirit in Jesus' life and in the life of the early church. The Gospel of John emphasizes the role and mission of the Holy Spirit as one sent from the Father (and the Son—see John 15:26) after Jesus' death and resurrection. Both John and the Acts of the Apostles give the Holy Spirit a prominent role in the missionary activity of the church. The Holy Spirit changes hearts, gifts people for ministry, and brings about the dynamic transformation of the world according to the values of the gospel.

The New Testament often speaks of God in triadic language that prepares the way for the later formulation of the dogma of the Trinity. We see this threefold pattern in Acts and the Pauline letters, where doxologies, greetings, and discursive passages refer to the roles of the Son, the Spirit, and the Father.[3] We see the same pattern in the letters ascribed to but not written by Paul himself, and also in the pastorals.[4]

The New Testament reveals the one God of the Hebrew faith, now acting in the world in the persons of the Son and the Spirit. The language used to describe the Son and the Spirit makes clear that they are of divine origin, are divine agents, and in some way share in the very life of the one God. But it took several hundred years for the church to formulate clearly its belief in a three-personed God and to find a language to express this mystery: God is one yet three, utterly beyond all creatures but completely present to them and engaged in the world.

That story is too complicated and lengthy to deal with here. However, it is important to note that in the early centuries of its existence, the church came to understand with greater clarity the *missionary* character of this three-personed God. In recent years, theologians have helped us understand that we come to know God through God's missionary activity in the world. One cannot think of God apart from the sphere of God's activity. The very nature of God is revealed to us in the missionary activity of the Son and the Holy Spirit.[5]

The Father Is Love

What is this very nature of God? It can be summed up in one word: love. It is overflowing, outreaching, and passionate. The Second Vatican Council calls it God's "fountain-like love."[6] It is this love that is the source of God's missionary activity.

Both Old and New Testaments speak about God's activity in the world arising out of his abundant love—outreaching, overflowing, and relentless. Renewed trinitarian theology helps us appreciate this passionate character of God's love. It tells us that God's very being is relational, reaching out to the other within the Godhead, to us, and to the world.[7] In fact, trinitarian theology has helped us redefine personhood in terms of identity-in-relation. The very being of God is to exist for the other. Personhood in God means self-donation, being other-oriented, and being toward-the-other rather than for oneself. This overflowing love originates in the Father, finds expression in the Son, who is love's word, and is communicated to us through the Holy Spirit, who is love's breath.

John tells us that God is love (1 John 4:8). And Augustine says: "Are you contemplating what God is like? Everything you imagine, God is not. Everything you put in your thoughts, God is not. But if you wish to savor something of God, then know that God is love, the same love by which we love one another."[8]

Although I come from Minnesota, the land of ten thousand lakes, I never had much interest in them. They bored me. A lake is just there; it doesn't come from anywhere or go anywhere. But I grew up on the banks of the Mississippi River—a five-minute drive from our house—and the river has always held a certain mystery for me. It came from another place and flowed past us on its way to somewhere else, far away. When I was a teenager, I had the opportunity to travel to the source of the Mississippi, at Lake Itasca in northern Minnesota, where one can walk across the "Father of Many Waters." Many years later, after I was ordained and stationed in Austin, Texas, I took a trip to New Orleans. I had more interest in following the Mississippi down to the Gulf than in going into New Orleans. It was a thrill: I had been to the source and was now going down to the mouth of this great river.

God's love is like the current of the river—always flowing outward, sometimes easy and gentle, sometimes powerful and relentless as it courses through our lives and through history. As one popular religious song expresses it: "Love is flowing like a river." Walter Kasper says that God the Father is the "unoriginated origin of divine love, a pure source, a pure overflowing."[9] Michael Downey tells us that to say that God is love is to say that God is not enclosed and not turned inward; rather, God is the life that "pours itself forth: constantly, abundantly, excessively, never-to-stop-coming-as-gift."[10]

Both the Old and New Testaments have wonderful images and stories of this overflowing, outreaching love of God. But it is hard to find a more touching image than the one offered by the prophet Hosea. He came to experience the depths of God's love through his relationship with his wife, Gomer. Although the sequence of events is unclear, apparently, after Hosea married Gomer, she became unfaithful and even became a temple prostitute. Hosea resolved to divorce her—but could not. His love for her wouldn't allow him to go through with it. And, just as Hosea could not give up his unfaithful wife, God could not renounce Israel, even when it turned away from him. Hosea boldly pictures God's relationship with Israel as a marriage.

In another part of Hosea, Chapter 11, there is an expression of God's tender love for unfaithful Israel that has no parallel in the entire Old Testament. The image of God changes from loving husband to loving parent, and the image of Israel changes from unfaithful wife to rebellious son. Like a loving parent, God teaches the child to walk, takes the child in his arms, feeds and heals him. But Israel does not recognize or return God's love, and is punished. Then, in a powerful change of heart, God says, "How can I give you up, Ephraim? How can I hand you over, O Israel?...My heart recoils within me; my compassion grows warm and tender. I will not execute my fierce anger; I will not again destroy Ephraim; for I am God and no mortal, the Holy One in your midst, and I will not come in wrath"(11:8–9). Why is God's heart moved? Why does God show such overflowing compassion for Israel? Because this is who God is. As Hosea could not stop loving Gomer, so God cannot stop loving Israel. This is who God is.

Although God is never mentioned in the Song of Songs, its very inclusion in the canon favors the interpretation that our relationship to God is like the passionate love between a man and his beloved. It is possible that this love poem may have originally been written to celebrate the wedding of a king.[11] It is interesting that the Bible begins and ends with the image of a marriage. Thus, in the Christian reading of the book, we see powerful support for Augustine's dictum that if we want to know who God is, we must talk about love—the same love that human beings have for one another. We come to know something of the love of God in the sexual love of man and woman.

The passion and depth of God's love are often symbolized in both the Old and New Testaments by the expression that God feels moved from the womb[12] (*rechamim* in Hebrew) or from the innards (*splanchna* in Greek). God's love strives to embody itself in flesh. This "bodily passion" of God's love as described in the Old Testament takes on a new reality in the incarnation.

Therefore, when the New Testament describes Jesus' compassionate love for the poor in terms of having his innards moved, we can see a strong connection to the passionate character of God's love as it is described in the Old Testament.

Nor can we overlook the frequent image of the Lord as a shepherd, an image immortalized in the twenty-third psalm. The shepherd cares for the sheep, leads them to restful waters, and guides them in right paths through the valley of darkness. In both Matthew and Luke, Jesus describes God as a shepherd who goes out in search of a lost sheep. The words of 1 Peter 5:7 about God's love reflect the shepherd's loving care: "Cast all your anxiety on him, because he cares for you."

The parables offer countless images of God's outreaching love. None, perhaps, is more touching than Luke's "prodigal father," who catches sight of his son from a long way off and is moved with compassion *(splanchniznomai)* that is extravagant, even excessive; for to be "prodigal" means not only to spend lavishly, like the son, but to *give* lavishly, like the father, who lavishly gives his love. He runs to his son and embraces and kisses him (15:20).

John's gospel makes the outreaching love of God a major theme: "For God so loved the world that he gave his only Son, so that everyone who believes in him may not perish but may have eternal life" (3:16). According to John, the ultimate revelation of God's love takes place on the cross. "No one has greater love than this, to lay down one's life for one's friends" (15:13). Jesus' hour of darkness is paradoxically the hour of greatest light because, in that moment, God's love is revealed to the world.

The Judeo-Christian tradition holds that God created human beings in his own image; we see this tradition expressed in the creation narrative in Genesis. There are many different interpretations of what that might mean. The late Thomas Merton has this to say about it: "To say I am made in the image of God is to say love is the reason for my existence, for God is love. Love is my true identity. Selflessness is my true self. Love is my true character. Love is my name."[13]

As human beings, then, we are love because God is love. And the root and source of the church's evangelizing activity must be

this same love. This contrasts greatly with an excessive emphasis on saving people from damnation, as if the outcome of salvation or damnation were simply two equal possibilities in
God's plan. Dermot Lane points out in *Keeping Hope Alive:*
"[H]eaven and hell do not enjoy the same philosophical or theological status within Christian eschatology." The promise of
salvation (heaven) and the possibility of the loss (hell) are not on
the same plane.[14] God's will is for our salvation; hell is not something God wills for us (Eph 1:1–19). God desires to save us in
love. Evangelizers, therefore, root their message in the saving
love of God, even as they acknowledge the possibility of refusal
of that love.

We cannot always adequately articulate the mystery of the
three-personed God and his loving plan for our salvation. But
evangelization immerses us in the mystery, leading us to contemplate the Trinity until it is not so much that we grasp the
reality but that we are grasped by it.[15] We are, as the preface of
Christmas so beautifully proclaims, "caught up in the love of the
God that we cannot see." Our evangelizing activity is a participation in the mystery of God's loving missionary activity on
behalf of the world.

The Son Is Love's Word

In a trinitarian perspective, God is the unoriginated source,
the unbegotten begetter, the invisible one who reveals himself to
us in the person of Jesus. The very being of God is communicated to us in the person of the Son. Thus, Jesus is love's word.
In the Son, God expresses, communicates, and reveals his own
loving self in the flesh of Jesus and in our human history. One of
the most compelling expressions of this is Pope Paul VI's designation of Jesus as the good news of God (*EN*, no. 7). Jesus is the
very expression of everything that God wants to say to the
world. This is what John means in his gospel when he says that
God was the Word and the Word became flesh.

Furthermore, this event—God expressing his loving self in
the Word—is not something that took place once in history; it is
an ongoing reality. The incarnation is not simply a reference to
a past event. The Word is love *expressing* and the Spirit is love

breathing here and now in our time. "In and through the Word, God communicates, speechifies, expresses God's love...God weeps and washes, God is silent and listens . . . God visits, eats and rests, feels pain, he touches, he suffers, he even dies."[16]

Theologians, borrowing from Philippians 2:7, speak of the *kenosis,* or self-emptying, of God in Jesus because Jesus pours himself out in love. Jesus, as love's word, brings to expression God's infinite love for us. He is utterly one with us in our human condition through the incarnation. Downey captures the meaning of the incarnation in the word *vulnerability*.

> Vulnerability may be understood as the capacity to be open, to be attracted, touched, or moved by the draw of God's love as this is experienced in one's own life or in the lives of others. It is vulnerability that enables one to enter into relationships of interpersonal communication and communion with others who recognize their own weakness and need. Vulnerability requires the integrity and the strength—indeed the power—to risk enormous pain, to bear the burdens of the darkest hour without avoidance, denial, and deception. It demands the stamina to be open in order to be touched in one's fragility. Vulnerability implies a willingness to lose oneself, to be knocked off center by the claim of the other upon one in the hope of finding one's true self. It demands readiness to die to one's self so that one might truly live.[17]

The expression of God's vulnerability is Jesus, revealed particularly in Jesus' self-emptying death on the cross. Jesus is vulnerable enough to undergo risk and loss for the good of the other. This is true compassion. Thus Jesus is love's word, love's expression of compassion. "Compassion is tenderness moved to action."[18]

The love of God that is the source of the sending of the Son and the Spirit is a suffering love, a love full of compassion. It leads ultimately to the Father's gift of the Son in love on the cross. "For God so loved the world that he gave his only Son..." (John 3:16). Yet this runs counter to the teaching of classical theology, which saw suffering only in the human nature of Christ.

The divine person of Christ could not suffer and God could not suffer. God was perfect and immutable—ideas imported from Greek philosophy—and could not change;[19] therefore, God could not suffer. This issue lay at the heart of the Arian heresy. The Arians accepted the suffering of Christ and so could not bring themselves to acknowledge him as divine, precisely *because* he suffered.

God is love. But does God suffer? This issue has become even more pressing in a post-Holocaust world. We human beings have come to realize that love and suffering are inextricably tied. We cannot understand a divine love that looks on our world and does not suffer. Unless a trinitarian theology can speak meaningfully to this issue of suffering, it has nothing to say to the modern world. As Kasper says, "The question of God and the question of suffering belong together."[20]

In one of its most significant contributions, modern trinitarian theology has tried to wrestle with this issue by bringing love's suffering into the very heart of God. Kasper says it is "impossible to dismiss all this as simple anthropomorphism, or to ascribe it solely to the human nature of Jesus, while leaving his divinity untouched by it."[21] He offers examples of how earlier church fathers asserted the suffering of God, and finds an especially fruitful path set out by Origen, who speaks of the suffering of God that comes from love:

> If God suffers, then he suffers in a divine manner, that is, his sufferings are an expression of his freedom; suffering does not befall God, rather he freely allows it to touch him. He does not suffer, as creatures do, from a lack of being; he suffers out of love and by reason of his love, which is the overflow of his being.... Because God is the omnipotence of love, he can as it were indulge in the weakness of love; he can enter into suffering and death without perishing therein.[22]

The God we know through salvation history and the three-personed God who exists for all eternity are one and the same. The Father loves us and so cannot be untouched by the human condition. In love, God sends us the Son, who dies on the cross for us. Yet how do we explain the suffering of God in light of classical theology's picture of God as immutable, perfect, and so on? LaCugna responds: "It is more sound procedure to revise or overturn the premise of God's impassibility in the light of the Cross, rather than to allow an axiom from Greek philosophy to predispose the conclusions of theology."[23]

The very nature of God is to love; God cannot be God without reaching out in love to us. LaCugna says that love is the basic and fundamental characteristic of God.[24] And the nature of this divine love is to suffer, because love entails suffering. Of course, the issue of suffering is only adequately addressed for the Christian when we reflect upon the cross as the ultimate revelation of God's love.

The Holy Spirit Is Love's Breath

Biblical tradition sees the Spirit as *ruah*—breath or wind— and this provides the basis for the image of the Holy Spirit as love's breath. The Spirit is God's life-giving principle. At the beginning of the world, according to the first creation story in Genesis 1:1, God's *ruah*—life-giving wind—hovered over the waters. In the second creation narrative, God formed Adam from the clay of the ground and "breathed into his nostrils the breath of life; and the man became a living being" (Gen 2:7). Perhaps the most vivid example of the life-giving power of the Spirit in the Old Testament is from Ezekiel where, in a symbolic action of spiritual revival of the people of Israel, God breathes a life-giving breath upon dry bones (chapter 37). In the New Testament, in John's gospel, the risen Jesus breathes on the disciples and gives them the gift of the Spirit (20:22), for "it is the Spirit that gives life" (6:63).

Love's breath gives life. Walter Kasper points out that the biblical concept of spirit was always associated with the transcendent, life-giving, and world-creating power of God.[25] In contrast, Greek philosophy saw the spirit as representing an inner side of the world, the unseen part of human beings (as in body and soul). The distinction in Christianity, though, is not between inner and outer, but between human and divine, temporal and everlasting. The Spirit is the life-giving power of God's eternal love. That power manifests itself not only in creation but also in history. Jesus, as the agent of the kingdom, is revealed as a man of the Spirit at his baptism and throughout his ministry (especially in Luke and John). He is filled with the *ruah* of God—God's life-giving power. All the gospels begin their account by giving testimony to the fact that, at his baptism, the Spirit of God came upon Jesus and, throughout his ministry, showed itself in his words and mighty deeds.

"By the mystery of the Incarnation, God's love is made manifest, present to the human reality.... In Word and Spirit, God is speaking and breathing divine life into the world."[26] The Holy Spirit is the experience of love. It activates itself in us and bonds us to Jesus and to the Father. The Holy Spirit not only brings Jesus to life in the incarnation, but also enables us to be open to what the incarnation is: the revelation of Jesus as the Son of God made flesh for us.

Through the Spirit, the transforming power of Jesus' death and resurrection is made real. The Spirit doesn't act on its own but comes to us as the Spirit of the Lord Jesus Christ. The Spirit teaches us and forms us in the image of Christ. The Spirit is love's power to change the world. It changes hearts through the power of love. It forms us into Christ's body, working in the world in wondrous ways to bring about reconciliation among peoples and the fullness of peace.

This brief summary of some insights of contemporary trinitarian theology helps us understand how our God is a missionary God. The passionate, overflowing, and outreaching love of God the Father expresses itself in the sending of the Son in the incarnation and the "missioning" of the Holy Spirit—both for the sake of our salvation.

Evangelization Is the Church's Deepest Identity

For evangelization to succeed, we need to see the church as missionary; in other words, we need a missionary ecclesiology, a missionary understanding of church. And we need to base this ecclesiology in a missionary theology.[27]

Since the Extraordinary Synod of 1985, something known as communion ecclesiology has enjoyed a great deal of favor. One of the values of this ecclesiology is that it roots the life of the church in the communal life of God—the very thing we are trying to do in this chapter. The communion of the church is "prefigured, made possible and sustained by the communion of the Trinity."[28] From the point of view of evangelization, however, a communion ecclesiology that is not sufficiently grounded in mission tends to be too static. Going back to the analogy of the lake and the river, I would say that communion ecclesiology tends to be too much like a lake and not enough like a river. While it is rooted in God's communal *being,* it doesn't sufficiently emphasize God's missionary *activity.*

Neil Ormerod proposes the kind of missionary ecclesiology to which I refer.[29] He says that what is first in our knowledge of the Trinity are the divine missions of the Word and the Spirit. We know them first by what they do—mission. Mission is prior to communion in our experiential knowledge; thus it provides a better foundation for our experience of ourselves, here and now, as a pilgrim church.[30]

Paul VI points the way to a mission ecclesiology when he says that "evangelizing all peoples constitutes the essential mission of the Church" and that it is the "grace and vocation proper to the Church, her deepest identity" (*EN,* no. 14).[31] Just as a communion ecclesiology roots itself in the life of the Trinity, so does a mission ecclesiology, but it relies on the missionary character of the communion of persons rooted in love as its organizing principle. Perhaps the church as a community of disciples can provide a model for a dynamic missionary ecclesiology for the future, particularly if adequate emphasis is given to the role of the Holy Spirit, who energizes disciples for mission by a variety of gifts.

Outreaching Love Is the Source of All Evangelizing Activity

We affirm that overflowing love is the source of God's missionary activity. Therefore, this love must also be the source of the evangelizing activity of the church.[32] Evangelization is a work of God; it is then, of necessity, a work of love. John Paul II says, "Love is the driving force of mission" (*RM,* no. 60). We seek to live our faith fully, share it freely, and transform the world in Christ because our hearts too overflow with the love of God. As Paul says: "For the love of Christ urges us on, because we are convinced that . . . he died for all, so that those who live might live no longer for themselves, but for him who died and was raised for them" (2 Cor 5:14–15).

Returning briefly to the image of the river, we can see in the pulsing, dynamic movement of the current the compelling force and power of God's love. This love makes things happen. The current has the same characteristic of all cosmic movement: it is bigger than all of us and is symbolic of the energy that keeps the world moving. One is reminded of Dante's image in *The Divine Comedy:* God's love is the energy that "moves the sun and the other stars."[33] The spheres of history and creation are moving with the explosive energy of God's love. Evangelization is part of that movement. It existed before us and will continue after us because it flows from God's eternal love like a fountain or a river.

David Bosch is fond of saying that the mission has a church,[34] not the other way around. Evangelization is God's work and we are privileged participants in it. We are invited to jump in and be swept away by the flow of God's outreaching love. Rosemary Haughton, in her book *The Passionate God,* describes the kind of energy that is released in the world, an energy whose moving force is love. The love that she writes of is passion. Like the coming of spring, the breakthrough power of love is not gentle or cozy. "It is an eruption of life so strong it can push bricks apart and make houses fall down."[35] She speaks of breakthroughs and exchanges, obstacles and new openings, times of stagnation and of explosion—all part of the unfolding, exciting story of God's love, where the unthinkable and unexpected (such as the incarnation) happen.

This is not a manageable universe; it is a world of *sturm und drang,* an adventure in which God enters human history with passionate love. If we picture the river of God's love coursing through history, flooding and passing through narrow canyons and steep cliffs as well as tranquil flowing valleys, then we get a better sense of the exciting journey we begin when we say *yes* to the evangelizing project. Our task is to jump into the flow and take the ride.

When I was growing up and considering my vocation to the priesthood, I was attracted by the prospect of being part of something important, something bigger than I was. I wanted to be a little player in an important enterprise. I wanted to make a difference in an important undertaking that was not of my doing. That is what evangelization feels like. It is a huge and impossible agenda from a human point of view. But from God's perspective, it is the plan that is being worked out in history through the Son and the Spirit, with all of us as bit players.

At a certain point in my vocational search, I realized that I had found what I was looking for and that this is who I am. Nothing else would satisfy—and, as a consequence, I was no longer free to choose something else. I had no other option. I was compelled by my free choice. It was, in Edward Schillebeeckx's words, the "existential inability to do otherwise."[36] This is different from seeing freedom—mistakenly, I believe—as having multiple options. Ultimately, the deepest meaning of freedom is having the capacity to decide how to give oneself in love. Once we come to know and understand that evangelization corresponds to our deepest identity, it is no longer optional. This is who I am. We freely embrace it because we have to.

Evangelization represents the deepest truth about us as a church. Thus, the challenge to live our faith fully, to share it freely, and to transform the world in Christ is deeply rooted in our freedom. We freely choose to evangelize because that is who God is and that is who we are. Paul urges: "Do not be ashamed, then, of the testimony about our Lord or of me his prisoner, but join with me in suffering for the gospel, relying on the power of God..." (2 Tim 1:8). Jesus promises that his yoke is easy and his burden light (Matt 11:30). When the burden of evangelization is taken up out of the depths of freedom,[37] in conformity with our deepest identity, the yoke is easy and the burden is light indeed. The desire to evangelize wells up from deep within us, not only in response to the Lord's mandate but from the movement of God's life within us. Evangelization is a profound privilege that arises out of my identity as a Christian.[38]

PART II

Go and Make Disciples

CHAPTER FIVE

A PLAN AND STRATEGY FOR CATHOLIC EVANGELIZATION

Insight: Go and Make Disciples *provides a practical tool that enables the church to move evangelization from vision to reality.*

Reflection

I am one of those strange creatures who always wanted to be a priest. Frankly, given the time and place where I grew up—in a large Catholic family in a mostly Catholic neighborhood in a small midwestern town in the 1940s and 1950s—this was not that unusual. Lots of children in the first grade at my Catholic school announced that they were going to become a priest or a nun. What is unusual is that I never gave up the idea.

I had this dream all my life, and I made many decisions and shaped many activities around it. The dream shifted and changed with the upheaval of the 1960s, but it remained largely intact right up to the time I was ordained to the diaconate. Then it all fell apart. I had had the idea that God was calling me to the priesthood because I was "perfect" for the job. After a dark night of the soul in which I almost gave up the idea completely, I received my vocation back, and it was sheer gift. I realized that I was "perfect" for the job *because* God was calling me to the priesthood. A very different matter indeed!

As a result of that transforming experience, I felt a strong responsibility to nurture and protect the gift of my vocation. I knew I needed to take the actions that would let me grow in the priesthood. I needed to pursue with a certain single-mindedness and resoluteness some of the goals that I felt were critical to being an effective priest. It required me to become intentional

79

about my life, rather than just sliding into the future in a haphazard manner.

I am not a planner by instinct. I have a fear of being too organized in life (I might get bored!). But I do believe that it is important to set out the important goals that are connected with our dreams and relentlessly pursue them, or they won't happen. We need to do some personal planning to achieve these goals, if we are to truly live out our dreams.

If it is an enormous challenge for you and me to turn our dreams into reality, imagine how difficult it is for the church to carry out its task: helping turn God's vision for the world into reality. This task—to evangelize all the peoples of the earth—is almost impossible to *conceive*, never mind *actualize*. Evangelization will not happen by accident or chance. The kingdom of God will not magically appear. We, the church, need to be intimately involved with, and committed to, this mission. In addition, we need a plan (a blueprint, a design, a framework) to coordinate and unify our many efforts. Thanks to the Holy Spirit and to the bishops of the United States, we have such a plan. Go and Make Disciples: A National Plan and Strategy for Catholic Evangelization in the United States **provides the practical tool that will enable the church to move evangelization from vision to reality.**

Introducing the Plan

Go and Make Disciples: A National Plan and Strategy for Catholic Evangelization in the United States was approved by the bishops in November 1992 and was published shortly thereafter. The document is divided into two parts, which are roughly equal in length and importance. The first half presents a vision of Catholic evangelization. The second half outlines the goals and strategies that are needed to implement this vision. The bishops intentionally gave us a detailed framework for carrying out the vision because, as they say, they hope that this plan "will lead Catholics to action" (*GMD*, no. 75). The vision of evangelization is meant to be not just a subject for prayer and meditation but also an impetus for movement.

In the past thirty-five years or so, the Catholic Church has been fully occupied in carrying out the renewal called for by the Second Vatican Council. At the same time, the Holy Spirit has led the church to articulate a vision of evangelization as the essential mission of the church. As the church in the United States prepared to enter the third millennium of Christianity, the bishops provided dioceses and parishes in the United States with a practical plan for implementing that great vision of evangelization.

Overview of the Plan

The bishops invite every Catholic to be part of the story of salvation. They invite all of us to take ownership of the plan (*GMD*, nos. 129–32). Inspired by Pope Paul VI, they define evangelization as "bringing the Good News of salvation into every human situation and seeking to convert individuals and society by the divine power of the Gospel itself. Its essence is the proclamation of salvation in Jesus Christ and the response of a person in faith, both being the work of the Spirit of God" (*GMD*, no.10).

In Part 1, the bishops look at the nature of conversion. For individuals, conversion means change, and it is ongoing, because "we can hold on to our faith only if it continues to grow." For society, conversion means the transformation of human existence. At times, this requires that we confront the world; more often, we are called to let our faith shine in our everyday lives (*GMD*, nos. 12–17).

The bishops reject trickery and manipulation in evangelization, asserting that the power of the good news will move all who sincerely seek God. And they describe the two directions of evangelization: the inward (our continued receiving of the gospel) and the outward (toward all those in need of the gospel). "Our relationship with Jesus is found in our relationship with the community of Jesus—the church," they write (*GMD*, nos. 23, 26). Finally, they explore why we evangelize—and the most powerful reason they give is, simply, our love for all people—and also how evangelization happens (*GMD*, nos. 28–44).

In Part 2, the bishops present the goals of evangelization. Together they form a tripod that supports the broad platform of Catholic evangelization:

Goal I: To bring about in all Catholics such an enthusiasm for their faith that, in living their faith in Jesus, they freely share it with others.

Goal II: To invite all people in the United States, whatever their social or cultural background, to hear the message of salvation in Jesus Christ so they may come to join us in the fullness of the Catholic faith.

Goal III: To foster gospel values in our society, promoting the dignity of the human person, the importance of the family, and the common good of our society, so that our nation may continue to be transformed by the saving power of Jesus Christ.

Part 2 is dedicated to the implementation, context, attendant objectives, and derivative strategies of these goals.

Overview of the Goals

Go and Make Disciples provides the invaluable service of making evangelization doable. It does this by breaking the vision down into manageable elements: the three goals. In essence, the bishops say that evangelization consists of these three elements of holiness, invitation/welcome, and transformation. All of our parish ministries and activities fall into one of these three categories. Then, for each goal, the bishops develop a set of objectives and strategies to help us implement it.

But all this is actually just the beginning of our evangelization efforts. The bishops point out that their document "can only suggest the richness of this ministry. In fact, at the end of this plan we explicitly invite additional responses to the objectives we are setting forth. We look for innovative responses, far exceeding the suggested strategies we offer in this plan" (*GMD*, no. 79). They realize that parishes in different parts of the country, of different sizes and with different ethnic and cultural makeups, will greatly increase the variety of what we do to make evangelization happen.

Pursue All Three Goals

Dividing evangelization into three main categories, then, is one of the true innovations of *Go and Make Disciples*. However, this approach does have a down side. It creates the hazard of separating the constitutive aspects of evangelization. Working on one goal at a time is a completely logical, not to mention manageable, concept. "We're already so busy, let's not try to kill ourselves." Divide and conquer is part of our efficiency-minded culture. It has led to the common practice of dedicating specific years to specific ministries: the year of the family, the year of stewardship, the year of evangelization, and so on. But in the evangelizing arena, this habit leads to real problems because, often, the added focus given to one specific area provides a handy excuse for not focusing on the other areas, or focusing on them only sporadically.

Father Philip Wilhite, former director of *Disciples in Mission* for the Diocese of Galveston-Houston, uses the following analogy when he encounters people who want to focus on the goals individually or in isolation. Imagine that you are a parent. You have the responsibility to clothe, feed, and educate your children. Do you clothe them for one year, feed them the next year, and educate them the third year? Of course not. You must meet all these needs for your children every year, or you are not fulfilling your responsibility.

Similarly, we must pursue all the goals simultaneously. The bishops state, "None of these goals is presented by itself; taken together, they challenge us to the full scope of Catholic evangelization" (*GMD*, no. 45). We are called to that full scope of evangelization. Pursuing the goals in isolation violates that full scope. We have all seen it happen.

Goal I calls us to live our faith fully. If we work on it in isolation or at the expense of the other two goals, this leads to a type of "club Christianity." In this mode, we are most concerned with the personal holiness and salvation of the church's members. We spend our time and effort consuming the sacraments, participating in activities within the parish community, devoting ourselves to prayer, and studying our faith. There is little interest or energy spent on nonmembers. This is not because we don't care about them. Rather, it's a matter of out of sight, out of mind. We're just too busy taking care of ourselves to worry about who's not here.

Sometimes we focus all our efforts on living our faith fully, with the notion that once we've become holy enough or knowledgeable enough, *then* we'll go out into the world to spread the good news. If the first disciples had waited until they perfected their faith before carrying out Christ's commission, Christianity wouldn't exist. Furthermore, an inward-focused pursuit of Goal I is too narrow; it doesn't respect the fullness of the goal. The enthusiasm for faith that the goal speaks about is not an end, but a step toward freely sharing that faith with *others*.

Goal II calls Catholics to invite others to hear the good news. If we work on it in isolation or at the expense of the other two, this leads to a type of "market Christianity." In this mode, we become caught up in a numbers game. With how many non-Catholics have we shared the gospel? How many inactive Catholics have we helped back to the church? How many catechumens did we have in this year's RCIA? Is our parish growing?

We ask ourselves these questions mindful of the competition we face in the marketplace of religions. We look at the statistics that show we are losing more Catholics through the proverbial back door (switching to other Christian denominations, becoming inactive, and so on) than we are bringing in through the front door (infant baptism, RCIA, conversions, and so on). Our solution? Better marketing, better signage, better messages, nicer buildings, more outreach, and so on. We focus on attracting people to the church, paying little attention to what happens to them once they arrive or how the church is functioning as an agent of social transformation.

Goal III calls Catholics to transform society through Christ. If we work on it in isolation or at the expense of the other two, this leads to a "social agency Christianity." In this mode, we concentrate almost solely on the church's social impact on the world. We lobby the government. We support charities with our time, money, and sweat. We stand in solidarity with the poor, the oppressed, the marginalized, the wounded. These are all good, even necessary—but it's easy to forget that it is God who will bring about the kingdom, not us. God is in charge, and we really don't know just how the kingdom will be brought about or what it will look like.

There's another pitfall, too: we can find ourselves neglecting God because we are too involved in doing God's work. Pursuing the church's social justice agenda without paying attention to the spiritual formation necessary can quickly lead to burnout. The opening words of *Communities of Salt and Light* make this point very clearly: "The most important setting for the church's social teaching is not in a food pantry or in a legislative committee room, but in prayer and worship, especially gathered around the altar for the Eucharist."[1]

Modern Catholic evangelization is a comprehensive vision. The goals of *Go and Make Disciples* are equally comprehensive, but they capture this vision in a concise and manageable way. Separating the vision into three parts does not mean we can split our vision three ways. Rather, the separation into realizable elements helps us link our vision with reality. To make this move, however, we must keep all three goals in balance as we proceed to implementation. We are a people accustomed to three-in-one phenomena. Like our theological understanding of the Trinity, surely we can understand the vision of evangelization in three goals with but one purpose.

What Have We Learned in Twelve Years of Implementing the Plan?

The PNCEA has been working with dioceses and parishes to foster the implementation of *Go and Make Disciples* since its promulgation in 1992. Every year, the PNCEA institutes workshops focused on the plan. Additionally, the PNCEA offered *Disciples in Mission,* a formation process designed specifically to help dioceses and parishes implement *Go and Make Disciples.*[2] Over a twelve-year period, two thousand parishes and more than two million parishioners have participated in some manner in *Disciples in Mission* through Sunday liturgies, small faith-sharing groups, family groups, and parish reflection days.

We learned a great deal in those twelve years about what works in this implementation effort. The vision of evangelization presented in *Go and Make Disciples* is compelling. The bishops' plan provides a way to implement it, but parishes need something much more concrete and structured in order to do it successfully. They need an implementation methodology, and the PNCEA has provided two of them: *Disciples in Mission* (*DM*, a formation process) and *ENVISION*[3] (a planning process). Parishes also need time to absorb this new vision, to form new attitudes, and to practice new behaviors for mission. *Disciples in Mission* and *ENVISION* are multi-year processes, and meet this need as well. Catholic laity are able to embrace the vision of evangelization with considerable enthusiasm.

Given a context in which to understand the far-reaching implications of evangelization as the essential mission of the church (and therefore of the local parish), Catholic people are willing to invest themselves in its implementation and are able to achieve considerable success. However, they must have adequate pastoral leadership. When that leadership is lacking, there is a great deal of frustration. The laity themselves are capable of providing outstanding leadership, and many come to discover that they have the charism of an evangelist. Oftentimes, evangelization brings new participants to the table, people who have not been active in parish ministry previously.

The goals hold up very well and are eminently doable. They provide an organizing principle that revitalizes all the ministries and gives parishioners a new perspective from which to view all the components of parish life. Furthermore, when given an opportunity, the three goals provide a simple framework and a wonderful stimulus from which the parish can become more missionary. Understandably, Goal II provides the greatest challenge. In many ways the implementation of Goal I and Goal III has already been taking place in the parish. But Goal II challenges Catholics to new attitudes and behaviors that require a conversion from their sense of baptism as entitlement to one of active discipleship and disciple-making.

There is a great deal of inertia in parish life, one that tends to keep parishes mired in maintenance. It is very difficult to move the entire parish to a more missionary posture. Yet, the fact is, evangelization is growing in acceptance. It is rising on the priority list of parishes and dioceses, and is becoming more and more the lens through which all ministry should be viewed and the organizing principle for all aspects of parish life. Once the *General Directory for Catechesis* made it clear that catechesis was part of evangelization, the last major holdout for the notion of evangelization as one priority or one program among many disappeared. Parishes and dioceses are now ready for a whole community evangelization, with evangelization as the integrating umbrella for all ministries.

Our experience at the PNCEA has yielded some key information that can help us form successful strategies for the future. Leadership is critical, both at the diocesan and parish level. Small groups are very effective in forming evangelizers. Catholics are open to evangelizing when they formulate their own faith stories and understand the importance of witness and proclamation. There is some evidence that healing can take place in parishes and dioceses under the unifying mission of evangelization. There can be a rebirth of effective pastoral leadership, a lessening of turfism, a rise in participation levels, a diminishing of fragmentation, and a heightened sense of ongoing conversion in the parish.

Finally, these years of implementation have made us very aware of the importance of diversity and multiculturalism as a core issue for evangelization. The call to hospitality requires parishes to look at the makeup of their congregations and the level of welcoming that is being extended to the different language and cultural groups within it. We have only begun to confront this challenge, but it has clearly gotten onto the agenda of the parish. How parishes respond to this challenge will determine in great measure their willingness to embrace the full message of evangelization. We cannot reach out beyond the walls of the parish if we haven't addressed the challenge of creating hospitable and inclusive communities among all those who make up the parish family.

These are some of the things that we have learned in the past twelve years in implementing *Go and Make Disciples*. We hope that at some time in the future, the bishops will gather the wisdom and experience of these years of implementation and update the entire document as a sign of their ongoing commitment to evangelization as the essential mission of the church and the ongoing viability of the plan.

The Planning Strategy

The national plan and strategy is so detailed that we can be overwhelmed when confronted with the sheer breadth of the tasks outlined for us. And what do we do as individuals, or as organizations, when we feel overwhelmed? Nothing productive! We get paralyzed. We procrastinate. We focus our attention on the easier or clearer things. Or, worst of all, we give up. I often see these varied responses to evangelization in my travels around the country. This is why we need a plan. This is the genius of *Go and Make Disciples*.

The Plan Won't Run by Itself

It is one thing to have a detailed and practical plan and strategy to make the vision of evangelization a reality. It is another thing to actually implement that plan and strategy. In order for us to carry out this implementation, we need an effective planning process. In the plan, the bishops offer a special word to pastors about this. "We recognize how burdened parish leadership is today; our hope is that this plan can actually clarify the purpose of parish leadership and thereby ease the burdens of already busy pastors" (*GMD*, no. 136). This sentiment could be similarly applied to individuals, families, institutions, and organizations. We are all busy. American culture esteems busy-ness and an overfull plate. Two parables from Luke offer a wonderful meditation to pastoral leaders as we contemplate the enormous challenge of systematically implementing the vision of

Catholic evangelization. The first is a parable on the importance of planning (14:28–32), where Jesus urges us to think ahead about whether we have the resources to finish what we start. The second is the parable about Mary and Martha (10:38–42). We can celebrate the Mary and Martha in all of us by being very careful not to be busy about many things but rather focus on the one important thing—evangelization as the essential mission of the church. Then let us prayerfully, carefully, and prudently align our many activities with this central mission.

In this society in particular, it is important that evangelization not be just one more thing to add to the pile, but a **way to look at, prioritize, and engage in the things that are already piled up.** Some activities may need to be discontinued. Some new ones may need to be added to fill in gaps. Some activities may need to be approached differently. We may need to find a way to become more systematic about our priorities. And, in all cases, when more work is called for, the vision of evangelization compels us to look for more workers, not just to dump new tasks on the backs of those already shouldering more than their fair share of the load. Evangelization is a call for everyone, not for a select few.

The last sentence of the concluding prayer in the plan summarizes this idea: "We pray that the fire of Jesus enkindled in us by God's Spirit may lead more and more people in our land to become disciples, formed in the image of Christ our Savior" (*GMD*, no. 141). Like the kingdom of God, *Go and Make Disciples* won't run by itself. It is not self-implementing. It requires the action of disciples who are consumed by the fire of Jesus, which comes to us through the Holy Spirit. As the parable from Chapter Three illustrates, Jesus' only plan is for his followers to spread the good news. That's us—all of us.

Rehabilitating the Notion of Planning

Why is parish planning necessary? While the complex and comprehensive nature of evangelization calls for a coordinated plan to implement it, the idea of planning triggers some negative associations and stereotypes. In certain church circles, *planning* has even become a dirty word. This can make the job of promoting and using *Go and Make Disciples* doubly difficult, because we have to overcome not one obstacle but two: resistance to evangelization and resistance to planning.

What has been your experience with planning? Many people's initial experience was with management by objectives model (MBO). It was based on the sound insight that we will accomplish our goals only if they are broken down into manageable steps (objectives) and have clearly articulated, achievable, measurable results. But when parishes tried to do MBO, for the most part they went through the external process without first going through an internal conversion—and this internal conversion is essential. You must do the work of discerning and developing your vision before you can even start to think about your goals. The whole planning process never made it off the paper for most of us; the only result was a drawerful of papers. Parishes are wary of planning, because their experience is colored by a history of endless meetings that don't seem to accomplish anything and ineffective planning processes that are largely unproductive. It's not surprising that we find a lot of resistance.

Planning has come a long way since the MBO model. The social sciences have created dynamic forms of planning, such as the Preferred Futuring[4] model of planning. This model engages participants in a forward-looking process; it is rooted in imagining the future rather than merely trying to solve the problems of the past.

The type of planning *Go and Make Disciples* espouses is quite open-ended and also very basic: study, reflection, and inspired action.

- "All this movement and all these documents call us to re-examine our hearts and recommit our wills to the pursuit of evangelization; they motivate us to issue this plan to make evangelization a natural and normal part of Catholic life and to give evangelizers the tools and support they need to carry out this ministry today" (*GMD*, no. 64).

- "We envision groups of Catholics reading this plan together, discussing its implications and being stimulated by the range of suggested strategies. We see these groups seeking to do things, both within and beyond their own Catholic communities, in ways that make sense for their locale and situation. This document should generate discussion about action: the possibilities and activities present in every Catholic parish and institution" (*GMD,* no. 76).

- "The ministry of evangelization does not consist in following a recipe but in letting the Spirit open our hearts to God's Word so that we can live and proclaim God's Word to others. So, let the Spirit work!" (*GMD,* no. 79).

- "All evangelization planning basically strives to make more possible the kind of everyday exchange between believers and unbelievers which is the thrust of evangelization" (*GMD,* no. 83).

- "Parishes, as part of their regular planning process, need to examine their activities in light of this plan. They should consider how to give their present ministry a clearer evangelizing focus and how new ministries might be formed to achieve the goals of this plan. Each parish should have an evangelization team trained and prepared to help the whole parish implement the goals and objectives of this plan. These teams could help train Catholics in evangelization and provide resources to individuals, families, and parish groups. Parishes might even consider designating a trained person as a full-time coordinator of evangelization" (*GMD,* no. 136c).

Parishes are gradually coming to accept the need for effective planning. They know that there are effective planning resources available. *Go and Make Disciples* challenges parishes to find ways to make evangelization more intentional in the parish so they can make progress in implementing the three goals. "Failing to plan is planning to fail." The challenge is to identify an effective planning process and begin to integrate it into the normal cycle of our parish activities.

There are many different types of planning that go on in a parish. We make the following helpful distinctions:

- **Functional or Operational Planning** has to do with making sure that the facilities and resources are available and functioning so that the fundamental work of the parish can happen. This type of planning deals with administration and answers the question: what do we need in order to function well?

- **Mission-based Planning** has to do with aligning resources and personnel so that the priorities of the parish can be selected and carried out. It answers the question: what do we want to do?

- There is another type of planning that we call **Planning for Full Engagement or Shared Vision Planning,** which answers the question: who do we want to become? This kind of planning engages a large number of parishioners in answering the questions: who are we as a parish? And how do we want to move together into the future? This type of planning makes profound, systemwide changes. It enables a parish to move from being maintenance-oriented to being mission-oriented. It can help a parish become truly evangelizing.

What are some of the characteristics of this kind of planning process, one that allows a parish to redefine itself as a missionary parish? First, it needs to be **integrated** into the church environment. Participants must be able to recognize it as a spiritual activity, one that is part of their overall experience of being part of the parish community. Such a process will be firmly rooted in prayer and reflection. Second, it is **mission-focused.** It helps participants work toward specific results and deliberate actions that answer the call to bring the gospel to the world. Third, a good planning process is **results-oriented.** It is designed to help the parish achieve continuous short-term cycles of results to accomplish long-term impact. Fourth, it is **inclusive** and **participatory.** It is based on the active involvement of all segments of the parish and encourages all parishioners to use their gifts for the mission of the faith community. Finally, it is **flexible** and **repeatable.** A parish will be able to use it in ways that accommodate its own unique strengths and needs over the long term.[5]

Conclusion

To summarize, *Go and Make Disciples* provides a comprehensive and practical tool that parishes can use to move evangelization from vision to reality—but it is not self-implementing! It requires us to engage in some kind of planning process to implement the goals.

CHAPTER SIX

GOAL I

Insight: Goal I challenges Catholics to a lifelong pursuit of holiness, which provides the essential foundation for inviting others to share the faith.

Reflection

My co-worker, Sister Susan Wolf, SND, relates the following experience.

A few years ago, I was returning from the National Council of Catholic Evangelization (NCCE) meeting in Phoenix. I had given a talk, had been involved in a number of meetings, and ran the display booth for the entire conference, so I was pretty exhausted by the time I took my seat on the plane. I was looking for a peaceful trip. I sat down, opened my newspaper, and was hoping no one would take the seat next to me.

In fact, shortly after I had expressed this thought to myself, a woman sat down. She wasn't there more than a couple of minutes when she said, "Excuse me, have you ever heard of putting your newspaper in the microwave? My husband gets newspaper print all over his hands and all over the kitchen tablecloth, and a friend of mine told me you could put the newspaper in the microwave and zap it for thirty seconds and the ink would dry. It has changed my life and I just needed to share that with you."

Then she asked, "Are you going home? Or is Phoenix your home?"

"I'm going back to Washington, D.C.," I said.

"What were you doing here in Phoenix?"

"I was at a conference."

"Oh, what kind of conference?"

"An evangelization conference."

There was silence for a moment, then the woman burst

forth. "Oh—For a hundred years we've gotten along without evangelism. Now, that's all they talk about. Everyone has to do it. My precious religion (she is becoming very upset)—it's nothing but marketing. That's all it is. And I won't have anything to do with it."

After pausing to reflect, I responded: "I think it is very unfortunate that some people have given evangelization such a negative image for you. I can personally tell you that I would never do anything to offend or manipulate someone into doing something they didn't want to do. I was born a Catholic. I consider it a great gift. I don't know what I would do without my faith. I don't know how people get through the difficult times of their life without God.

"Do you know there are 98 million unchurched people in this country who hunger for some spiritual nourishment in their lives? Where are they going to get it? From the television? From the movies? The newspaper? If we don't witness to them what a genuine Christian faith is, they will fill the vacuum with phony substitutes like Jonestown, Waco, New Age. People are desperately looking for some spiritual dimension to their lives. Where are they going to find it?

"Just a minute ago, you shared the happiness you found in discovering a little thing that improved your life. Why should you be angry when people share their faith?"

After a pause, the woman said, "I never thought about it like that." She calmed down and we had a nice conversation.

At the end of the flight, just when she was about to leave, she said, "Excuse me. I am going to tell my husband about this conversation with you. I just want to tell you that I think we had it all wrong. I think you are doing a wonderful work. God bless you."

This story illustrates an important truth about evangelization. People love to talk about the things that they are passionate about. Everybody has certain things that generate energy and enthusiasm in them, even if it is something as mundane as microwaving a newspaper.

Enthusiasm for our faith is a good place to begin our reflection on the three goals of *Go and Make Disciples*. It is a foundation for the arduous task of carrying out Catholic evangelization in the parish.

Pathways to Holiness

Goal I challenges Catholics to be enthusiastic about their faith, just as the woman was enthusiastic about her discovery of what microwave ovens can do for newspapers. Unless we are enthusiastic about our faith, we will never share it.

> **Goal I:** To bring about in all Catholics such an enthusiasm for their faith that, in living their faith in Jesus, they freely share it with others. (*GMD*, no. 89)

Goal I, then, seeks to bring about a deepening of faith in *all* baptized Catholics. Yet we know there are many Catholics who haven't experienced the kind of conversion to Christ that is necessary to live one's faith fully. How do the bishops address this challenge?

They begin by taking a closer look at what is meant by a life of faith. First, they describe it as a deepening process. It does not stay the same over time; it is not static but dynamic. Second, they explain that this is a call to *holiness,* a call that is given to every Catholic through baptism. Third, faith in Jesus calls Catholics beyond personal holiness to outward openness and action. Faith cannot be contained within an individual. Holiness is not for personal consumption alone. The call to holiness "consecrates each one to God *and* to the service of the kingdom." It "fosters a desire to involve *others* in that faith, until God will be '*all in all*' in a transformed *world*" (*GMD*, no. 89; emphasis added).

The objectives and strategies for this goal—what the bishops propose as ways to meet it—aim at both individual and communal renewal. All have this twofold dimension. They are also familiar, straightforward, and within the grasp of today's Catholic. Most of the strategies can easily be part of ordinary parish life. Goal I presents parishes with a variety of objectives aimed at individual and communal conversion and growth in holiness. I will focus on several that I have found promising, based upon my experience in implementing *GMD* over these many years.

Conversion and Renewal

The next chapter will investigate outreach to the inactive Catholic. Here, in discussing Goal I, I am concerned with the faithful Catholics, people who are already in the pew. Some studies have shown that the Catholic population can be reasonably grouped into three categories: nuclear (25 percent), modal (55 percent), and dormant (25 percent).[1] These categories are helpful for our current discussion. Nuclear Catholics are solid, core Catholics who regularly attend mass and participate actively in the life of the parish. Modal Catholics attend mass about once a month. The church is important to them, but they have a significantly weaker attachment and involvement than the nuclear group does. Dormant Catholics rarely or almost never attend mass and are weak in their commitment level. Obviously, most parishes don't see many of their dormant Catholics.

Evangelization begins with the people in the pew. This is what the first objective of Goal I is touching on, when it calls the parish to "foster an experience of conversion and renewal in the heart of every believer, leading to a more active living of Catholic life." On any given Sunday, there would be a large representation of modal Catholics. Parishes would find it fruitful to focus on them, in order to move them into the category of nuclear Catholics. The objective offers a number of different strategies for doing this, including retreats, parish renewals, RENEW, Cursillo, involvement in the Charismatic movement, encounter weekends, and marriage-encounter weekends. We might add small faith-sharing groups to that list.

Many Catholics have not had the fundamental kerygmatic experience of basic conversion to Jesus Christ. Catholics baptize infants and rely upon the family to form their children in the faith. Any number of factors might account for the fact that some baptized Catholics never come to the point of adult commitment in the practice of their faith. Having such a basic conversion experience could transform these people—modal

Catholics—into solid nuclear Catholics. It might not take much, since they already have a significant level of involvement with the church. All the strategies for this objective could be very effective in bringing modal Catholics to a new level of commitment.

Early in *Go and Make Disciples,* the bishops offer a rich definition of conversion that explains the purpose of the strategies just mentioned.

> Conversion is the change of our lives that comes about through the power of the Holy Spirit. All who accept the Gospel undergo change as we continually put on the mind of Christ by rejecting sin and becoming more faithful disciples in his Church. (*GMD,* no. 12)

The definition makes the important point that while change comes through the power of the Spirit, we ourselves have an essential and active role in the process. Conversion doesn't just happen while we're doing other things. Putting on the mind of Christ, rejecting sin, and becoming a more faithful disciple: we must intentionally choose to do these things if we are to be converted. And it can be a difficult, even painful process, as the word *undergo* suggests. Conversion is neither convenient nor easy.

Additionally, we typically think of conversion as what happens when we first come to faith, or when someone joins the Catholic Church from another religious tradition—a convert. We see conversion as a one-time event for the newcomer. But *all* disciples of Jesus experience conversion, which is a never-ending process in the life of faith.

The experience of conversion takes many forms. The bishops point out that it can be sudden or gradual; it can happen through the RCIA, through family and friends, through Catholic schools or religious education programs, or through episodic events such as ecumenical encounters or retreats (*GMD,* no. 13). These are all pathways to conversion.

Conversion, in fact, is the metastrategy for Goal I. All its strategies focus on bringing Catholics to conversion. It is the priority in the lifelong journey of a disciple. Why? Because "we can only share what we have received; we can only hold on to our faith if it continues to grow."[2] And, finally, the reason for all our efforts: we work for ongoing conversion because it is crucial to our lifelong pursuit of holiness. "Conversion is directed to holiness, since conversion 'is not an end in itself but a journey toward God who is holy.'"[3]

Appreciation of God's Word[4]

The third and sixth objectives focus on increasing an appreciation of scripture. Four developments in the church since Vatican II relate to these two objectives: the laity are now encouraged to read scripture regularly; scripture study may use scientific methods of biblical criticism; small faith-sharing groups have become prevalent in the church; and the renewed appreciation of the role of the homily in Catholic worship. Catholics are urged in many different contexts—communal and individual, liturgical and personal—to come alive to the power of God's word in their lives. We have come a long way, but we have a long way to go.

We have all the official documentation needed to reinforce this as a priority area for the church's evangelization efforts. What is needed is continued serious implementation of *GMD*'s objectives. How can we foster a love and appreciation of the word of God that leads preachers to deliver effective homilies and laity to deepen their dependence on scripture for their day-to-day spiritual renewal and mission outreach? Research suggests that we have made progress: preaching is good but not great; Catholics are growing in their love of the word. Let me focus briefly on what is arguably the most critical strategy, which is the improvement of the homily.

Interestingly, one of the things we learned from *Disciples in Mission* is that, during the Lenten season, when *DM* small faith-sharing groups were in session, the homilies were rated higher than usual. We don't know if the receptivity of the listeners is heightened when they have already done faith-sharing around the Sunday readings, or if the preacher has worked harder on the homily, knowing that the expectation of the congregation has probably been elevated. Or maybe the preacher has improved the quality of his preaching because of his participation in a small faith-sharing group before preparing his homily. All of these are reasonable interpretations of the data. In any case, there seems to be an important correlation between the existence of small groups in a parish and the improved quality of the homily—a correlation worth exploiting.

Another fruitful strategy is to increase accountability by making the improvement of preaching a conscious, intentional, and focused objective of parish planning. Whole community evangelization suggests that everyone is accountable for an integrated implementation of the evangelizing mission. Why not make the entire community accountable for improved preaching? Why is this area an untouchable sacred cow? Why can't the entire community commit itself to a process of getting adequate feedback on the preaching, finding out how to improve it, and establishing focused objectives and strategies to start doing it? Such a process would allow the entire community to hold itself accountable for growth in the quality of preaching. This would be a great test of how serious we are about improving the preaching in our parish communities.

This approach makes clear that improving the quality of the homily is not simply the responsibility of the preacher, but also of the community. Perhaps we must reckon with the fact that communities get the preaching they deserve. If we don't demand better preaching, we won't get it. If we don't commit the entire community to do what is needed to improve the preaching, it won't improve.

The year 2004 witnessed the loss of Bishop Kenneth Untener, someone who was truly committed to improving preaching in the Catholic Church. He not only wrote a fine book on preaching *(Preaching Better: Practical Suggestions for Homilists)*, but also instituted a very practical process for working with his priests systematically to improve their preaching. It is refreshing to see a bishop who seriously takes preaching as his *primum officium*, and who is committed to giving sustained leadership to improve the quality of preaching in the local church. Unfortunately, there aren't many of them. Even as the bishops have failed to provide leadership for improved preaching, they have allowed their own leadership in liturgy to be preempted by the dictates of Roman congregations. It is depressing to witness the inability of the Catholic Church to take clear, focused, serious action on this highest of priority issues.

The Sunday Eucharist

The Second Vatican Council called the liturgy the source and summit of Christian life. The Sunday Eucharist is our finest moment as Catholics and is unlimited in its evangelizing power. The Sunday Eucharist, then, must also be the source and summit of evangelization. The power to evangelize ourselves and others comes from God, and most profoundly in the celebration of the Eucharist. Some years ago, when I was conducting a PNCEA parish mission in a small rural parish west of Philadelphia, I was having a conversation with the Baptist minister who lived next door to the rectory. He said: "If I believed what you Catholics believe about the Eucharist, I would crawl to church on my hands and knees!" Truly, the Eucharist is one of the most powerful evangelizing tools that we Catholics have.

The bishops urge us "to make the evangelizing dimension of the Sunday Eucharist more explicit." I like that formulation. Evangelization is not an add-on dimension of the Eucharist; rather, it is in and of itself an evangelizing experience and we need to let its evangelizing power shine forth clearly.[5]

Let me highlight some of the promising strategies that can intensify the evangelizing power of the Sunday Eucharist. These are things we have learned from our implementation efforts. First, the level of hospitality of the gathered community matters a great deal. The council included it among the various ways we experience the presence of Christ. Making sure that the community practices hospitality in its fullest and broadest dimension, especially in welcoming diverse and multicultural populations, is crucial.

A second evangelizing element is the quality of the eucharistic celebration itself. How well do we celebrate the gathering and dismissal rites, the Liturgy of the Word and the Liturgy of the Eucharist?[6] Vatican II helped us to experience the liturgy in a more holistic fashion than before. Its reforms presume that each part of the rite builds on the preceding one, leading us from the gathering to the breaking open of the word to the climax of the eucharistic offering and communion and concluding with the missioning in the dismissal rite. All aspects are important to the complete celebration. This contrasts with the isolating and truncated theology of the Eucharist that came before, which focused on the importance of the offertory, consecration, and communion, ignoring the centrality of the word altogether and the importance of the gathering and dismissal rites.

Liturgy is never an action that takes place only within the church building. We eat and drink the body and blood in order to become the body of Christ in the world. The dismissal rite reminds us to go live what we have celebrated. The missionary focus of the Eucharist is not limited to the dismissal rite, but certainly the renewed focus on this rite as a missioning of the people that ends our celebration is an important aspect of the renewal and a key evangelizing dimension of the Eucharist.

Finally, we cannot speak about an authentic celebration of each element of the Eucharist without focusing on the full, conscious, and active participation of the assembly, which is the council's criterion for liturgical renewal and the test of the authenticity of any celebration. We are not talking only about external activity but about the interior disposition that is expressed in this participation. Such full participation of an assembly in the action of worship is surely a most powerful evangelizing event. Through such participation, the worshiper experiences the transforming power of the Eucharist as praise, redemption and forgiveness, communion and mission. The evangelizing power of the Eucharist comes from the fact that we have been engaged in and entered into the mystery that is God and are thereby made holy. We have united ourselves with Christ in worship, have eaten the body and thereby become the body of Christ. What could be more evangelizing than participating in the celebration of the mystery of the Eucharist? All we have to do is allow its evangelizing power to shine forth.[7]

The Challenge of Diversity and Multiculturalism in the Parish

The last objective under Goal I states: "to foster greater appreciation of cultural and ethnic spirituality." Embracing the multicultural nature and diversity of our parish life is not optional; it is an essential aspect of the call to holiness. Why? Because how we relate to the stranger, the other, the minority person, the person on the margins, is central to the quality of our community life in Christ. The best illustration of this objective comes not from ecclesial documents, but from an ecclesial event: *Encuentro* 2000.[8]

The theme of *Encuentro* 2000 was "Many Faces in God's House." It brought together "people of various cultures to share their stories and dreams, voice concerns, grow together in unity, celebrate the Catholic faith, and come to a deeper understanding of the church's identity and mission."[9] The convocation accomplished just that: a powerful spirit of unity arose through the celebration of diversity. The *Encuentro* featured a great variety of presentations, workshops, liturgies, music, film, exhibitions, and food, yet everyone there claimed one faith in one God as members of one church. It certainly contradicts the idea that uniformity breeds unity. We are now seeing pluralism not as a weakness or an obstacle to unity, but as the richness of a unity rooted in diversity.

It is one thing to celebrate this unity in diversity in a one-time national event. It is quite another thing to work through the painstaking challenge of creating parishes where homogeneity has given way to diversity. Spiritual unity in the parish, therefore, can no longer be built on a common cultural or ethnic heritage, or on one way of expressing our faith. It must be based on a new foundation, one that nurtures unity in diversity and includes respect for and celebration of our differences. This kind of foundation is much stronger than a unity built on uniformity, because it must be chosen and nourished to persist.

Probably the most challenging task facing many pastors of multicultural parishes is to find a way to make each cultural group feel part of the one parish. Too often, the dominant group considers itself the owners and the minority group space-renters, rather than full-fledged members of the one parish community. How do we find a way to break through the cultural barriers so that we achieve this mutual acceptance and interaction? How do we go beyond token events to a long-lasting, shared existence as

Anglo, Hispanic, Vietnamese, and African American communities in one parish?

Perhaps it is sufficient here to note the centrality of this endeavor.[10] It is not an incidental issue. Failure to address it will simply contribute to the growing numbers of inactive Catholics who cannot find a home in the Catholic Church because their basic needs are not being addressed. Having one's faith nurtured in ways that respect one's culture is not an add-on but an essential aspect of Christian life. As a matter of fact, all of us need to experience spiritual nourishment in ways that respect our cultural situations. This brings us to the final topic in our reflection.

Adult Formation and Inculturation

There are several important objectives under Goal I that touch upon the broad area of adult formation and catechesis. We cannot possibly address them all. However, the salient and promising focus for evangelization might be identified as the following: people need to encounter Christ in the light of their specific circumstances and cultural contexts. Whether we are talking generational characteristics, ethnic, racial, and language considerations, lifestyle and social standing, or urban or suburban location, what seems to stand out in our experience is that we all need to find Christ in our own life circumstances. Failure to address people in context seems to guarantee irrelevancy.

As with the other topics, there is much documentation on the importance and centrality of adult catechesis as the chief form of all catechesis. There is new guidance in the form of a pastoral plan on adult formation called *Our Hearts Were Burning Within Us*. There is no need to repeat the teaching in these documents. What do we know from our experience in this important topic? I believe it can be reduced to a very simple point: people are hungry to be fed. To the degree that we find a way to nourish them in their spiritual hungers, we will succeed in stemming the outflow of people from the Catholic Church. We will open the gates wide to those who are seeking meaning in the midst of a variety of life situations that they find challenging, if not downright destructive, to their spiritual and physical well-being. Whether we are talking about compassion and forgiveness for the sinner, justice for the oppressed, food for the starving, companionship for the lonely, a word of truth for those who seek it, an experience of the transcendent for those who are unable to find God in their lives—any and all of these contexts cry out for food for hungry hearts.

Many people don't believe that religion can deliver. They look for spirituality elsewhere—in the church basement rather than in the sanctuary, at the Alcoholics Anonymous meeting and not at the Sunday Eucharist. Our experience over the years seems rather clear: to the degree that the Catholic Church is able to offer spiritual nourishment, spiritual treasures, and a spiritual path, we will be able to break through to the hearts of people and manifest to them a dimension of church that is currently being overshadowed by the church as institution, maker of laws, keeper of structures, practitioner of ancient rituals, guardian of morality, and preserver of authority and tradition. Valuable as all these dimensions of religion are, unless we can show how they serve to nourish people spiritually, Catholicism will continue to be seen by many people as an uninviting option among the smorgasbord of offerings (religious and nonreligious) that are laying claim to their lives today.

Conclusion

There is still much room for growth in enthusiasm, deepening of faith, and pursuit of holiness. Mercifully, the challenge is lifelong. Like the rest of Christ's disciples, we are in process. We must be aware, however, of the danger of stagnating or even of abandoning this challenge. The bishops caution, "We can only share what we have received; we can hold on to our faith only if it continues to grow. 'But if salt loses its taste,' Jesus asked, 'with what can it be seasoned?'" (*GMD*, no. 14). This sobering admonition moves us along our pursuit, as it should compel all Catholics. "If faith is not transforming each heart and life, it is dead" (*GMD*, no. 16).

CHAPTER SEVEN

GOAL II

Insight: Goal II challenges Catholics to invite into the fullness of the Catholic faith all those who do not share it.

Reflection

Every once in a while, we human beings experience a break-through idea or discovery that forever changes the way we look at things. One such paradigmatic breakthrough was Copernicus's realization that the sun does not revolve around the earth, but that the earth revolves around the sun. Originally dismissed by many people as nonsense, the theory gained credence as irrefutable evidence was accumulated to prove it, and it eventually was accepted. Now, those breakthrough ideas that dramatically alter the way we look at things are called Copernican revolutions.

Since Copernicus's time, there have been many revolutionary ideas that merit the name *Copernican* because they have dramatically altered our landscape. One example comes to mind: the founding of Alcoholics Anonymous in 1935. In diagnosing alcoholism as a disease and offering a proven remedy, AA changed forever the way the world deals with the alcoholic. Since then, many other new understandings about addiction have followed from this original breakthrough. Something similar occurred in the area of interreligious relations, when the church arrived at the breakthrough understanding that Jesus came to save all people, not just the Jews. Paul, after Jesus appeared to him, became the apostle to the Gentiles, taking Jesus' message of salvation to the world. Since that time, Christianity has struggled to absorb the profound implications of the truth of universal salvation. It has been a complicated journey, with many ups and downs. Recently, since the Second

Vatican Council, we have come to a new breakthrough under-standing, and it is to be found in the Vatican document *Dialogue and Proclamation,* which states: "The Old Testament testifies that from the beginning of creation God made a covenant with all peoples (Gen 1:11). This shows that there is but one history of salvation for the whole of humankind."[1]

This means that there is not one salvation history for Catholics, another for other Christians, and still another for Jews and other religions. There is only one universal plan and one history of salvation and one church. And we have to figure out how all the elements fit together. The Vatican Council looked for new ways to express this profound conviction that there is one plan for all people by breaking down age-old exclu-sionary distinctions between the Catholic Church and other churches (no longer called *sects*) and the Christian religion and other religions (no longer simply regarded as unbelievers). Those facile exclusionary distinctions do not serve us well. They do not help us understand God's one plan of salvation, and how there is one history of salvation that in some way coincides with the history of the world.[2] In other words, there is a new context for evangelization, and it is called *dialogue.*[3] We must proclaim Jesus Christ as universal savior *in dialogue with other religions.* We must proclaim that the Catholic Church has the fullness of the means of salvation *in dialogue with other Christians,* who also form part of the one church of Jesus Christ.

The landscape for evangelization has changed dramatically because of the developments begun in the Second Vatican Council and the deepening understanding of God's universal will for salvation. Rather than the exclusive claims of the past that focused on membership in the Roman Catholic Church, we have come to a much more inclusive understanding of salvation for all. God has only one plan of salvation and one salvation history and one church. Therefore, we have to figure out how all of us are part of that one plan. The exclusionary claims of the past that found their most exquisite expression in the lapidary phrase *extra ecclesiam nulla salus est* (most narrowly construed by Leonard Feeney to mean that there is no salvation for those who are not visibly members of the Roman Catholic Church)[4] have yielded to a much more complex situation of tension and dialogue. Today, we struggle not only with how Christians relate to the one church of Jesus Christ, but also how all humanity can be said to find salvation through Jesus Christ. This is the landscape in which I wish to reflect upon Goal II of *Go and Make Disciples,* which reads as follows:

> **Goal II:** To invite all people in the United States, whatever their social or cultural background, to hear the message of salvation in Jesus Christ so they may come to join us in the fullness of the Catholic faith. (*GMD,* no. 104)

The Beneficiaries of Evangelization

However, one plan of salvation and one salvation history does not translate into a monolithic, one-size-fits-all way of doing evangelization. This is, as I mentioned earlier, a complex situation. The old "either you're in or you're out" perspective no longer holds. The new landscape has resulted in a new appreciation of the richness and diversity of all people's backgrounds and faiths. Everyone is different; everyone has his or her own history. We do believe that all people can benefit from hearing the story of salvation in Jesus Christ and the Catholic Church— but we must tell the story with the listener in mind. In other words, the beneficiary of evangelization will affect the mode of evangelization.

The Nonbeliever

The 2001 American Religious Identification Survey estimates that 14.1 percent of our adult population—29.5 million adults—fall into one of the following categories: atheist, agnostic, humanist, secular, or no religion. While this is a comparatively small segment of the U.S. population, its size has more than doubled since 1990.[5] We apply the theological label *nonbeliever* to these people, but there is much we do not know about them. Have they heard the good news of Jesus Christ? Were they once believers or members of a church—perhaps during their youth? Are they hostile to religion? Do they seek faith?

The appropriate mode of evangelization for the nonbeliever is mission *ad gentes,* literally, *to the nations.* This takes its name from the Vatican II *Decree on the Church's Missionary Activity (Ad Gentes).* It is directed to those "'who do not yet believe in Christ,' 'who are far away from Christ,' in whom the church 'has not yet taken root' and whose culture has not yet been influenced by the Gospel" (*RM,* no. 34). It is the quintessential proclamation of the good news, the message of salvation in Jesus Christ.

The mission *ad gentes* is the model for all the church's missionary activity.[6] It is the template for all invitation, regardless of the beneficiary. Bridge players say, "Lead with your longest and strongest suit." For the Catholic evangelizer, the mission *ad gentes* is our longest and strongest suit. There is nothing more powerful than the good news, unvarnished and presented in its fullness. Inviting people to hear the message of salvation in Jesus Christ is the best we have to offer. If that doesn't have an effect, little else will.

Non-Christians

An estimated 7.74 million adults in the United States (3.7 percent) belong to a non-Christian religion; most of them are Jews, Muslims, Buddhists, and Hindus.[7] While this is a comparatively small number, their presence fuels a healthy sense of religious pluralism in society and within the Catholic Church. We not only accept members of other religions, we also respect them for their convictions and their contributions to society. Authentic pluralism is not a grudging live-and-let-live stance; it is more than indifference, equivocation, or toleration. It sees the real richness in diversity and accepts that people participate in God's plan for salvation in different ways.

Pluralism, however, points up the inherent tension between dialogue and proclamation.[8] On the one hand, we Catholics begin with the foundation that Jesus Christ is the way, the truth, and the life, and that the Catholic Church possesses the fullness of the means of sanctification and truth. This is what we proclaim. On the other hand, we are called to dialogue, which has as its purpose not the conversion of others to Christ but mutual openness to truth. Authentic dialogue is not a veneer for prose-lytism, a hidden attempt to make converts through manipulation or pressure tactics. It is a privileged opportunity to strive for religious understanding, peace among all peoples, and enrichment of our own Catholic faith with all that is true and holy in other religions.

How do we approach this tension? John Paul II, in *Redemptoris Missio,* helps us by pointing out: "Interreligious dialogue is a part of the church's evangelizing mission" (no. 55). It is one of the expressions of the mission *ad gentes.* We cannot separate the two. Moreover, as one writer has recently put it, to believe that we do not need to evangelize Jews, Muslims, Hindus, or Buddhists is to suggest that they are not invited to hear the good news. This attitude is the worst form of discrimination. Dialogue, then, does not replace but accompanies the mission *ad gentes,* which is "directed toward that 'mystery of unity,' from which 'it follows that all men and women who are saved share, though differently, in the same mystery of salvation in Jesus Christ through his Spirit.'"[9]

Another way to understand the connection between proclamation and dialogue lies in that phrase *mystery of unity.* We must accept that we cannot know the form that unity will take; we can only be faithful to working toward it. Indeed, the evangelizer must reckon with the distinct possibility, as *Dialogue and Proclamation* insists, that the conversion to which people of other religions are called is not to explicit faith in Jesus Christ, but to the truth as God reveals it to them, which may be through their own religions.

Other Christians

An estimated 75.5 percent of the adult population in the United States—159 million people—is Christian, and close to a third of them are Catholic.[10] This means that nearly two out of every three non-Catholic adults we encounter already believe in and follow Jesus Christ, although to different extents. Other Christians, if grouped together, are numerically the largest potential beneficiaries of Catholic evangelization. The 2000 edition of *Statistical Abstracts of the United States* lists over seventy religious bodies that fall under the large umbrella of Christianity.[11]

This division among Christians is not only a grave offense against the unity willed by Christ, it is a public scandal that compromises the church's mission to all people and complicates interreligious dialogue. Consequently, restoring Christian unity was one of the main concerns of Vatican II and continues to be a constitutive dimension of modern Catholic evangelization.

As Catholics, however, we have a unique perspective on unity. There exists a real but imperfect communion between the Catholic Church and all who believe in Christ and have been baptized. They possess the scriptures, the life of grace, gifts of the Holy Spirit, liturgical actions, and the means of salvation in Christ. But, and this is a pivotal caveat, they do not enjoy the *fullness* of the means of salvation—for example, the apostolic faith and the sacraments (especially the Eucharist).[12] Hence, we regard the Catholic Church as the reference point for Christian unity.

So if unity is the objective and the fullness of that unity is grounded in the Catholic Church, to what are Catholic evangelizers inviting non-Catholic Christians? The answer is in Goal II: we invite them to join us in "the fullness of the Catholic faith." This can happen in two ways: ecumenical dialogue and conversions.

Vatican II defined the *ecumenical movement* as, essentially, promoting Christian unity. The hoped-for result of this movement "will be that...all Christians will be gathered, in a common celebration of the Eucharist, into the unity of the one and only church, which Christ bestowed on his church from the beginning."[13] It is important to stress that *unity* is the goal, not a theological lowest common denominator. The various dialogues between the Catholic Church and other denominations are not negotiations. Rather, the "principle underlying these dialogues is that reunion is effected not by compromise but by common biblical and historical study to find a ground of truth which transcends the historic division, by the power of the Spirit working in the ecumenical movement."[14]

Given the grandness of ecumenism's scope, and our association of dialogue with something official experts do, ordinary

Catholics may believe that they have no role in it. This would be a mistake. There is much needed and valuable work to be done in local communities, in families, in neighborhoods, and in workplaces. Catholics need to develop a fresh ecumenical spirit, if for no other reason than to avoid further injury to the cause of Christian unity! A new sense of respect, sharing, and collaboration is required.

The second way we invite other Christians to join the fullness of the Catholic faith is by reaching out to and welcoming people who want to become Catholic—or, as some might say, people who want to convert on their own initiative. These seekers are often baptized Christians from other denominations. The U.S. bishops' report on the RCIA in 2000 found that 61 percent of RCIA participants fell into this category, which was larger than the other two categories combined: never baptized (25 percent) and baptized Catholic (14 percent). Interestingly, the most common reason given for starting the RCIA was to unify an ecumenical or interchurch marriage; 83 percent of married participants had Catholic spouses.[15]

In pastoral practice, there is a tension between ecumenism and invitation that requires a delicate balance. Ecumenical sensitivity should not close the door on individual Christians who wish to join the Catholic Church. Neither should ecumenism be applied as a veneer for proselytism. As the *Decree on Ecumenism* states, "It is evident that the work of preparing and reconciling those individuals who wish for full Catholic communion is of its nature distinct from ecumenical action. But there is no opposition between the two, since both proceed from the marvelous ways of God."[16]

Inactive Catholics

Many of us have loved ones who have drifted away from the church or from their faith. It is impossible to count all the inactive Catholics in this country, but sociological research helps us to estimate the number at about 21 million people—41 percent of the nearly 51 million adult Catholics in the United States. At these levels, active Catholics constitute the single largest Christian denomination in the country (31 million) *and* inactive

Catholics constitute the second largest. Southern Baptists come in third, at an estimated 16 million members.[17] These are staggering estimates that demand the attention of Catholic evangelization. If we, as a church, cannot reconcile with and invite back Catholics who no longer fully practice the faith, what hope do we have of reaching out to non-Catholics?

Who are these inactive Catholics? *Go and Make Disciples* links inactivity to not participating in communal worship. Mass attendance is, indeed, a leading criterion used by sociologists of religion to measure people's commitment to the institutional church. We could also consider their observance of the Easter duty (annual confession and communion), level of volunteering, financial contributions, devotional activity, observance of days of fasting and abstinence, participation in parish activities outside of liturgy, or living gospel values in daily life. All of these are observable and measurable *activities* that we associate with the Catholic faith, and which Catholics practice to varying degrees.

For all the research and writing in this area, however, there is little consensus on how to define an inactive Catholic. There are other adjectives applied to this group of Catholics—nonpracticing, fallen-away, disaffected, marginal, cultural—but *inactive* is the most frequently used in ecclesial and theological writings.[18]

I offer the following definition: *An inactive Catholic is a member of the Catholic Church who does not actively practice the Catholic faith; that is, who has not attended mass in the previous six months other than for special holy days (Christmas and Easter), weddings, funerals, or the like.*[19]

Using this definition prevents us from judging fellow parishioners or family members too quickly. It is only a measure of *one* externally observable behavior; we cannot draw any conclusions about a person's level of faith, state of sin, or intentions of the heart.

This definition also does not reference a person's commitment to the teachings of the Catholic Church. As mentioned in Chapter One, many Catholics openly disagree with or dissent from certain tenets, particularly in the area of sexual morality. While this phenomenon may be related to inactivity, it would be a pastoral error to presume the link. I believe formation and not invitation is the best way to address the issue of Catholic dissent.

The definition also does not turn on the issue of parish registration. While inactive Catholics are usually not registered with a parish, many registered Catholics are inactive as well. Registration is a weak indication of inactivity.

It is important to note that the group of Catholics defined as inactive is broad. Consider two examples. Because of a new job, a single college graduate has recently moved to an area where she has no family or friends. She attended mass weekly and was involved in regular ministry projects during college. In the first six months of her new job, however, she has been overwhelmed with work and has not made it to mass except for Christmas morning. But she intends to get back into regular practice when life settles down. Now compare this first person to a second example. A man was raised in a Catholic family and participated fully in his parish through high school—was even an altar boy for many years. He was married and divorced in his twenties. He remarried outside the church to a non-Catholic and raised a family. One day he was told in confession that he could not receive communion because he was in a perpetual state of adultery. He hasn't been back to mass in forty years. These examples are worlds apart and illustrate the sheer diversity that evangelizers are likely to encounter when inviting inactive Catholics to return to the community.

The bishops state, "Every Catholic can be a minister of welcome, reconciliation, and understanding to those who have stopped practicing the faith" (*GMD,* no. 40). We don't have to go looking for this beneficiary of evangelization. Inactive Catholics are our family members. They are our friends and co-workers. They probably share the pew with us at Christmas and Easter. And if we, the Catholic community, do not reach out to them, there are many other communities who will.

The Mode of Evangelization Corresponds to the Beneficiary

Beneficiary	Mode of Evangelization	Appropriate Goal
The Faithful	Ongoing Growth and Renewed Conversion	Goal 1
Inactive Catholics	Reevangelization,[20] Outreach, Reconciliation	Goal 2
Other Christians	Ecumenical Outreach	Goal 2
Members of Other Religions	Interreligious Dialogue	Goal 2
Nonbelievers	Mission *Ad Gentes*	Goal 2

Invitation

In the 1989 movie *Field of Dreams,* an Iowa farmer hears a voice whisper to him one evening as he is standing in his cornfield: "If you build it, he will come." The "it" is a baseball diamond; the "he" who ultimately shows up is his father, long dead, along with Shoeless Joe Jackson and seven other Chicago White Sox players who had been banned from baseball for throwing the 1919 World Series. It is a delightful fantasy. But it is also a telling metaphor for many Catholics' approach to evangelization: "Build it (the church) and they (inactive Catholics and unchurched people) will come!" In this mindset, there is no need for invitation and little emphasis on welcoming. All we need to do is witness with our lives.

Christian witness is indeed an indispensable element of evangelization—but it is only a first step. We also need to do explicit welcoming and inviting. The second goal of *Go and Make Disciples* challenges us to augment a *Field of Dreams* perspective with the outreaching action we see in Jesus' parable of the wedding feast (Matt 22:1–14). In the parable, Jesus likens the kingdom of heaven to a king who gives a wedding banquet for his son. When the feast is ready, however, the invited guests decline to attend, for various reasons. Some of them even persecute the king's messengers. The king is angry. He punishes the murderers and then tells his servants: "Go therefore into the main streets, and invite everyone you find to the wedding banquet" (Matt 22:9).[21] The servants bring in everyone they find, both bad and good, and fill the wedding hall.

Unlike in the movie, the king built it (prepared the feast) but they (the invited guests) would *not* come. Offering a great feast was not enough to attract people. The king had to go out to the highways and byways. We have here a different metaphor for looking at church: it is not a field of dreams but a banquet table, and to attract guests we need to go beyond our walls and reach out to those who are not present. We have a heavenly feast to share with all peoples, yet many people do not come to the table because we fail to extend an invitation.

The bishops write, "People can know they are invited to experience Jesus Christ in our church only if they are really and effectively asked and adequate provisions are made for their full participation. We want our Catholic brothers and sisters to effectively ask and to really invite" (*GMD*, no. 54). Yet we rarely get around to inviting others! Goal II challenges Catholics to invite into the fullness of the Catholic faith all those who do not share in it.

Inviting is such a common word that its significance in Goal II may be overlooked. Think about what inviting is *not*. It isn't pressuring, manipulating, proselytizing, forcing, tricking, duping, strong-arming, or using guilt. "Such tactics contradict the Good News we announce and undermine the spirit of invitation that should characterize all true evangelization" (*GMD*, no. 55). Invitation does not presuppose acceptance or expect reciprocation. It respects the freedom of the recipient. Genuine invitation is open to rejection; hence the goal states that hearers "*may* come to join us." Through us, Jesus invites others: "Follow me" and "Come and see."

Given this open-endedness, we might believe that invitation is an impotent or ambiguous method of evangelization. Quite the contrary; personal invitation is a powerful force, not to be underestimated. Being invited makes people feel wanted, welcomed, needed, and valued. Even when I must decline, it makes my day to receive the invitation. Being excluded makes people feel left out, rejected, passed over, and hurt. We have all had painful experiences of being left out and memorable experiences of being invited in.

I remember a rather bizarre experience I had when I was a student at the North American College in Rome. It was my second year of theology and I felt pretty left out, for lots of reasons. In desperation, one evening about ten o'clock I went to the room of one of my classmates, knocked on the door, and said—without any introductory remarks—"I want to be your friend." Needless to say, I nearly scared him out of his wits. He didn't know how to respond. Curiously, it didn't much matter to me. I desperately needed an invitation, but I couldn't wait for someone else to invite me! It felt like I was in jail, and I needed to break out of my isolation. After taking that desperate action, I felt free to try something more effective. Actually, a year or so later, he and I did become friends. I don't recommend my method, but I know there are many people in the world who feel the same loneliness and desperation, which can sometimes result in far more bizarre behavior. God made us to be part of the whole. Invitation is a powerful way to communicate to someone else the life-saving message that we are wanted.

The fifth objective of this goal draws attention to the importance of inviting people during their formative years: to use special times in parish and family life to invite people to faith. Experience has shown that premarriage and prebaptism preparation is an excellent opportunity to reach out to inactive Catholics. Similarly, for years parishes have offered various "come home" programs at Christmas, Ash Wednesday, and at Easter with high degrees of success.

Strategies that reach out to age groups rely upon principles of generational and life-cycle models of sociology.[22] These principles give us insights into the various age groups and their openness to religion at different times in their lives. For example, generational sociology tells us that we cannot approach generation Xers—people in their twenties and early thirties—with an appeal to institutional loyalty, which is a dominant feature of another group, the pre–Vatican II generation. Similarly, based on the life-cycle model, we might expect the birth of a child to be a time when inactive Catholics might consider returning to actively practicing their faith.

The seventh objective offers practical methods of invitation. Unlike all the other strategies for the other goals, however, the bishops separate the strategies for this objective into national and local levels.

The national-level strategies center on coordinated public relations, particularly through the media. As *Thy Kingdom Come* asserts, "Mass evangelization requires mass communications—the media.[23] While the most effective evangelization may always be person-to-person or mediated through small groups, there is a definite and growing place for proclamation to the society at large."[24] It makes sense to run large-scale media campaigns from the national level; parishes and perhaps even dioceses may not have the financial and personnel resources to take on such projects. The local-level strategies are ideally suited to the parish and perhaps the diocese, but ill-suited to the national church. One of these local strategies, since it is what we most commonly think of as evangelization, deserves further exploration: home visitation. Due to the dedicated missionary work of the Mormons and Jehovah's Witnesses, evangelization still triggers visions of going door to door—an off-putting idea for many people. Nonetheless, in our modern society, which is highly diverse and highly mobile, home visitation "helps substitute for the ties of blood, proximity, family, and culture that once bound parishes together."[25]

Home visitation has distinct advantages and disadvantages, and the former outweigh the latter. It is labor intensive and somewhat out of fashion today. But it helps Catholics meet people they otherwise are not likely to encounter; it puts a human face on the institutional parish and shows vitality in the parish community. The visit itself typically takes one of four forms. The first is the *census visit,* either to everyone in the parish boundaries or only to registered Catholics. The second is the *social visit,* where parishioners visit people in their neighborhood. The third is the *witness visit,* when Catholics share their faith so as to elicit a response from those they visit. The last is the *pastoral visit,* such as to people preparing to baptize a child. Beyond these, the "key to the visit is the response that people make to the visitors. Visitors must be sensitive enough to be able to know what others are asking when the visit starts to go a little deeper, when others are reaching out for some kind of help, enlightenment or direction."[26]

It is the job of all Catholics to invite all people to hear the message of salvation. People's responses, however, are up to God. We Catholics actually have the easy part. The bishops remind us that both the proclaiming of the message of salvation and the response of the listeners are works of the Spirit of God (*GMD*, no. 10). The power of God is what converts. We do not convert; we proclaim. When we have the courage to proclaim the gospel of Jesus Christ in our pluralistic, post-Christian age, the power of the Spirit will work. Many of us fail to let God work because we assume that we can't change people's hearts, especially in our current culture. This misses the point; we never had that power. It is God's. We must learn to trust in God's power to evangelize and play our part. In our weakness, God is strong.

Welcoming

A Tale from Catholic Folklore

A single Catholic man just moved into town and wants to go to mass. He finds his local parish in the phone book and calls for information. He gets a recorded message from the pastor with weekend mass times and a number to call in emergencies. He jots down the information and looks forward to attending mass and meeting some new people on the weekend.

On Sunday morning the man leaves his house early because he doesn't know exactly where he is going. It's a good thing, too, because he gets lost looking for the church. It doesn't help that the parish's sign is small and easy to miss, especially with all the cars trying to leave after the earlier mass. He finally finds a spot in the back lot and tries to enter the church through a side door, which, unfortunately, is locked. He has to walk all the way around the building and go in the main entrance.

The vestibule of the church is packed with parishioners from the previous mass. Some of them crowd around the priest. The man looks around and decides to go into the sanctuary and pray silently before the next mass begins. On his way in, an usher smiles and hands him a one-page, folded worship aid and an envelope for the second collection. The pews are mostly empty. A few families are hanging around talking to one another. Some children are running up and down the aisles. Up front, the choir from the earlier mass is clearing out, and the choir members for the upcoming mass are tuning their instruments and warming up their voices. Looking for a little quiet, the man sits toward the front of the sanctuary, away from the choir, on the end of a pew.

After a few minutes, an older woman comes up to the man and strikes up a conversation. She asks if the man is new. Thrilled to be recognized, the man says that he is and asks her if she is on the parish staff. She says no. One of the ushers? No. Part of some hospitality committee? No? At a loss, the man then asks how she knew that he was new. "Well," she replies, "it's just that you're in my seat."

Do you see anyone or anything familiar in this story? It is not a fantasy. It's quite real and is being played out every week around the country. By and large, Catholic parishes are just not that welcoming, even of fellow parishioners. Then how do newcomers and non-Catholic visitors perceive our parishes? Ultimately, they are the final judges of a parish's welcoming spirit. Welcoming, or hospitality, is a necessary part of any outreach. When we invite others to join us in the fullness of the Catholic faith, to what are we really inviting them? How prepared are we to receive the people who respond to our invitation?

Mindful of this situation, the bishops include welcoming as one of the components of Goal II. "This goal means not only that people are invited but also that an essential welcoming spirit is present in Catholic institutions" (*GMD*, no. 104). We want people, parishioners and visitors alike, to feel at home in our parishes. But there is a big difference between being one parish family and being families who attend one parish.

It is important to say upfront what hospitality is all about. We are not talking about a hail-fellow-well-met, back-slapping kind of friendliness. Hospitality, rather, falls under the virtue of accepting and reverencing people because, as human beings, they have worth and dignity. We are talking about giving all people a warm welcome simply because they are brothers and sisters in God's family, no matter their race, sex, culture, sexual orientation, culture, or social status.

The Decline of Hospitality in Our Society

The practice of hospitality has lost currency in contemporary society.[27] *Hospitality* is what we extend to invited guests: family, friends, and business associates. These are people whom we know, directly or indirectly, and trust. By way of contrast, *hostility* is our default reaction to uninvited visitors: strangers, door-to-door salespeople, door-to-door evangelists (Mormons, Jehovah's Witnesses, and so on), fundraisers, and scammers. Other unwanted intrusions into our homes come from telemarketers, junk mail, and dozens of spam e-mail messages. We might even consider how we react to insects, spiders, and rodents that dare enter our homes. Often, instead of a welcome mat, houses today display ARMED RESPONSE! security signs and ABSOLUTELY NO SOLICITORS! plaques near the doorbell.

On one occasion, while I was a pastor in Los Angeles, I was on my way to visit a parishioner and I got lost. I had the address and phone number but couldn't find the street. I was dressed in my clerics. I spotted a couple of women chatting in front of a house. I asked them if they knew where the street was. They didn't. Then I asked if I could use their phone to call the family. One of the women looked at me as if I had come in from another planet. She said: "Excuse me, sir. But this is Los Angeles in the 1990s! You give me the telephone number; I will make the call!" I was an unwelcome intruder and not to be allowed in the house.

We teach our children never to talk to strangers, accept gifts from strangers, open the front door to strangers, or get in a stranger's car. Helping out the stranger stranded on the side of the road, giving a ride to a hitchhiker, or giving cash to a stranger are considered acts of folly, not virtue. Pondering the modern condition and the need for a spiritual movement from hostility to hospitality, Henri Nouwen observes, "Our society seems to be increasingly full of fearful, defensive, aggressive people anxiously clinging to suspicion, always expecting an enemy to suddenly appear, intrude and do harm."[28]

To understand why, we need look no further than the daily news: violence, crime, cons, injuries, and killings are daily fare, brought vividly into our lives through modern communications. The cumulative impact over time is that fear and self-preservation crowd out welcoming and hospitality. As Nouwen summarizes:

> In our world the assumption is that strangers are a potential danger and that it is up to them to disprove it. When we travel we keep a careful eye on our luggage; when we walk the streets we are aware of where we keep our money; and when we walk at night in a dark park our whole body is tense with fear of an attack. Our heart might desire to help others: to feed the hungry, visit the prisoners and offer a shelter to travelers; but meanwhile we have surrounded ourselves with a wall of fear and hostile feelings, instinctively avoiding people and places where we might be reminded of our good intentions.[29]

Our busy-ness, too, is an obstacle to welcoming and hospitality. Our lives are overflowing with commitments, activities, and responsibilities. The unexpected visitor is a distraction, a delay, an inconvenience. Welcoming the stranger or someone new opens us up to the possibility of new relationships and commitments. Since there are too many demands on our time and energy as it is, the lack of hospitality is a preemptive defense against this so as to preserve what precious free time we have left.

In this social context, advancing our parishes' spirit of welcoming will take great effort and a conversion in our thought patterns. It will be a difficult, though not impossible, task, for in this work we have a strong ally in human nature: we all yearn to be welcomed and belong ourselves! The trick will be connecting this desire for ourselves with action for others. To create the parish environment we seek, we must do unto others as we would have them do unto us. Furthermore, we must extend to others the hospitality that we have received from the Lord: "Welcome one another, therefore, just as Christ has welcomed you, for the glory of God" (Rom 15:7).

Making Catholic Parishes More Welcoming

Welcoming is the very first objective listed under Goal II. A wonderful restatement of this objective comes from a parish in the archdiocese of Louisville: "May no one visiting our parish for the first time ever leave as a stranger."[30] This motto echoes the New Testament understanding of friendship *(philoxenia)* as "making the stranger a friend," and it provides a vivid image of what a truly welcoming parish can achieve.

Of all the strategies for this objective, designated ministers of hospitality receive the most attention in the literature on Catholic welcoming. The three most commonly referenced ministers are receptionists, greeters, and ushers. They are often the first points of contact in the parish for parishioners and visitors alike. As such, theirs is a ministry of first impressions for the newcomer, inquirer, or returnee. They don't simply *tend* the entrance points to a parish; they *are* the entrance points. "The hospitality ministers, much more than doorkeepers, are doors themselves, giving open access to the warmth of holy fellowship in the spirit of Jesus."[31]

Hospitality ministers are on the front lines of welcoming, presumably (it is hoped!) because of their warm personality and friendliness. But, more often than not, they mirror the attitude of the congregation. If the greeters and ushers are friendly and outgoing, the worshiping community is likewise enthusiastic and hospitable. Unfortunately, the opposite is also true. If greeters and ushers appear distracted, unfriendly, or rushed, the worshiping assembly is often similar.[32] Ministers of hospitality can put the parish's best face or voice forward, but they can neither manufacture a welcoming spirit that isn't present in the broader community nor compensate for the lack of welcoming newcomers may experience once through the front door. Accordingly, it is not enough to delegate welcoming to the select few. The whole community must be endowed with a hospitable spirit.

Welcoming: The Community's Responsibility

Arising out of a consumer mentality, many Catholics see themselves as guests in their own parish. They support the parish financially and then expect certain services in return. When they come to mass, they are passive participants, trying to refuel spiritually for the week ahead. In this mindset, welcoming is the job of the priest, the parish staff, and the parish ministers. Moreover, they themselves are the people to be welcomed! It is true that all of us are guests in God's house, Christ's guests at the table of the Eucharist, and should behave accordingly. We must further admit that parish leaders ought to be models of hospitality.[33] Nonetheless, learning from African American spirituality, we must *also* see ourselves as hosts and the parish as our home.

> African Americans see the primary function of the ministry is to welcome people into our church home. This is, as in any home, a place where someone receives you; rejoices in your coming; extends their happiness in your presence; shares themselves in your happiness, sorrow, counsel, and comfort. It is a place where the person is important and is called to contribute their gifts in the continuance and nurturing of the church family.[34]

An immediate outcome of developing a spirit of hospitality is that parishioners will be more welcoming toward each other, which is an important ingredient in building the parish community. Frank DeSiano asserts, "There is no point in discussing how we welcome visitors and strangers if we have not looked at how we welcome ourselves—namely, how the assembly gathers and what kind of welcome we give each other when we come together."[35] Do we know our fellow parishioners? Do we greet those around us at mass? Would we notice if a regular weren't there? These are simple questions that have serious implications. As pointed out in Chapter One, many Catholics are leaving the church. While the reasons differ, an easy one to identify—and solve—is the perception that people aren't welcome. "Does anyone care when I'm here?" "Would anyone miss me if I left?"

To have parishioners welcome each other is essential, but it is not enough. True Christian hospitality compels us to welcome the stranger, the newcomer, the visitor, and the returnee. Admittedly, the "most challenging aspect of being a welcoming community is getting parishioners to go beyond welcoming the regulars."[36] This may require a moment of conversion for

Catholics, who, before Vatican II, held, and projected, the image of the church as a closed society. "So often regular churchgoers put on 'blinders' that enable them to see only people they already know or, even worse, to ignore just about anyone else. When this is a collective mentality, visitors and strangers can be little more than onlookers."[37] Overcoming this tendency is the responsibility of the whole community.

Welcoming the Newcomer to Our Land

The tenth objective of Goal II talks about cultural diversity, but its strategies are all about welcoming foreigners.

It is important to note that this objective is important enough that it is specifically included in Goal II itself: "To invite all people in the United States, *whatever their social or cultural background....*"

Welcoming the newcomer, foreigner, or stranger is a fundamental Christian calling, for in the stranger we welcome God. Abraham welcomes the Lord, who appears as three men, and in return for Abraham's hospitality, the Lord foretells the birth of Isaac (Gen 18:1–15). The two disciples on the road to Emmaus invite a stranger to stay the night with them, only to have the stranger reveal himself as the risen Christ through the breaking of the bread (Luke 24:13–35). Jesus teaches his followers: "Whoever receives one whom I send receives me; and whoever receives me receives him who sent me" (John 13:20). Jesus lists the welcoming of strangers as one of the criteria of the final judgment, because whatever we do for the stranger we do for Christ (Matt 25:31–46). Hospitality is listed among the qualifications for bishops (1 Tim 3:2; Titus 1:8). Lastly, the author of Hebrews warns, "Do not neglect to show hospitality to strangers, for by doing that some have entertained angels without knowing it" (13:2). The way the community expresses its hospitality to strangers, particularly in meals, is a matter of fidelity to the gospel. As Nouwen summarizes, "Old and New Testament stories not only show how serious our obligation is to welcome the stranger in our home, but they also tell us that guests are carrying precious gifts with them, which they are eager to reveal to a receptive host."[38]

Another motivation for Catholics to welcome the immigrant is that Catholics too come from immigrant families. We have always been an immigrant church, a fact that we need to remember as successive waves of immigration continue to roll onto our shores. We are "a witness at once to the diversity of people who make up our world and to our unity in one humanity, destined to enjoy the fullness of God's blessings in Jesus Christ."[39] This reminder can help us overcome the pervasive xenophobia, our fear that the foreigners will displace us and our parish traditions, and lead us to welcome the newcomers, old immigrant to new immigrant. In this regard, God's consistent reminder to Israel seems an appropriate message for us: "You shall also love the stranger, for you were strangers in the land of Egypt" (Deut 10:19).[40]

From an evangelizing perspective, a notable consequence of the new immigration from non-Western European countries is that the distinction between foreign missions and home missions is being erased. Previously, the mission territories were far-off nations in Africa, Asia, or the Pacific Islands. Priests and religious traveled there to spread the good news to those who had never heard of Jesus Christ or his church. The mode of evangelization in these encounters was mission *ad gentes,* the primary proclamation of the gospel and the calling to initial conversion. Now, with all the immigration from these continents, the United States is receiving an influx of non-Christians and comparatively new Christians. Catholics don't need to go to distant lands to evangelize, because the peoples of the distant lands have moved into their neighborhoods.

In welcoming the newcomer, we must not fall into the trap of trying to make the "other" one of "us." As Nouwen cautions, "Hospitality is not a subtle invitation to adopt the lifestyle of the host, but the gift of a chance for the guest to find his own."[41] Welcoming is not a cover for rapid assimilation into the dominant parish culture so that unity can be quickly achieved in uniformity. Its purpose, as Pope John Paul II reminds us, is mutual enrichment.[42]

True welcoming will shed any vestiges of *nativism,* which is the belief that there is only one image of the real American and that any embrace of foreign traditions, culture, or language threatens the unity of our society. Nativism manifests itself in parishes when "established members insist that there is just one way to worship, one set of familiar hymns, one small handful of familiar devotions, one way to organize a parish community, one language for all—and that immigrants must adapt to that way of doing things."[43]

If we can transcend nativism, then we will experience the fruit of truly welcoming the foreigner into our parish life: mutual enrichment.

> When we welcome a stranger to our midst we are welcoming him or her to an unfamiliar world. Hospitality allows us to open up our own worlds. Strangers have stories to tell which we have never heard. These stories trigger our imagination. They can enrich or even transform our lives.[44]

Both the established communities and the incoming cultures have gifts from their rich histories to share. In this exchange, a balance must be struck where each side embraces the other's contributions. There will be defensiveness on both sides, but also change, for it is an inevitable result of an open, respectful encounter between the old and the new.

This change can be not only enriching but purifying. The U.S. bishops write:

> Change, however, is inevitable as immigrants set down roots in this country, enriching American culture while adopting aspects of it themselves. Indeed, it would be a mistake to regard any culture as fixed and immutable. All cultures are in constant processes of change as their members seek new ways to address individual and group needs and as they encounter new situations and other cultures. Indeed, no culture is either permanent or perfect. All constantly need to be evangelized and uplifted by the good news of Jesus Christ. The encounter between cultures that is an everyday affair in the incorporation of immigrants into the church and the communities of the United States should provoke not only adaptation on

both sides but a critical discernment of the strengths and failings of each culture in the light of the Gospel.[45]

Virgil Elizondo, founder of the Mexican American Cultural Center in San Antonio, Texas, employs a wonderful metaphor to describe this process: the stewpot.[46] The people and gifts of the many cultures are like stew ingredients mixed in a great big pot, which is the parish. The ongoing interaction and friction among the cultures applies heat to the pot and can, at times, bring it to a boiling point. Yet, in the cooking process each ingredient gives up something of itself to enrich the stew. Moreover, the carrots, potatoes, meat, and so on, all take on the flavors shared by the other ingredients. In the end, the delicious stew is a joint creation, greater than the sum of the individual ingredients. Unlike the melting-pot analogy, the individual ingredients maintain their original identity.

Conclusion

The thrust of Goal II is what Catholics most readily associate with *evangelization*. Goal I activities appear under a number of other names, such as renewal, catechesis, formation, ongoing conversion, discipleship, Christian life, and holiness. Goal III, as we will see in Chapter Eight, goes under the names of social justice, political advocacy, community organizing, and public service. The ministries associated with Goals I and III are well-established. Hence, since the Second Vatican Council, evangelization committees and ministries have been charged mainly with Goal II initiatives.

A similar narrowing exists within Goal II activities. Ministry with diverse ethnic and cultural groups, which we have grouped under the main category of welcoming, is carried out mainly by offices or committees comprised of representatives of those groups. Moreover, there are separate offices or committees for each constituency: Hispanic, African American, Vietnamese, Korean, Filipino, deaf, disabled, and so on. Ecumenism and interreligious dialogue are carried out by specialists in each of those fields, and tend to further subdivide, depending on the dialogue partner: Anglicans, Lutherans, Evangelicals, Jews, Muslims, and so on.

So what is left that is purely evangelization? Looking at the objectives and strategies of Goal II, the answer is clear: invitation. Invitation has several phases, including formation of active Catholics for outreach, inviting, and welcoming those who respond. Using the language in Chapter Three, we might identify invitation with *disciple-making,* which helps further explain why we feel that Catholics must embrace disciple-making in order for the church to fully embrace evangelization as its essential mission.

CHAPTER EIGHT

GOAL III

Insight: Goal III challenges Catholics to actualize their faith in society.

Reflection

In recent years, we have become increasingly aware of just how interrelated our physical universe is. We look at things such as pollution, global warming, and weather systems like El Niño, and realize that nothing happens in isolation. Some time ago, I was fascinated to read about a phenomenon called the "butterfly effect," which explores this tightly knit ecosystem. It gets its name because it describes how a butterfly flaps its wings on one side of the globe and causes a major change in the ecosystem half a world away. I don't understand the scientific basis for this claim, but it strikes me as a fascinating symbol of a very startling reality: we live in one, highly interconnected universe.

We have also become keenly aware that, as a human society, we live in a global village. We are inextricably tied to each other, economically, politically, and socially. We can see this manifested everywhere. One example that has been in the news recently is outsourcing: companies based in the United States move jobs to other countries, where labor costs are less, to increase their profits. In this country, the result is lower prices for some goods, but also, in some cases, less employment. There is a particular concern that this will begin to affect higher-level service and technical jobs. In the countries with the new jobs, employment is higher, but the employees sometimes find themselves forced to work long hours in dangerous and unhealthy conditions. In another example, increased international trade and travel means that deadly viruses can easily move from one continent to another; the outbreak of the SARS virus sharply highlighted this.

Yet not all aspects of interconnectedness are negative. The global network that is the World Wide Web has truly changed the way we live. One fascinating use of it is by political dissidents in some countries, who are able to communicate with each other and with the outside world in ways that were impossible before. The communications media, too, helps to bring all parts of the world closer together.

The notion that we are all connected is not new, however. This is exactly what Paul was writing about in 1 Corinthians, in his discourse on the body of Christ.

> As it is, there are many members, yet one body. The eye cannot say to the hand, "I have no need of you," nor again the head to the feet, "I have no need of you...." If one member suffers, all suffer together with it; if one member is honored, all rejoice together with it. Now you are the body of Christ and individually members of it. (12:20–21, 26–27)

Paul was not just expressing a pious hope, but describing a reality. We are all connected to each other in ways we don't fully understand but that are nonetheless real.

Interestingly, modern physics—especially that branch known as quantum mechanics—is exploring this same idea. Scientists did experiments where they first paired molecules, then separated them. After that, they discovered that anything they did to one half of the pair also affected the other half—even though they were not physically touching, not connected, and were separated by significant distances. They were connected in ways that could not be explained by traditional science.

This interconnectedness helps explain why we are called to take part in the reordering of society according to the values of God's kingdom: by doing so, we are simply trying to right the balance of, and heal, the body of Christ, of which we are all a part.

In Chapter Twelve of this book, I will propose that we view the three goals of *Go and Make Disciples* through the threefold lens of the priestly, prophetic, and royal character of our baptism. This focus on the trilogy, which enjoyed considerable prominence in the documents of the Second Vatican Council, offers a rich spirituality for both lay and ordained. Viewing Goal III through the royal lens reminds us that we are called to participate in the reordering of society according to the values of God's kingdom—a kingdom that has already been inaugurated in the world by Jesus' death and resurrection. It is not, then, a matter of changing the world by our own efforts; rather, it is a matter of participating in the transforming power of Christ already at work in the world through the Holy Spirit.

Catholic social teaching—and the entire Christian faith, for that matter—does not accept the apathy and defeatism that make individuals feel powerless to change things. We are participants in God's plan to save the world. Salvation history has turned on the lives of individuals such as Noah, Abraham, Moses, David, Mary, Jesus, and Paul. A living example of the power of one is John Paul II; though old and frail now, his personal impact on the world continues to be enormous. The example of saints, official and unofficial, is testimony to what individuals can do to change the world, Mother Teresa being a recent example. Nor should we limit our perspective to a few select, larger-than-life heroes. The civil rights movement was fueled by the courageous actions of one, rather ordinary, woman, Rosa Parks, who on December 1, 1955 in Montgomery, Alabama, refused to go to the back of the bus. History is full of stories of world-changing actions by quite ordinary individuals. There is a list in the Holocaust Museum in Washington, D.C., of righteous Gentiles, people who acted to save Jews during the Holocaust. This is a powerful reminder that there are individuals who make a difference by acting with courage to make the world a better place to live. The book (and now the movie trilogy) *The Lord of the Rings* gives us a fictional account of individual commitment and courage in the face of overwhelming evil.

Salvation history also shows us that communities of faith such as Israel, Jesus' disciples, and the church are forces to be reckoned with in the world. There is a wonderful story of a small village in the south central area of France called Le Chambon. The village was populated largely by Huguenots—French Calvinists—a group severely persecuted in Catholic France almost since it first appeared in the time of the Reformation. During the Second World War, under the leadership of its pastor, Andre Trocme, the entire community established itself as a place of refuge for Jews. Virtually all the residents participated in sheltering Jewish refugees of all ages. When that became increasingly difficult, the villagers led them across the Alps to freedom in Switzerland.

The book that tells the story of Le Chambon[1] is *Lest Innocent Blood Be Shed,* written by Philip Hallie, a French Jew. Some years after he had written the book, Professor Hallie was giving a talk in Minneapolis. After the talk, a woman stood up and asked if the village of Le Chambon was in the region of Haute-Loire in south central France, where the great river Loire has its origins. Mr. Hallie said it was.

> "Well, you have been speaking about the village that saved the lives of all three of my children," she said. She then thanked him for writing the book so that Americans could understand those days better than they have. Then she paused briefly and said, "The Holocaust was storm, lightning, thunder, wind, rain, yes, and Le Chambon is the rainbow...the rainbow."[2]

Goal III—the struggle to transform society in Christ—is an integral part of evangelization. As John Paul II asserts, Catholic social doctrine "pertains to the Church's evangelizing mission and is an essential part of the Christian message" because it "points out the direct consequences of that message in the life of society and situates daily work and struggles for justice in the context of bearing witness to Christ the savior."[3] Practical works of justice, charity, and peace "fully authenticate our message" (*GMD,* no. 60). That is to say, we cannot proclaim a gospel we do not live, and we cannot carry out a real social ministry without knowing the Lord and hearing his call to justice and peace. Henri Nouwen states: "[Jesus'] appearance in our midst has made it undeniably clear that changing the human heart and changing human society are not separate tasks, but are as interconnected as the two beams on the cross."[4]

If every parishioner would carry the Christian values of social justice into the family, the neighborhood, the workplace, and society, then the world would be transformed in Christ. The light of Christ would shine through these people and the parish would become a rainbow of hope, for all to see and give praise to their heavenly Father. I think of Goal III as the *hallmark* of Catholic evangelization, because the church did not limit its vision of evangelization to the spiritual, but rather insisted upon an integral vision that embraces the temporal as well. The Catholic vision of evangelization is broad and complex, as this goal clearly shows.

Goal III reads as follows:

Goal III: To foster gospel values in our society, promoting the dignity of the human person, the importance of the family, and the common good of our society, so that our nation may continue to be transformed by the saving power of Jesus Christ. (*GMD*, no. 117)

The wording of this goal is more complex than that of the previous two, which opens it to varying interpretations. I read the statement in the following way. The heart of the goal is to "foster gospel values in our society...so that our nation may continue to be transformed by the saving power of Jesus Christ." We foster gospel values in society through promoting three specific goods: (1) the dignity of the human person, (2) the importance of the family, and (3) the common good of our society. The implication of this reading, then, is that "fostering gospel values in society" serves as an umbrella concept for the other three elements (the dignity of the individual, the importance of the family, the common good). When we promote those three elements, we are working to promote gospel values.

It is noteworthy that there are significantly fewer objectives and strategies for Goal III than for Goals I and II. To be sure, quantity does not trump quality. Nonetheless, Goal III is comparatively underdeveloped. Consequently, readers would do well to rely on a companion publication by the U.S. bishops, released a year after *Go and Make Disciples* was approved: *Communities of Salt and Light: Reflections on the Social Mission of the Parish (CSL)*. This document helps parishes as they work to implement Goal III at the parish level. As the introduction to *CSL* confirms,

"This focus on the social mission of the parish complements and strengthens the call to evangelization found in our statement *Go and Make Disciples*."[5]

In short, this goal is the third leg of the tripod that supports the platform of Catholic evangelization in the United States: holiness, welcome/invitation, and transformation.

While Goal III is often referred to as the social justice goal, "fostering gospel values in society" has a much broader perspective, one that encompasses our work for justice but is not limited to it. The goal is geared toward "having a greater impact on society's values" (*GMD,* no. 120). This leads to a two-pronged approach. It means supporting those cultural elements in our country that reflect Catholic values: instinctual religiousness, freedom and religious liberty, openness to immigrants, and idealism. At the same time, we challenge those elements that reject these values: materialism, sexism, racism, consumerism, individualism, selfishness, neglect of the poor and weak, disregard for human life, and empty fads (*GMD,* nos. 58, 118). Hence, fostering gospel values in society must be about more than fighting injustice.

Catholics cannot pursue holiness (Goal I) in a social vacuum. Nor can we invite and welcome newcomers to our church (Goal II) while ignoring the culture in which we swim like fish in the sea. Holiness and missionary outreach demand that we take the third step and seek to transform society. As the bishops summarize, the pursuit of Goal III "must accompany the pursuit of the other two because evangelization is not possible without powerful signs of justice and peace, as the Gospel shapes the framework of our lives" (*GMD,* no. 117). In short, Goal III challenges Catholics to actualize—to realize in and through action—their faith in society.

After an overview of the goal, I will explore the major challenge of fostering gospel values in our society, touching especially on the issue of inculturation. Then I will explore, in turn, each of the three major avenues listed in the goal as ways to foster gospel values in society—promoting the dignity of the human person, the importance of the family, and the common good of our society—so that the nation may be transformed by the saving power of Jesus Christ. Before I begin, however, some comments on the relationship of the church's social teaching to evangelization are in order.

In the 1971 Synod on Justice in the World, the bishops stated: "Action on behalf of justice and participation in the transformation of the world fully appears to us as a constitutive dimension of the preaching of the gospel, or, in other words, of the church's mission for the redemption of the human race and its liberation from every oppressive situation."[6] After the document was promulgated, there was a bit of a firestorm in some conservative circles over the word *constitutive*. They resisted the term because they saw the evangelizing mission of the church as primarily "spiritual."[7] However, it became clear that Paul VI's vision of evangelization included a strong emphasis on a kingdom-centered evangelization and a message of liberation that included both spiritual and temporal transformation. A vision of Catholic evangelization that embraced social justice was thus ensured. This strong connection between evangelization and justice had already been emphasized by the Latin American bishops at Medellin in 1968, and reinforced again in 1979 at Puebla. John Paul II has continually emphasized the strong connection between justice and evangelization in all of his writings.

Standing behind all the objectives under Goal III is the wealth of Catholic social justice teaching, which goes back at least a hundred years to Leo XIII's *Rerum Novarum*. The body of teaching is contained in encyclicals, apostolic exhortations, and council documents such as *Gaudium et Spes* and *Dignitatis Humanae*. And, in addition to these pronouncements from the universal church, the U.S. bishops have added to this body of work in important ways, particularly with their teachings on the death penalty, the economy, and peace. A recent publication has called this Catholic social justice teaching "our best kept secret."[8]

This body of social teaching is not a fixed set of tightly developed doctrines but, as scholars DeBerri and Hug suggest, a collection of key themes that are rooted in biblical teachings and have evolved in response to the challenges of the day.[9] Some of the themes have taken on a clear and concise formulation, such as the principles of human dignity, common good, subsidiarity, and solidarity. Others are the products of considerable development, changes in perspective, new methodology, and reformulation over the years. For example, views on private property, the state, capitalism and socialism, labor and the economy, have undergone considerable change since Leo XIII. In 1999, the USCCB distilled this teaching into seven general principles.[10] Hug and DeBerri offer the following synthesis:

- **The Dignity of the Human Person**
  Major Areas of Concern:
  - Authentic Human Development
  - Love of God and Love of Neighbor
  - Love and Justice
  - Dialogue

- **The Dignity of Work**
  Major Areas of Concern:
  - The Priority of Labor over Capital
  - Religious and Social Development

- **The Person in Community**
  Major Areas of Concern:
  - Common Good
  - Human Freedom/Social Structures
  - Structures of Sin/Structures of Grace
  - Liberation
  - Participation
  - The Role of the Church

- **Rights and Responsibilities**
  Major Areas of Concern:
  - Human Rights
  - Responsibilities
  - Private Property/Social Mortgage
  - Resisting Market Idolatry
  - The Role of Government
  - The Principle of Subsidiarity

- **Option for Those in Poverty**
  Major Areas of Concern:
  - Biblical Justice

- **Solidarity**
  Major Areas of Concern:
  - •Unity of Humanity
  - •Peacemaking
  - •Pacifism or Nonviolence
  - •Just War

- **Care for Creation**

This body of teaching is responsive and relevant to our world today, yet it also has been tested by time. It enjoys different levels of authority, depending upon the exact teaching. However, all the objectives of Goal III are rooted in this body of teaching and depend upon it.

Transformation of Culture

The subtext of Goal III is inculturation: inserting gospel values into our contemporary culture. In the introduction to Goal III, the bishops state:

> This goal means supporting those cultural elements in our land that reflect Catholic values and challenging those that reject it. Catholics, who today are involved in every level of modern life in the United States, have to address our society as a system and also in particular situations.
>
> The transformation of our society in Christ particularly calls for the involvement and skills of lay men and women who carry the values of the Gospel into their homes, workplaces, areas of recreation—indeed to all aspects of life. (*GMD,* nos. 118–19)

These two paragraphs touch upon the heart of the challenge that we face in Goal III and offer the best place to begin our reflection. The theme of inculturation of the gospel was inspired by the Second Vatican Council's groundbreaking treatment of the subject in the *Pastoral Constitution on the Church in the*

Modern World, which then strongly influenced Paul VI's treatment of it in *Evangelii Nuntiandi.* Dermot Lane states, "The central non-ecclesiological issue at the Second Vatican Council and in the postconciliar church is the relationship between faith and culture."[11] Both the council documents and Paul VI make the point that this transformation of culture has to take place dynamically, from within. It cannot be imposed from outside; it is a question of transforming the culture's basic values.

Let us reflect on the larger challenge of inculturation, since it is so crucial to Goal III and such an important contemporary issue.[12] Vatican II began the modern-day discussion in the Catholic Church on the relationship between faith and culture in the *Pastoral Constitution on the Church in the Modern World.*[13] The word *culture* comes from the Latin word *colere,* meaning "to cultivate the soil." The task of inculturating gospel values, then, suggests that they need to be dynamically absorbed into the soil of the culture.

Culture is not being used in the restrictive sense of the arts, but in the much wider sense of "everything by which human beings refine and develop their various capacities of mind and body."[14] The council fathers proved prophetic in their treatment of this topic, because they began a reflection that has since taken on great prominence in evangelization, particularly in *Evangelii Nuntiandi* and in the writings of John Paul II.

Living out our faith in the modern world is not easy. Sometimes it would appear that the secular culture has made more headway in converting Christians than the other way around.[15] Pope Paul VI seems to focus on the negative side of the relationship between faith and culture when he states that the split between the gospel and culture is the "drama of our time" and of every other time as well (*EN,* no. 20).[16] He also makes the point that the process of bringing gospel values to all strata of humanity could not be merely decorative, but had to impact dynamically the culture at the levels of "judgment, determining values, points of interest, lines of thought, sources of inspiration and models of life" (*EN,* no. 19).

Michael Gallagher notes that John Paul II announced early on in his papacy that the relationship between faith and culture is one that he has "pondered much . . . as a scholar, a Christian, a priest, a bishop, and now as pope."[17] Gallagher cites the speech John Paul gave to UNESCO in June 1980 as the cornerstone of his thinking on the subject. His central thought seems to be that the human person in his or her self-transcendence is shaped by, and shapes, culture. The Holy Father captures the challenge succinctly when he says, "Faith must become culture."[18]

We are, indeed, products of our culture; it is inevitable that it should affect us. And this is not necessarily a negative thing, for the diversity of human culture surely reflects the incredible richness of God, the creator of human beings in their great variety. The church has moved a long way from its earlier blanket condemnation of the world and its cultures. However, Catholics also are not to accept unthinkingly all aspects of culture, to merely swim in the ocean that surrounds us. We are called to look at it through the lens of the gospel, to discern critically what in it reflects gospel values and what does not—and then work to shape it to fit better those values. John Paul II offers powerful language to make this discernment when he speaks of a culture of life and a culture of death.[19] To the degree that we can, we utilize the wisdom tradition of the church and prayerfully, carefully, but decisively determine which are those elements of our culture that are life-giving and which are death-dealing in promoting a truly authentically human world.

The fact is, there is no ahistorical Christianity waiting to be inculturated. "Faith itself is culture," as Cardinal Ratzinger says.[20] John Paul II is keenly aware of the challenge that cultural modernity poses to faith and of the need to make the message of the gospel accessible to all cultures. Perhaps the most famous phrase that seems to sum up his thinking on the matter is the call that we all have to create a "civilization of love."

A final note in our brief reflection on this subject is the importance of stressing a mutuality in the relationship between gospel values and the culture in which those values are incarnated. It is not a one-way street, but rather a process of mutual enrichment, as the bishops state in *Our Hearts Were Burning Within Us*.[21] Inculturation can be defined as a mutual process that occurs between faith and culture. Each one shapes and influences the other.

I might offer the following examples of inculturation. Today, the twelve-step movement is widely experienced as a form of secular spirituality practiced by millions of people. It adheres to no particular religious tenets, nor is religious adherence required in order to participate. The twelve-step movement is clearly a secular spirituality, unaffiliated with any religion. However, it is not widely recognized that Alcoholics Anonymous, the father of all twelve-step movements, has its spiritual origins in the Oxford Group (later named Moral Rearmament), a nondenominational evangelical effort to recapture the impetus and spirit of primitive Christianity. The "five procedures" espoused by the Oxford Group were: (1) give in to God, (2) listen to God's directions, (3) check guidance, (4) restitution, and (5) sharing or telling one's sins.[22] Rowland H., Ebby T., and Bill Wilson, one of the founders of AA, were greatly influenced by these five procedures, which form the basis of what ultimately would be the twelve steps of AA. Out of this background Bill W., in writing the big book of AA, was able to offer alcoholics hope through a spiritual conversion to a higher power not specifically identified with religion.

Three religious personalities, two of them Catholic, figure prominently in the development of AA as well. The first was Sister Ignatia of the Sisters of Charity at St. Thomas Hospital in Akron, Ohio, where Dr. Bob, the cofounder of AA, carried out his medical practice. She provided support and offered a venue where alcoholics could be treated in those early days.

The other two were Rev. Dr. Samuel Shoemaker, the head of Calvary Episcopal Church, which was the national headquarters of the Oxford Group in the United States, and Father Edward Dowling, a Jesuit.[23] In 1955, at the twentieth anniversary of AA, both men were standing with Bill W., as he spoke of his debt to the Oxford Group and how he learned from them what to do and what not to do with alcoholics. Dowling's place on the platform that day makes clear his importance to Bill W., as a personal friend and supporter. It also reflected his key role in helping make AA acceptable to the Catholic Church at a time when its early association with the Oxford Group would have made it difficult for Catholics to participate. The formation of AA is an example of how religion influences and shapes culture.

Inculturation is a process of mutual enrichment between culture and the gospel. Our second example is a gift from the secular culture to the church: *participation.* John Paul II has identified participation as a "sign of the times," that is, a cultural value in the world that to the eyes of faith is the work of the Holy Spirit in history and, to the nonbeliever, a reinforcement in the choice of human values.[24] When something good happens in history, like the growth of participation, for Christians this is a sign that the Holy Spirit is at work. For the nonbeliever, it is simply evidence of something good happening in society. A general affirmation of the importance and value of widespread participation on the part of all people in deciding their own destiny is the product of centuries of development in democratic values. Recently, the importance and value of participation are being acknowledged as essential to the life of the church, even as it grows in importance in the secular sphere. The ancient secular dictum *quod tanget omnes, ab omnibus tractari et approbari debet (what touches all must be treated and approved by all)*[25] has far-reaching implications in the ecclesial world as well. It has to do, essentially, with how adults want to be treated. In matters of importance, they don't want things decided for them. Now, clearly, the Roman Catholic Church is not a democracy or an egalitarian community, but can it be a faith community where the faithful participate (as appropriate) in those decisions that significantly affect them? That is certainly a critical question that is being worked out in the church today, especially in countries where the right to participate is taken for granted. The growth of the value of participation in the Catholic Church is a good example of how culture shapes religion.

Three Themes of Goal III

Promoting the Dignity of the Human Person, the Importance of the Family, and the Common Good of Our Society

How can individuals, families, and parishes make an impact in promoting the dignity of the individual, the importance of the family, and the common good of society so that our nation may continue to be transformed by the saving power of Christ?

The Catholic Church has a simple, clear, and powerful message about humanity to share with society. The formulation of Goal III enshrines two truths that represent the twin pillars of its social justice teaching: the dignity and worth of every human person and our solidarity in the human family. Catholicism recognizes that society is based upon both the bedrock value of the individual person and the inherently social character of human life. We need to continue to hold aloft these two truths as the foundation for building a civilization of love. Their compelling clarity and simplicity are no guarantee that they will be taken seriously. This must not keep us from proclaiming these truths in season and out and hammering home their application in all areas where they are at risk. But we must continue to emphasize the dignity and worth of the individual from birth to death, and the truth that we are responsible for one another.

The family is the place to begin, and the family is at risk. It desperately needs the support of society and the church in order for it to thrive in the midst of so many forces that tend to undermine healthy family living. Goal III challenges parishes to promote the importance of the family because it is a fundamental building block of society. It is the place where people come to experience their worth and dignity as human beings, because they are loved and valued unconditionally. When that doesn't happen in the family, individuals spend their whole lives looking for something to fill them.[26]

It is not possible, nor is it helpful, to try to delineate all the ways that parishes might help foster healthy family life. The document offers a number of helpful strategies. By singling out family life along with the twin pillars of human dignity and solidarity (common good), the bishops make clear the importance of the family as the place where these basic values are first learned. When they are not learned in the family, individuals are often irreparably at risk as they move into adulthood. The family is the most basic unit of society, where we foster both the dignity and worth of the individual and the communal well-being of society's smallest community structure. There is obviously a great need to focus on the family, given the rise of divorce, the growth of family diversity, and the changing character of the family in modern society. Recently, a newspaper reported that some generation X couples wind up in divorce court so early that these unions are being labeled *starter marriages,* because they don't last longer than five years.[27]

Family life concerns all of us. It can be either a blessing or a curse. It is difficult to walk away from family or neutralize its impact. We must deal with it. Today, we have come to understand, more than ever before, that our relationships in our families of origin are a forceful reality that needs to be attended to well into adulthood. So, clearly, support for healthy families is an important way of fostering the dignity of the individual and the well-being of community at the most basic level of society.

Nor should we ignore the potential of family-to-family ministry in modeling and assisting one another in developing healthy family life. Families are challenged to make their faith real in society. I remember in my own family life, one of the prime values was extending the hospitality that we felt in our own home to all of our friends, many of whom came from difficult family situations. My mother had a tremendous gift of hospitality— probably because, as a child born out of wedlock, she grew up without a home of her own. Her stepfather would not allow her to live with him and her mother, so she was shuttled back and forth between her grandparents and aunts and uncles. When she grew up, she had a unique ability to welcome people, make them feel at home, and, most important, value them as individuals no matter who they were. She did not make a fuss over them. She gave people a loving welcome through the most ordinary actions. She fostered ecumenism long before it was fashionable. We can help one another as families by encouraging, supporting, and modeling family life as the most important place where human dignity and solidarity get their solid foundations.

What about the parish in all of this? Increased social justice activity has been characteristic of most Catholic parishes since Vatican II. However, parishes don't often exploit the possibilities of collaboration in this area that exist among Catholic parishes, and along ecumenical and interreligious lines. God has only one plan of salvation, and it involves all people of all different religious traditions. How all peoples come together in God's plan of salvation in Christ is a subject of much-needed dialogue. However, even if different religions have not reached agreement at the theological level, action for justice is still possible and necessary. Goal III is an important area for collaboration with other churches and other religions, as well as with civic institutions. Efforts to build a civilization of love must include the entire human family because we have a common origin and a common destiny.[28] Therefore, implementing the objectives of Goal III cries out for interfaith and interreligious effort.

One of the best experiences in my priestly ministry—something that exemplifies this type of collaboration—occurred in West Los Angeles through an organization called PATH, People Assisting the Homeless. Christian and non-Christian religions and civic and business community representatives (especially the motion picture industry) came together to create a very successful outreach to homeless people who had experienced temporary setbacks, but were capable of reintegrating into society with a little helping hand. They were given free housing, job training, and initial employment opportunities, and they were able to get on their own again. PATH is still thriving.

When parishes work together at the ecumenical and interreligious level, much can be accomplished. However, collaboration among neighboring Catholic parishes or along deanery lines also can be a very successful way of carrying out direct outreach efforts. Again in West Los Angeles, Catholic parishes came together, pooled their resources, and worked actively with Catholic charities to develop more effective outreach to the poor and needy by providing food, clothing, shelter, and social work services. By collaborating with other parishes and other churches, parishes avoid unnecessary duplication of services and also expand their own limited resources by uniting with others in a common cause.

By dividing the comprehensive evangelization task into three broad but functioning goals, *Go and Make Disciples* intends the reader to understand those goals dynamically and interactively. As Paul VI warned, there is always a temptation to identify evangelization with a partial and fragmentary definition (*EN*, no. 17). Goals I, II, and III must be implemented together in order to capture authentically the vision of Catholic evangelization. *Communities of Salt and Light* gives us a good example of how the social ministry of the parish must be carried out in an integrated fashion. Thus, it begins by speaking of prayer and worship as the foundation of social justice activity. Mother Teresa was once asked why her sisters spent two hours in the chapel praying when there were so many needy people out on the streets of Calcutta. She answered that if they didn't spend those two hours in the chapel, they wouldn't go out and minister to the people on the street.

In recent years, the Catholic Church has spoken about the importance of translating the concept of social justice as a constitutive dimension of the gospel by its preferential option for the poor.[29] The Catholic world first heard this language at Medellin in 1968 and Puebla in 1979, and liberation theologians have continued to give voice to this idea. It can be found among the seven key social justice themes of the U.S. bishops.[30] By making an option for the poor, the church commits itself to change the structures of injustice that marginalize and dehumanize people. *Communities of Salt and Light* encourages us to make the social ministry an integral part of parish ministry and evangelization. "We need to build local communities of faith where our social teaching is a central, not fringe activity, where social ministry is integral, not optional; where it is the work of every believer, not just the mission of a few committed people and committees."[31] Furthermore, at a time when the rich are getting richer and the poor are getting poorer, the document establishes a decisive criterion by which to test the well-being of our society, namely, "how we treat and care for the weakest among us."[32] Social justice principles such as the dignity of each individual and the commitment in solidarity to the common good require us to reach out to individuals and seek ways to strengthen society's safety net, in order to protect individuals from the dehumanizing experience of abject poverty.

Conclusion

Vatican II opened up the church to embrace the world *(Gaudium et Spes)*. We seek to transform this world, instead of just getting everybody to the next one—rerouting the waters, not hiding in the Ark waiting for the flood. Goal III reminds us that the ultimate focus of evangelization is the kingdom, not the church. The Catholic faith is intensely personal, inevitably communal, and ineluctably social in its scope. The three goals of *Go and Make Disciples* encompass a comprehensive vision of evangelization, one that calls every Catholic to personal holiness in a communal context, to living their faith fully and sharing it freely with others, and to transforming the world in Christ.

I began my reflection on this goal by emphasizing how important it is for each individual not to underestimate his or her capacity to be an agent for good in the world. We can make a difference. I conclude this reflection on Goal III with a parable from the Gospel of Matthew. Jesus tells of five wise virgins and five foolish virgins, who were all awaiting the master's return to begin the wedding celebration. The five foolish virgins had brought no extra oil, and the master was a long time in coming. Everyone was awakened with the announcement that the bridegroom was arriving, and the oil lamps of the foolish virgins went out. They immediately sought to borrow some oil from the wise virgins, who promptly refused. Why did they refuse? According to John Donahue, SJ,[33] the parable is basically an allegory and the oil lamp is a symbol of the good deeds of the disciple. In effect, the allegory states: the foolish virgins couldn't borrow oil from the wise ones because no disciple can borrow anyone else's good deeds. Goal III calls all of us to perform our own good deeds—bringing gospel values to the world by the way we live our lives as active disciples in the family, the neighborhood, the workplace, and society, both as individuals and as a community.

PART III
The Evangelizing Parish

CHAPTER NINE

THE PARISH—AN IDEAL VENUE FOR EVANGELIZATION

Insight: The parish is where the vision and plan for evangelization become real.

Reflection

In 1858, Isaac Hecker founded the Paulist Fathers to be a missionary society that would convert all America. One of the society's first actions was to establish a parish in New York City, which was named St. Paul the Apostle. In fact, taking on a parish in the city was a condition imposed on the fledgling group by Archbishop John Hughes before it could establish its base there. St. Paul's was to function both as a territorial parish and as a base from which to carry out the society's missionary activity.

The early years of the community witnessed a great struggle between the people who felt that the Paulist Fathers should carry out a more traditional parish ministry and those, like Hecker, who viewed the parish as a mission base for the society. In fact, there were times when a shortage of manpower forced the Paulists to discontinue the missions for brief periods of time in order to meet parish demands. This debate—over whether Paulist parishes could carry out the missionary purposes of the society without consuming the energy their priests needed to meet the demands of the parish—still goes on today.

In 1986, the Paulist community created a new mission statement, which refocused its energies on evangelization, reconciliation, and ecumenism. The question arose again, with a new urgency: can the ordinary parish carry out the evangelizing work of the society? And the question has broadened significantly since the Paulists' early days. For one thing, in this post–Vatican

II church, it is not just Paulist missionaries who are being entrusted with the task of evangelization; it is the entire parish. Second, the question is being asked about all parishes, not only Paulist parishes. Can the parish itself become missionary?

Since joining the society in 1975, I have been privileged to pastor Paulist parishes in Greensboro, North Carolina, and Los Angeles, California. I experienced firsthand the evangelizing possibilities in the parish. I believed then, and still do, that the parish not only can evangelize, but also is uniquely suited to it. It is an ideal place from which to carry out the church's mission of evangelization.

Some years ago, Andrew Greeley wrote a book called *The Catholic Myth: The Behavior and Beliefs of American Catholics.* In it, Greeley affirms that the parish is the focal point of Catholic life. Even if the pastor lacks leadership skills, or the religious education program is weak, or something else is not perfect, Catholics still love their parish because it is the place where their faith is nourished. Nothing else, no other place, can do this for them. And this is true, Greeley says, because the parish is a sacrament of God's presence.[1] People instinctively feel at home there in their Catholic faith. There is ownership, identification, and an array of rich relationships, something that James S. Coleman calls the "social capital" of a parish. The insight statement for this chapter—that the parish is an ideal venue for evangelization—is based on this realization.

The History of the Catholic Parish

Early History

The word *parish* comes from the Greek word *paroikia*. By the fourth century, this term meant "those living near or beside," and it became the official term in church documents for the local Christian community we now know as the parish.[2] These were the years following the peace of Constantine (313 AD); the persecutions had ended and Christianity was growing at a great rate. James Coriden estimates that at the beginning of the fourth century, Christians made up six or seven million of a total population of fifty million. Within a century, they became the dominant religious force in the Roman Empire.

Local churches began to multiply in the fifth and sixth centuries and, interestingly, they came in many different forms. There were urban parishes, small rural churches cared for by itinerant pastors from the cities, stable rural parishes with their own presbyters, monasteries, shrines or oratories built over saints' burial places, and estate churches established by owners of large estates. Certain important churches in central locations were designated as baptismal churches, headed by an archpresbyter. Baptisms took place only there.

In later years, major changes occurred that affected local churches. Europe became feudal territory, meaning that there was no central government and many different people and groups held power. The church, drawn into the middle of things, found itself struggling to maintain both temporal and spiritual jurisdiction. For example, a system of "proprietary churches" developed, in which the church building was the personal property of the local landlord, prince, or lord. He assumed the right of hiring and firing church personnel, and these priests (and bishops and abbots) thus owed allegiance to him. The consequences of this breakdown of church authority, according to one source, were corruption, cynicism, and general demoralization.[3] The church struggled for centuries to free itself from this system of local ownership, and it wasn't solved until well into the Middle Ages.

Over the centuries, the church instituted different reforms designed to renew parish life. The Carolingian reform (750–900) established parish churches in every village. These churches were the center of all community life. They were the storehouse of the history of the community. There, baptisms, marriages, and deaths were recorded. Charlemagne's church officials even provided sermon outlines for pastors. The Fourth Lateran Council (1215) made several reforms in parish life that continue to this day: annual confession, Easter communion, observance of marriage regulations, better preaching and pastoral care, improved education for priests, observance of clerical celibacy and moral integrity, and a regular parish visit by the diocesan bishop. The council also attempted to correct the abuses that had grown up around the benefice system, in which a parish functioned as a source of income for the clergy. In summarizing these reforms, Coriden makes the key point that while there were abuses, the reforms show that the magisterium was aware of the importance of sound parish life and a healthy relationship between pastor and people.[4]

The Council of Trent (1545–63) made preaching and catechetical instruction obligatory every Sunday and holy day for parish priests, and sacramental and moral education for the people. Pastors were required to maintain residence in the parish assigned to them so they could adequately care for their people. An effort was made to assign people to clear and distinct parishes in order to facilitate the reform.

These reforms improved parish life in many ways. However, an unfortunate result was that they emphasized the hierarchical authority and clerical leadership to such an extent that it left the lay members of the church in a purely passive role. From the fourth century on, an imbalance had been building in the Catholic Church in lay-clergy roles. That imbalance was institutionalized in parish structures and would not be addressed until Vatican II and the renewal of the laity's role in the church.

In 1906 Pius X, in *Vehementer Nos*, gave extreme expression to this view:

> It follows that the church is essentially an unequal society, that is, a society comprising two categories of persons, the Pastors and the flock, those who occupy a rank in the different degrees of the hierarchy and multitude of the faithful. So distinct are these categories that with the pastoral body only rests the necessary right and authority for promoting the end of the society and directing all its members toward that end; the one duty of the multitude is to allow themselves to be led and, like a docile flock, to follow the Pastors.[5]

Two developments in Europe had a major impact on parishes—the evolution of the modern absolutist state and the onset of the Industrial Revolution. The power of the monarchy placed the church at the service of the state in many ways.

During certain periods in its history, the church suffered a great deal because of its subservient status. The state interfered in ecclesiastical appointments, appropriated church property, and restricted its freedom in many ways. Eventually, with the establishment of church-state agreements called concordats, the church gained certain privileges deriving from its special relationship to the state. This model of church-state relations was regarded as most favorable and desirable up until the Second Vatican Council.

The Industrial Revolution (1750–1900), with its invention of modern means of transportation, communication, and industrial production, led to tremendous changes in the social setting of the parish. People migrated to the cities in vast numbers. The size of the typical urban parish grew proportionately, changing the way pastoral care was delivered. Pastors faced enormous challenges resulting from the huge growth in the number of people they served.

Parish Life in the United States

Jay Dolan, in his introduction to the historical portion of the Notre Dame Study of Catholic Life, says that a key to understanding the history of American Catholicism is the *parish,* which was the central gathering place for the people and the foundation upon which Catholics built their entire lives. The primary institution that nurtured the faith of Catholics was the parish (and the parish school). "The marrow of Catholicism is concentrated at its most localized and accessible level—the parish—which continues to be the most significant, most vital structure in Roman Catholicism."[6]

The Committee on the Parish of the United States Conference of Catholic Bishops stated in 1983: "The parish is for most Catholics the single most important part of the church. This is where for them the mission of Christ continues. This is where they publicly express their faith, joining with others to give proof of their communion with God and with one another."[7]

The Catholic parish has had a vital—and diverse—history in the United States. The first parish on the continent was established in St. Augustine, Florida, in the sixteenth century: a Spanish parish. The earliest parishes were Spanish and French, in territories ranging from Florida to Louisiana and California and then north to the northeastern United States and Canada.

In colonial America, which had mostly English and German settlers, there was widespread hostility to "papists." Catholics, therefore, tended to gravitate to southern Maryland and Pennsylvania—two states where they were not persecuted. In addition, despite the hostility, Catholics were able to make early incursions into Virginia under the patronage of George Brent of Woodstock, and into New York where, despite an antipriest statute that wasn't repealed until 1784, the first permanent Catholic community was organized under Ferdinand Steinmeyer, a German Jesuit missionary. He traveled throughout the northeast as "Father Farmer."

Parishes were few and far between and priests were scarce. We don't tend to think of Catholic priests as circuit riders, but that is exactly what they were in those early decades. And they covered enormous distances, which meant that Catholics often went months between visits from a priest. Bishops in the colonies were hard put to find competent, faithful clergy to staff the fledgling church. This shortage continued for many years. James Hennesey points out that, after the Revolution, there were two sacraments—confirmation and holy orders—that were never conferred, because the oils needed had to be obtained from Europe![8] For a good part of American Catholic history, an adequate supply of priests was a real issue.

So Catholic laymen and women gathered together in community on their own, without priests. Eventually, they began to establish parishes; in fact, this is how most parishes started. What resulted was a degree of lay involvement in the parish that would surprise many Catholics today. As historian Jay Dolan puts it: "So the laypeople were on their own—do-it-yourself Catholicism.... Later laypeople began to incorporate parishes. They established boards of trustees who bought the land, put the land in their name, built the church, and brought the priests in.... The board ran the church with the priests, and they all worked together like this up until 1830 or so."[9] This was known as lay trusteeism: a system where ownership and control of the parish lay in the hands of the laity. There were certainly problems that arose from this system, but it does reflect the vitality of Catholic laypeople and Catholic parishes in the early years of the country.

Parishes also struggled with serious problems, however. For one thing, the number of Catholics in America was very small. At one point in the beginning of American Catholic history, the superior in Maryland and Pennsylvania sought permission for Catholics to marry first cousins in order to maintain their religious identity among the Protestants.[10] Many Catholics were lost to the faith through active proselytizing by Protestants or intermarriage. Catholics rarely saw a priest because there were so few of them. Some parishes were torn by strife because of unstable leadership or lay trusteeism issues. Parish life, in the early decades, was a matter of trying to survive.

What changed this picture dramatically was the massive immigration of Catholics into the United States in the early nineteenth century. The impact of this immigration on American parish life, on the growth of the church, and on the role of Catholicism in the country cannot be overestimated. For one thing, the numbers were enormous. By the 1850s, the Catholic Church was the largest denomination in America, with 1.3 million members.[11] During that decade, along with this growth in the number of Catholics, we also see a parallel growth in the number of priests, religious orders, parishes, and schools, an increase that more than matches the size of the Catholic population. Thus, the decade from 1850 to 1860 was a watershed, giving institutional Catholicism a prominent place in the United States.

In addition to the Sunday mass and catechesis, the Catholic Church began to look to parish revivals or missions as a tool to gather Catholics together and reinforce their Catholic identity. By the 1850s, missions would become a regular part of parish life. The importance of the missions cannot be overestimated. They were an occasion when people renewed their faith, returned to the sacraments, and often had their marriages blessed by the church.

The American parish changed radically during this time period. The system of lay trusteeism no longer existed, and control of the parish had moved to the hands of the pastor. In addition to that, his role changed, from one who primarily cared for souls to one who acted as builder and administrator. There was a pressing need to build and finance more parishes and schools to serve the huge numbers of Catholics coming into the country, and this new role brought with it a great deal of power for the pastor. Overall, the power and status of the clergy grew while, at the same time, the role of the laity declined. Most often, the priest was the best-educated person in the parish. Laypeople who wanted to serve the church were directed into religious vocations. This situation would prevail until the onset of the Second Vatican Council.

Father Paul Robichaud, in writing about Paulist missionary efforts, notes that when Hecker and the Paulist Fathers established St. Paul the Apostle in New York City, there was no fixed way of doing parish. "No one exactly knew what an American parish was to look like in the mid-nineteenth century. The concept of parish was in transition from the Trusteeship period of earlier in the century to the Victorian parish of the latter part of the century."[12]

The history of the Catholic parish in the United States from this time on is a story of unity in diversity. Much of that diversity results from regionalism. The urban ethnic parishes of the northeast differed considerably from parishes in the southern and western areas of the country, which were limited by the small Catholic population. In fact, the South remained missionary territory for a hundred years or more. Catholics were few, personnel and resources were scarce, political and economic clout was almost nonexistent, the black population was beleaguered, the clergy were poor, and many parishes had only one priest but many missions and stations attached to them.[13] Anyone who worked in the South even as late as the early 1960s will recognize the truth of this description.

In addition to the dominant cultures of German, Irish, Italian, and Polish churches, one must take into account the legacy of Hispanic, French, and African American Catholics in the south and southwest. Southern Louisiana, for example, is one of the few areas of the country where the Catholic culture— and it was a French Catholic culture—put down strong early roots. It has had a tremendous impact on the self-image of

Catholics there, even black Catholics, in that they did not grow up as members of a minority group with the resulting inferiority complex. French Catholicism's historical roots in this part of the country have had an impact that lasts to the present day.

Mexican American Catholics

The legacy of the Spanish colonization of the southwestern United States is still with us, with one result being that Catholicism there contrasts greatly with Catholicism in the rest of the country. Once the Southwest was made part of the Continental United States in 1848, the Mexican Catholic population experienced a tremendous displacement in "being Mexican in an Anglo society."[14] By the twentieth century, the history of ministry to the Mexican American in California and Texas was a "history of neglect."[15] Mexican Catholicism was neither appreciated nor understood by many in the hierarchy. Often, the Mexican population was relegated to second-class citizenship in the Anglo parish, and there was little or no effective ministry directed to them. It was inevitable, then, that Mexican Catholics had little reason to identify with the parish and, by and large, maintained their faith through popular religion, which they practiced in their families. All of that changed with the large immigration of Mexicans into the country in the mid-twentieth century. They became such a force that they could not be ignored; thus began their growing influence. There were more Hispanic priests and bishops. Parishes became more responsive and made an effort to reach out to Hispanics in language, culture, and liturgies. Today, the church's Hispanic population is still growing dramatically—more than half of all Catholics will be of Hispanic origin by 2010—and its influence continues to be felt.

Native Americans

The history of Indian Catholic missions is a complex one, and that history still seriously impacts current pastoral and missionary efforts with Native peoples. For one thing, the church's attempt to "convert" and Christianize Native Americans by turning them away from their culture had, in general, very negative results. Religion cannot be separated from culture. In addition, Native Americans find it difficult to forget the church's past association with government policies and behaviors: broken treaties, land grabbing, corrupt policies, the misguided and even cruel reservation strategy, and the very mixed blessing of Indian missions and schools. Consequently, the current relationship between the Catholic Church and Native peoples continues to suffer from this history. Today, in some instances, that history is being rewritten by a more enlightened approach. By and large, however, it continues to be a great struggle to forge a new path.

Black Catholics

Cyprian Davis's *History of Black Catholics in the United States* makes the important point that blacks have been part of Catholicism in this country from the very beginning. However, by and large, black Catholics survived, and stayed Catholic, by drawing on their own inner resources, not because they had a great deal of support from the institutional church. That they did survive is one of the miracles of our Catholic history.

The following story, recounted in Dolan's *The American Catholic Parish*, illustrates what blacks were up against. Historian Albert Raboteau tells of this childhood experience:

One summer, when I was eight years old and lived in the Midwest, my family took a trip South to a small town on the Gulf Coast. I was born there and most of my relatives had been settled there for generations.... For some reason we had missed mass at the black church and went instead to the white church, which my grandfather, a carpenter, had helped build years before. We crowded into a half pew in the back with the only other black worshipers. The pew was too small to seat us all, so during mass we had to take turns kneeling and sitting.

In front of us two white men had a whole pew to themselves. The message was obvious: they belonged there; we didn't. Hot, tired, and angry, I couldn't understand how something so unfair could happen in a church.

Then we went to Communion. Since we were seated in the back, we brought up the rear of the line to the altar rail. But as we knelt, there were still some white communicants waiting to receive the Host. To my amazement, the priest passed me by, not once, but twice, until he had distributed Communion to all the whites. Then he returned to me. That mass, my mother commented afterward, hadn't done her a bit of good since all she felt during the service was hate. I didn't say anything. I just felt humiliated and betrayed.[16]

One of the few good things that can be said about Catholicism and African Americans is that the church never split into two denominations along racial lines. That being said, Catholics were generally soft on slavery; with few exceptions, they were slow to support its abolition. Pope Gregory XVI, in 1839, condemned the slave trade, but few American leaders raised their voices to apply this teaching to slavery in this country. After emancipation, little was done to reach out to African Americans in pastoral care or social outreach.[17] And, not only did the church fail to give adequate pastoral care to African Americans, it also refused to encourage or support the ordination of African American clergy.

In the church's dealings with African Americans, we have an example of an instance where universal teaching and leadership in Rome provided more support for racial equality than the national church. The history of African Americans in the church is a story of gritty survival, until changes in the mid-twentieth century brought about conditions conducive to new growth and vitality. These changes led to increased representation of African Americans in the hierarchy, more black clergy and religious, and vital parishes with an inculturated black worship.

Looking back at Catholic African Americans, we see a story of survival and even success. Looking ahead, we see a story of promise for the future.

Changes in Parish Life

Perhaps the predominant element in the entire history of the parish is the system of parish schools and the religious women who ran them. The schools were considered so essential that the

Third Plenary Council of Baltimore in 1884 mandated that every parish have a parish school within two years of its founding. This goal never was achieved. In the African American community, the schools were more important than the churches in carrying out evangelization. There is no need to document their importance among other ethnic communities. The history of Catholic schools is not only a story of an institution that kept the faith alive, but also an incredible story of the courageous women religious who ran them.

Another pervasive element in the parts of the country with large Catholic populations was the phenomenon of the pastor as a builder and administrator. Catholic immigrants loved their parishes, and pastors were charged with raising the funds and building the edifices to house them: schools, convents, rectories, and churches. An innovative money-raising technique was invented in 1910 that is still with us today: envelopes! St. Stanislaus Koska, the Polish parish of my childhood in Winona, Minnesota, is a marvelous testimony to the immigrant Catholic faith of this era. The Romanesque steeple overshadows all the other buildings in that small river city and proudly announces itself to all who travel up and down the Mississippi.

Charles Morris identifies three periods of American Catholic history: rise, triumph, and crisis. During the triumphant period, from the 1930s to the 1950s, the parish was the center not only of Catholics' spiritual lives but their social lives as well. The parish provided for all aspects of Catholics' physical, spiritual, and social well-being. This was a natural result of the role Catholic parishes played throughout history, functioning in a variety of ways to help American immigrants not only hold on to their faith but find their place in their new country. Urban Catholics referred to their inner-city neighborhoods by the name of their parish, rather than by street names, a habit still followed by some Catholics today.[18]

Morris puts the crisis period of American Catholic history as beginning with the Second Vatican Council. However, he, along with other historians, notes that the changes that took place in the church in the 1960s were part of a larger cultural change that was already well under way in the 1950s. One of the most important of those changes was the growth of the suburban parish. The exodus from the cities signaled an important transformation: the movement of a large segment of the Roman Catholic population from a blue-collar, urban, ethnic lifestyle to an upwardly mobile, educated, middle-class, suburban way of life. Catholics became more independent, more mainstream, and, for the first time, upwardly mobile.

With this demographic shift came a major change in parish life. The all-embracing function of the parish came to an end. Catholics had become inculturated. Well-integrated into the mainstream, Catholics no longer looked to their parishes to be their entire support system or to meet all their social needs. The parish did not need to be the foundation on which all else depended. It was no longer a "haven from the outside community, but rather a vehicle for relating to and transforming that community."[19]

The Second Vatican Council, too, brought tremendous changes in the role and function of parishes and in the way Catholic life is nourished. Today, Catholic schools no longer have the same indispensable role they once had in parish life. The rich and varied devotional life, annual missions, forty hours, bingo, parish bazaars and dinners, a wide assortment of parish organizations such as the Altar Society, the Holy Name Society, the Legion of Mary, the Knights of Columbus, the Catholic Daughters—many of these elements of the Catholic parish have been replaced by new forms of Catholic life.

Yet the parish remains a vital element of Catholic life. Today, Catholics *choose* to be involved in their parishes, and it's for spiritual reasons. The parish is where they get the nourishment society can't provide. Modern parishes are organized primarily around ministries that nurture the spiritual life of their parishioners and that contribute to their outreach efforts. Education, worship, family life, social outreach, finance, and administration are the standard committees of parish life.

While the vitality of parish life has been constant, the personnel that staffed parishes are dramatically different. Priests are in short supply and their job description is all but unrecognizable, compared to what it was in years past. The religious men and women everywhere in evidence before have been replaced by lay professionals and volunteers. This explosion of lay ministers was a largely unforeseen, but singular, grace of the council. It is, perhaps, this emerging role of the laity, more than anything else, that defines the evangelizing potential of the post–Vatican II parish. Today's parish is not a place where Catholics come to survive in a largely hostile world. It is a spiritual center that nourishes them and sends them forth to carry out the mission and ministry of the Lord Jesus. The parish is where God's people are gathered and the place from which they are sent!

The Parish—An Ideal Venue for Evangelization

What is the implication of this history for today's parish, in terms of its evangelizing mission? What the history suggests is a tremendous vitality and diversity in parish life throughout its existence. At the beginning of this chapter, we pointed to a number of authorities who told us of the centrality of the parish in the history of American Catholicism. The "marrow of Catholicism," Jay Dolan says, is concentrated in the local faith community that we call parish. It continues to be the most significant structure in Roman Catholicism. To paraphrase the Committee on the Parish of the United States Conference of Catholic Bishops, this is where the people are, where they nurture and express their faith, and where they celebrate their communion with God and one another.

What do we learn from this history? The parish has been central in the life of Catholics. The story of the parish is one of continued vitality, widespread diversity, unabated struggles, triumphs and transitions, power struggles and priest shortages. Through it all, the faith of the Catholic people has somehow found its dynamic focus in that local community. For much of its history, the parish was a community in search of a priest to staff it. The centrality of the Eucharist and the sacramental life requires the presence of a priest. In this respect, our current shortage of priests is consonant with our history. How this will be addressed in the new millennium remains to be seen.

The story of the Catholic parish is also largely a story of how we have dealt with successive waves of immigration. In the beginning, in the first Catholic settlements in Maryland,

Pennsylvania, and New York, the Catholic Church struggled to survive as a persecuted minority. By 1840, all that had changed and, for the most part, the rest of our history, right up to and including the present, is a story of the parish ministering to immigrant populations. As was true in the past, how we welcome the newcomer and the stranger continues to be something of a test of the quality of our *Catholic* faith, despite the changed context.[20]

Our history has shown as well how pervasive and vital has been the role of the laity. African American Catholics survived largely through the tenacity of a faith-filled laity, supported by a small but vibrant band of women religious. For a good part of their history, they were barely tolerated as a people, deprived of adequate pastoral care by priests and bishops, and denied the opportunity to have their own clergy. Yet they survived. Similarly, Mexican Americans kept the faith in their homes, without much help from the institutional church. Among the dominant European majority, the laity put themselves at the service of the bishops and priests to build the Catholic Church as a triumphant institution. Now, they have taken their place as Americans and Catholics in the larger society.

Another lesson that our history reveals is the strength of the Catholic Church as both a universal and a local church. For a good part of its early history, the church in America was mission country, under the protection of Rome. Today, it is no longer mission territory, and our relationship with Rome has changed; it has both positive and problematic dimensions. For better and for worse, however, the Catholic Church is a network of parishes within the larger local church, the diocese, and a union of many diocesan churches in union with the Holy See. Sometimes these larger relationships are perceived as a blessing, sometimes as a burden. But that larger connection is part of what it means to be Catholic, even if those larger institutional connections do not define Catholic experience at the parish level. At times, this larger connection has had a tremendous positive impact on the Catholic Church in the United States. Dynamic growth through immigration of other Catholics into the United States, which transformed the Catholic Church here early in its history, was possible only because we are part of a larger family of churches. Catholic parishes are not Congregationalist gatherings of believers. The parish, the central gathering of believers, is always part of something bigger—the universal church.

When it comes to pastoral care, the story is uneven at best. Prior to the renewal of the Second Vatican Council, Catholics' faith was rooted in a supernatural system of sacraments and devotions, doctrine and authority. Catholics focused on doing what was needed—what they were told was needed—in order to gain eternal life. It was a fear-based system, and there weren't many options for the ordinary Catholic to step outside it. If you didn't conform, you were cast aside. The place of the separated and divorced Catholic and the pastoral care of African Americans and Native Americans are examples of inadequacies of that earlier era. Many people were lost to the church in this earlier system. It also didn't always translate into the pastoral care that nurtured a vital spiritual life. What we expect in the Catholic Church today by way of preaching, sacramental celebrations, adult formation, and pastoral care is a far cry from what most people received throughout its history. Catholics kept the faith because of their schools and their local parishes, with all their strengths and weaknesses. History challenges us to do as good a job at making those same parishes spiritual communities and schools of faith and missionary outreach in a very different world.

The last issue I wish to address is the challenge of creating missionary parishes. In large measure, for a good part of our Catholic history, the church's mission was found in the huge number of immigrants that came ashore to find a new home. The Catholic Church spent a good deal of its energies from 1840 on in coping with that situation as best it could, and did very well as long as it was dealing with an immigrant, blue-collar, uneducated population. It formed these people in the faith, and also fed, housed, educated, and in general helped them survive. Now we have a very different situation and a new challenge. Almost half of our nation's population is without any church affiliation. Twenty million of those unaffiliated people are inactive Catholics. Moreover, many of our Catholic faithful are highly educated, upwardly mobile, and very inculturated into our secular, consumerist culture with its emphasis on choice. Today, we need a way of communicating the good news both within and outside of the church.

The early Paulists sought to establish parishes that would function as bases for their missionary activities. The big difference in the missionary character of the post–Vatican II parish is that all the baptized share in the evangelizing activities of the parish. However, unless those baptized Catholics can be set on fire as active disciples in this modern world, we will not succeed in carrying out our mission. It can happen—if the church helps them find spiritual significance in using their considerable gifts, talents, and resources in doing God's work. It is the most fruitful avenue we have with our lay faithful. Fear of going to hell will not motivate them. They are not looking for the parish to take care of their physical and social needs. But they *are* looking for the meaning that comes from using their gifts in God's service.

Because of the explosion of lay ministries, parishes are now in an ideal position to carry out God's evangelizing mission in ways they were never prepared for before. Baptism is being understood as a call to share fully in the mission and ministry of Jesus. Catholics are discovering that they have gifts to share. As the 1980 document of the bishops on lay ministry stated, they are "called and gifted." Since the council, these gathered faithful have come to see themselves more and more as active disciples called to carry out Jesus' mission and ministry. The parish is the place where the most important resource to carry out evangelization is gathered—the "assembly of the faithful."[21]

The parish is not only the place where this most powerful resource for evangelization is gathered; it is also a spiritual powerhouse. It is the expression of the local church. When the Vatican II documents speak about the parish, they use language that helps us realize that the parish is the church of God, made present in a specific geographic location. Each parish represents the universal church and is a unit of the entire church, because it is united with the local bishop. Each parish has everything it needs to experience itself as church, in its own particular form. Moreover, each parish makes the universal church visible in its locality and contributes toward building up the whole body of Christ in that locality.[22]

Thus, evangelization has the best chance of taking place in the parish, and from the parish, because the parish is the universal church made concrete and local, where the word of God is proclaimed and the sacraments are rightly celebrated. The Lord is present and active among his people, gifting them for works of ministry (Eph 4). So, not only does the parish have the people power, it has the spirit power, because it is the church in action. The parish has all that it needs to carry out the mission of evangelization. The critical challenge is to nurture and form the community for that mission.

There are many challenges that must be faced in order for Catholic parishes to reach their evangelizing potential. However, it is enough for us to note here that we have a vision and a plan, and we have the resources to implement that plan in the millions of women and men who come together in gathered local communities called Catholic parishes. We have an ideal venue in which to implement the evangelizing vision of the church, namely, the local parish. What is needed is leadership and widespread participation of all the faithful, the subject of our next chapter.

CHAPTER TEN

THE CHALLENGE OF COLLABORATION

Insight: The more a pastor involves parishioners in decision-making, the greater the release of gifts for mission.

Reflection

From my perspective as a priest, the awakening and empowering of the laity for ministry has been one of the most satisfying outcomes of the renewal of Vatican II. Increasing laypeople's participation at all levels of church life greatly enriches their experience of church and creates enormous satisfaction for them as they use their gifts for the mission of the church. Liturgy is an excellent example of this. We have moved from an almost exclusively priest-centered celebration, in which Father did everything (including count the collection!) to one where a variety of liturgical roles has been restored and countless people have been nurtured in their faith by ministering to others as lectors, eucharistic ministers, cantors, and so on. It has deepened their experience of the liturgy and their own spirituality, and has enriched the celebration immensely. More important, the real joy of the liturgical renewal, modeling the theological vision of the people of God, is the experience of the entire congregation joined as one body in prayer, worship, and praise.

Unfortunately, much of our current pastoral experience is not one of clergy and laity working together harmoniously for the well-being of the body of Christ. There are many built-in obstacles that inhibit this collaborative experience, some of which are beyond our control at the present time. However, there is still much that we can do to improve the situation within the current structures. I would like to draw on my own experience to make some suggestions as to how this could happen. In 1979, I was made pastor of a fairly new suburban parish in Greensboro, North Carolina, and later went to a much larger, more complicated urban parish in Los Angeles. In both places I began to accumulate an experience of pastoring that I would summarize in the following fashion.

Most Catholic pastors have a bifurcated job description. On the one hand, they spend a good deal of their time in what we might name traditional direct ministries, such as administering the sacraments, preaching, attending to the sick and dying, counseling, and administration.

These traditional ministries are usually very rewarding to priests and the favored way they express their love and care for their people. They establish relationships with the people through the celebration of the sacraments (especially at baptisms, funerals, and weddings), weekly preaching and celebration of the Eucharist, counseling, and the ministry of presence. These activities establish unbreakable bonds of love between priests and people. As Andrew Greeley points out in *Parish, Priest and People,* for effective leadership in a parish, people must love their priest, and they come to do that by the way they experience his love for them through these traditional ministries. By the way he comforts and challenges them, Greeley says, the priest is exercising "lovable troublemaking."[1]

Admittedly, the way we do some of these traditional ministries has changed. Because of the RCIA, priests no longer spend countless hours giving instructions to would-be converts. Because of lay ministry to the sick and dying, priests' visits to homes and hospitals have changed considerably. Other activities, such as preaching and presiding, are much more demanding than in the past. Nevertheless, these direct ministries, while changed to some degree, continue to occupy a good portion of the priest's time and energy.

I would make the following argument: the better that a priest becomes at performing these tasks, the worse life gets, for him and for everyone else. By this I mean that to the degree that we priests are diligent, competent, and effective in carrying out these ministries, we will continue to get more work. Even in single-priest parishes, the work load can tend to increase or decrease based upon performance. In multipriest parishes, this is even more true. The wonderful wedding I celebrated for John Smith means that I will probably be asked to do weddings for his brothers and sisters. The better a job I do at funerals, the more requests I will get to do more of them. The more people appreciate the quality of my ministry, the more I will be asked to exercise it, and the busier I will be. Hence my half-facetious statement: the better a priest becomes at his ministry, the worse life will get for him.

On the other hand, because of the explosion of lay ministry, pastors have had to take on new roles as managers. They must oversee the necessary activities that enable a parish community to function well and successfully carry out its mission: pastoral planning, personnel management, administration and financial stewardship, and facilities management. In analyzing this dimension of his job description, my observation is that the better that a pastor does these things, the better life gets for him and all concerned.

In the post–Vatican II world, with fewer priests to take care of parishes, not only is the pastor unable to carry the parish's mission by himself, he also needs to direct successfully the ministerial efforts of the parish staff and the parishioners. These are the managerial skills that most of us priests were not given in the seminary. Some pastors are good leaders; most are not good managers. They were not trained for it and some lack the innate skills. Consequently, their life gets worse instead of better.

Now consider this situation, which we see in many parishes. We have pastors who have wonderful direct ministry skills and, because of that, they get busier and busier and their life gets "worse." They become tired, stressed, and burned out. In addition, since they probably do not have the requisite managerial skills, as their parishes grow and become busier, their life gets worse yet. Thus, priests who are successful in direct ministry can become increasingly frustrated. They are getting more and more busy with their ministerial responsibilities and, at the same time, they are failing to provide adequate leadership for the effective ministry of the entire faith community. There are too many meetings—many of them ineffective. There isn't enough organization, leading to increasing frustration. It is a recipe for large-scale discontent. Hence my statement that to the degree that a priest fails to be a good manager, life gets worse for him and for everyone else.

Growing in competence in the traditional roles of ministry—such as preaching, presiding, and confession and counseling—is always a great challenge for priests. However, these are roles that they were educated to carry out. Exercising leadership of a complex organization, which is what the parish has now become because of lay involvement, is a challenge for which priests were not really trained. But it *is* one that, if adequately dealt with, can make priestly ministry immeasurably more fruitful and satisfying. Fostering a collaborative leadership style is one critical element of successfully leading a contemporary parish.

In this chapter, I make the claim that the more a pastor involves parishioners in decision-making, the greater the release of gifts for mission. Both are essential aspects of a collaborative approach to ministry, but it is important to note that the first must happen before the second can take place. The greater the collaboration, the higher the participation in the mission, because people then feel part of the mission.

Lay Ministry

What Is Lay Ministry?

Lay ministry[2] can be divided into two broad categories: lay ecclesial ministry and parishioner ministry. The USCCB Lay Ministry Subcommittee, in its publication *Lay Ecclesial Ministry: State of the Question,* restricts the term *lay ecclesial ministry* to fully initiated persons (baptized, confirmed, and received the Eucharist) who carry out some kind of public, authorized ministry as a competent professional or volunteer within the communion of the church.[3] Philip Murnion and David DeLambo, in a 1999 study of parish lay ministry, widen the term to include people who are formally authorized but not necessarily professional; that is, they may not necessarily have a formal education for ministry.[4] Basically, these are the folks who are working for the church in some formal, authorized position. Examples of lay ecclesial ministers are professionals or trained personnel who are called to serve in a parish as director of liturgy, religious education, and so on.

The second group Murnion calls *parishioner ministers*. They are the baptized disciples who carry out various ministerial activities without any recognized official position. The USCCB document cited above recognizes in this wider sphere of parishioner ministry all the laypeople who are participating and collaborating in the church's life and mission in the broadest sense. The document acknowledges that there is no single definitive way to categorize and distinguish the many ways in which laypersons participate in lay ministry in the latter sense. An example of this is the person who serves at the local homeless shelter, visits the sick or imprisoned, and so on. This type of ministry is what faithful disciples do within the church and in the world as part of their baptismal calling.

Both forms of ministry flow from the sacraments of initiation, which incorporate individuals into the body of Christ and call them to mission. *Dogmatic Constitution on the Church*[5] and *Decree on the Apostolate of Lay People*[6] speak of the laity's share in Christ's mission being based in their baptism. Pope John Paul II, in *The Lay Members of Christ's Faithful People*, states that the lay faithful carry out their ministerial roles on the basis of "baptism in which these tasks are rooted."[7] Canons 204.1 and 225.1 acknowledge that God calls the laity to the apostolate through their baptism and confirmation.[8]

All church documents carefully distinguish lay ministry from the ministry of the ordained. Pope John Paul II points out that the ministerial priesthood essentially has the royal priesthood of all the faithful as its aim and is ordered to it.[9] In other words, these two dimensions of the one priesthood of Jesus Christ are not to be in competition or conflict. There is one priesthood of Jesus Christ; lay and ordained share in that one priesthood in distinct but complementary ways. Post–Vatican II documents repeatedly assert that one of the roles of the ordained priesthood is to support and encourage the priesthood of the laity.[10]

An Explosion of Lay Ministry

Thomas O'Meara speaks of an "explosion" of lay ministry that took place after the Second Vatican Council.[11] He goes on to point out that this growth in ministry was enhanced by the cultural climate of the United States, where delight in belonging to groups, a tradition of helping and service, and a natural activism are all part of the American mentality.[12]

Philip Murnion and David DeLambo report that in 1999 almost 29,146 laypeople were involved full- or part-time in formal pastoral roles—an increase of 35 percent from 1992.[13] Zeni Fox, in an article titled "Ecclesial Lay Ministers: An Overview,"[14] tells us that a huge percentage of those ministers are women, many of whom began as parish volunteers. These lay ecclesial ministers are well-educated and most are happy in their ministry. Most important, they are already exercising considerable levels of leadership in parish life.

In addition, countless numbers of laypeople engage in parishioner ministry or discipleship by the way they actively live out their baptismal call in their daily lives. All of these people—lay ecclesial and parishioner ministers—provide the human resources to carry out the evangelizing ministry of the church. As we continue to equip Catholics to think of their baptism as a call to discipleship and disciple-making, these numbers will no doubt increase. Although now somewhat dated, in *Parish, Priest and People,* Andrew Greeley and his colleagues offer a description of a typically active Chicago suburban parish where the laity participate in a wide variety of ways in numerous organizations and groups: liturgical ministries, family support groups, Bible study, faith sharing, retreat programs, outreach, care ministries, bereavement programs, prison ministry, religious education at all levels, parish committee works, and neighborhood outreach.[15]

Lay Ministry: A Singular Grace

O'Meara regards this explosion of lay ministry as an event arising out of the interaction of grace and culture—a providential occurrence that was "unique in the past millennium,"[16] neither foreseen nor "dictated by the Council."[17] In the United

States, this explosion of ministry took place as the church sought to vigorously implement the decrees of the Second Vatican Council.

The restoration of the communal character of worship; the call to full, conscious, and active participation of the laity; and the restoration of liturgical roles all contributed to the huge growth of liturgical ministries. The implementation of the RCIA alone accounts for the creation of numerous roles that never existed before in recent church life. Social justice activities in the parish and various forms of religious education and formation all contributed to the expansion.

Parishes have changed their way of functioning in order to accommodate this explosion of ministry. By adding professional staff and enabling parishioner ministry at all levels of the church, parishes have expanded the scope and depth of parish ministry. For example, more than two hundred laypeople are involved in parish visitation and eucharistic ministry at UCLA hospital, thus changing the level of pastoral care that was being given to the large patient population. Rooting itself in baptism as the sacrament of ministry, we are in the process of creating a ministering church. David Power summarizes the experience of the church in these post–Vatican II years when he says that the key thing we have learned is that ministry is rooted in the church and there is only one ministry.[18]

Judging by the growth in the number of ecclesial lay ministers, and by the enthusiasm of parishioner ministers, this rich resource for evangelization will only grow. Pope John Paul II is surely right when he says that one of the signs of the times is the growth of participation, and that one of the most important functions of the ordained priest is to foster the ministries, offices, and roles of the laity.[19]

Yet, for all its growth and energy, lay ministry, if it is left to itself, if it is not harnessed, will be unfocused and ineffective. A collaborative leadership spirit is needed to harness it. People feel called; they are willing. But the parish must create an environment in which they can effectively use their gifts. Collaboration provides that hospitable context for the exercise of their gifts. Without that welcoming spirit, we will not achieve the kind of parishwide participation that is needed to carry out the mission of evangelization.

Parishes experience a great deal of frustration and anger when priests and laity cannot find a way to work together. This, of course, is not new. The history of the Catholic parish is replete with stories of major difficulties between priests and laity, going back to the days of lay investiture. Nevertheless, much more is riding on this issue now because today's parish is meant to be a ministering parish. How many times have new pastors been appointed to parishes and, because their leadership style is radically different from that of their predecessors, the parish falls into great disarray? In urban areas, we often see widespread movement from one parish to another because of these kinds of disturbances. This is not simply a matter of frustration and anger among the laity over a priest who is not collaborating. Sometimes it is a matter of priests struggling to deal with laity who are being unreasonable and unrealistic. It is a complex problem and, invariably, the mission suffers.

Collaboration

The Theology of Collaboration

One of the contributions of the Second Vatican Council was to reemphasize the role of the Holy Spirit in the life of the church. The gospels identify the mission of the community of disciples with the risen Lord's bestowal of the Spirit. Paul is very explicit about the role of the Holy Spirit in Christian life. In Romans he tells us "anyone who does not have the spirit of Christ does not belong to him" (Rom 8:9), so central is the gift of the Spirit to the Christian life. By the Holy Spirit, God fashioned us into the body of Christ that is the church and empowers all the baptized with gifts for ministry (Rom 8, 12:3–8; 1 Cor 12:4–11; Eph 4:11–16).

The *Decree on the Laity* states emphatically:

The Holy Spirit sanctifies the people of God through the ministry and the sacraments for the exercise of the apostolate, gives the faithful special gifts besides.... From the reception of these charisms, even the most ordinary ones, there follow for all Christian believers the right and duty to use them in the church and in the world for the good of humanity and the development of the church, to use them in the freedom of the holy Spirit who "chooses where to blow" (John 3:8), and at the same time in communion with the sisters and brothers in Christ, and with the pastors especially. It is for the pastors to pass judgment on the authenticity and the good use of these gifts, not certainly with a view to quenching the Spirit but to testing everything and keeping what is good (see 1 Thess 5:12, 19, 21).[20]

In other words, the council established the theological setting and the scriptural context for collaboration. The Holy Spirit is working in the church, not only to sanctify all the members but also to enable them to live out the missionary character of the church. It bestows on all the baptized gifts with which to serve, in the church and in the world. Collaboration, then, is not merely an issue of tactics or strategy; it is a matter of our ecclesiology. We must not "grieve the Holy Spirit,"[21] with which we were anointed.

The Role of the Pastor

Pastors, too, are obligated not to grieve the Holy Spirit, who has anointed all of us to be a ministering church. The *Decree on the Ministry and Life of Priests* states:

They [priests] should unite their efforts with those of the lay faithful and conduct themselves among them after the example of the Master, who came among humankind "not to be served but to serve, and to give his life as a ransom for many" (Matt 20:28). Priests are to be sincere in their appreciation and promotion of lay people's dignity and of the special role the laity have to play in the church's mission.... They should be willing to listen to lay people, give brotherly consideration to their wishes, and recognize their experience and competence in the different fields of human activity…. While testing the spirits to discover if they be of God, they must discover with faith, recognize with joy, and foster diligently the many and varied charismatic gifts of the laity, whether these be of a humble or more exalted kind.[22]

In the Synod on the Laity in 1987, the bishops strongly emphasized the role of pastors in fostering the Holy Spirit's activity in the laity. The *New Code of Canon Law* reflects Vatican II's theology of the laity. It says, in can. 275.2, that "clerics are to acknowledge and promote that mission which lay persons exercise in their own way in the church and in the world." It is noteworthy that in listing the duties of the pastor, a prominent one is acknowledging and promoting the proper role of the Christian faithful in carrying out the church's mission (can. 529.2).

Release of Gifts for Mission[23]

Loughlin Sofield, ST, and Carroll Juliano, SHCJ, have done a great deal of work to foster collaboration at all levels of parish life. They emphasize the importance of identifying and releasing the gifts of all the baptized and uniting them in ministry for the sake of mission.[24] The authors cite approvingly Bishop John Bathersby's definition of collaboration as the "utilization of our gifts in partnership with one another to carry out the mission of Jesus in the world."[25] His definition has the advantage of emphasizing that collaboration is not merely an in-house matter; it is our use of God's gifts for ministry in the church and in the world.

Collaboration, according to Sofield and Juliano, is a way of functioning that pervades the entire parish so that all baptized persons are called forth to use their gifts for ministry. Recent research by the Gallup Organization, however, indicates that 53 percent of those Christians asked responded that they do not have the opportunity in their congregations to do what they do best.[26] There is clearly a need here.

We can glean the following observations from Sofield and Juliano's approach. By fostering a collaborative leadership style, the pastor strives to foster a sense of ownership of the common mission, minimize turfism and competition, and foster a mutual partnership among all parishioners. This partnership manifests itself in a desire to work together for common goals. Particularly important in the process is the identification and release of the gifts of all the baptized to carry out the mission.

Through baptism, all the members have gifts to share. And they do not keep these gifts inside themselves, but give them freely for the common good. This is exactly how Paul describes a charismatic church (1 Cor 12:1–11). At its heart lies a profound and deeply satisfying experience of mutuality and interdependence—a giving and receiving that enlarges the members' capacity to serve the wider community.

Prayer is an essential component of a collaborative leadership style that calls everyone to conversion and to move beyond an ego-centered way of functioning. Very often, the form of prayer that is most appropriate is one based on people sharing their faith. Some parishes use the upcoming Sunday readings as a basis for common prayer among all the ministry groups in the parish. This enables the people who are united in ministry to be united in prayer as well. Coming together this way in prayer helps people overcome self-centeredness so they may freely give of themselves in ministry.

Shared ministry has a profound theological foundation, not only in the giftedness of baptism but also in the very partnership of salvation. God invites our participation and partnership in the kingdom through our free response to his grace. Freedom is one of God's greatest gifts to us. When we respond to God's invitation to use our gifts in ministry, we enter into partnership with him in bringing about the salvation of the world. Collaboration gives glory to God, because it too is a partnership and thus reflects an important dimension of God's plan of salvation.

A collaborative leadership style works to promote parish-wide participation in the mission precisely in terms of people's gifts. This enables us to empower a wide variety of people for ministry. One example in particular comes to mind. During my first few years as a campus minister, I witnessed the marriage of a young couple. The groom came from a very troubled family situation. His father, Pete, was severely damaged—psychologically because of his family background and physically as a result of serving in World War II. Pete was married to a woman named Alice, who had been a Jehovah's Witness. Little by little, because of the involvement of the young couple, the parents began actively participating in the parish. Alice began by attending mass with her son and daughter-in-law on Sundays. Then she and her husband got involved in the St. Thomas More Newman Center. Soon, I was able to bless the marriage and receive Alice into the church.

About twenty years later, I came back to do a mission in the parish near the college. I was delighted when Alice walked into the church with several severely disabled adults in tow. Her husband had died, and she had taken up this ministry. Her patience in dealing with her husband and his children by his first marriage equipped her very well to deal with these suffering adults. What came through strongly was her love for them, expressed in kindness and joy. It was an impressive sight. The parish had made her feel welcome, encouraged her to use her gifts, and helped her to feel confident that she had much to offer, even though she was not professionally trained or highly educated. Most important, five adults suffering from severe disabilities were the beneficiaries of her love and kindness.

Her story points as well to the wide expanse of lay ministry beyond the confines of the church. Laity are experiencing the call to ministry in the family, neighborhood, workplace, and larger society. Social justice activities are a major area of individual and communal ministry. Only a small number of ministers are needed to carry out activities within the community itself. Most lay ministers are called to use their gifts in the world.

Alice's story is multiplied many times over in the thousands of laypeople who have found great satisfaction in responding to Christ's call to ministry. The explosion of lay ministry is a great gift that has the power to unleash the evangelizing potential of the parish. It is a phenomenon that has changed the shape of the parish *ad intra* and *ad extra*. It is, by and large, the laity who live in the world and who have the potential to be a light to the world by virtue of being rooted in it.

Sofield and Juliano point out that when we empower people for ministry by helping them use their gifts, certain things are required of us. The parish needs to work to foster the values, habits, and behaviors in the community that support and lead to this kind of empowerment. In turn, the empowerment promotes ownership of a common mission, as well as the necessary communication and commitment to achieve true collaborative ministry. The authors offer a detailed picture of some of the challenges that this involves. Gratitude, appreciation, encouragement, and increased levels of communication are all examples of the Holy Spirit at work in a community to enable a parish to foster collaboration.

Whether one adopts a collaborative leadership style or not has a significant impact on the resources available to carry out the evangelizing mission of the church. It is a simple matter of numbers: do we want to use the gifts and abilities of all members of the church, or only a few? But more than this, collaboration—real participation—is, according to John Paul II, one of the true "signs of the times,"[27] a marker of the worth and dignity of all people. If we can work out this issue in the church, we have a powerful message to offer a world where millions of people are not allowed to participate fully and use their gifts to serve others. Currently, the lack of such collaboration is a source of alienation and sometimes a cause of disaffiliation and pain. Literally, the church grieves the Holy Spirit in failing to work through this issue.

Collaboration Depends on Shared Decision-making

The second aspect of a collaborative style of ministry, beyond facilitating participation through the use of people's gifts, is shared decision-making. The previously quoted dictum from Roman law is apt here: *quod tanget omnes, ab omnibus tractari et approbari debet (what touches all, must be treated and approved by all).*[28] Many writers are critical of the Catholic Church, alleging that true shared decision-making is impossible in a hierarchical system that allows only consultation. There is often a feeling that there is no accountability coming from the top down, and thus no commitment to take seriously what comes from the bottom up.

According to canon law, the pastor (or several priests in a team ministry: can. 517) is ultimately responsible for running the parish. The pastoral care of the parish has been entrusted to him as its shepherd, under the authority of the diocesan bishop (can. 515; 519). I will not go into the special circumstances of parishes that are not directly under the pastoral care of a pastor. Any form of shared decision-making has to reckon with the fact that the ultimate responsibility for the parish lies with the pastor. I am not talking about changing the structure of the church, but exploring and demonstrating how the current structure can be responsive to the challenge of collaborative leadership.

The form of shared decision-making that can take place in a parish whose ultimate care is entrusted to the pastor comes under the rubric of consultation. The practice of consultative decision-making is very old in the church. Cyprian writes: "I have made it a rule, ever since the beginning of my episcopate, to make no decision merely on the strength of my own personal opinion without consulting you (priests and deacons)."[29] A collaborative leadership style within the framework of consultation will always be clear about the parameters of the shared decision-making. It will respect and affirm the participants, dialogue with them, and ultimately, if necessary, communicate clearly the reasons why a certain decision does not follow the advisement of those being consulted.

In *That All May Be One,* Terrence Nichols has written an interesting book on the subject of what he calls participatory hierarchy. His conclusions are relevant to our subject. He asserts that hierarchy is a legitimate social and ontological structure in the universe. The situation where the pastoral care of the parish is entrusted to the pastor is a hierarchical structure. But Nichols also makes the point that the relationship of the hierarchical authority to its subjects does not have to be one of domination or subjugation; it can be participatory, allowing influence from the bottom up.

Nichols invokes the scientific notion of a *wholeness* as a way of understanding a participatory hierarchy. Nature is full of examples: something is a part of a larger system but also exists in itself, with an autonomy and an integrity that are not swallowed up by the larger system. Arthur Koestler speaks of a *holarchy,* in which something functions both as a part and as a whole. The whole does not dominate the part, but allows the lower parts to function according to their structures and abilities. In such a system, the parts influence the whole as the whole influences the parts. There is a "top-down" causality and a "bottom-up" causality.[30] In other words, life is a two-way street.

As an example, Nichols points to the cell, which is a holon within the body. The cell is influenced by its constituent parts, especially the DNA, which controls the cell's development. But the whole cell also seems to organize, constrain, and control the activities of its parts. Thus, there is a two-way influence of the part to the whole. Within the body, the cell's activity is controlled by the needs of the whole body. The growth of human tissue cells, which takes place randomly in tissue cultures, is controlled by the whole organism. The whole governs the part, yet every cell also makes a contribution to the whole.[31]

Let's apply this analogy to parish life. In the consultation that takes place through participatory hierarchy, clearly the influence comes from the top down *and* the bottom up. Consultation is not a one-way street. It is truly a process where there is mutuality, respect, and reciprocal influence. Subsidiarity and legitimate autonomy are appreciated values. There is a profound experience of the parishioner participating in the authority of the pastor, and the pastor participating in the experience of the parishioner. When consultation functions this way, the result is real wisdom.

Mark Fischer gives an elaborate example of this kind of participatory hierarchy[32] when he recounts how Bishop John Cummins of Oakland, California, dealt with one of the committees of the Diocesan Pastoral Council, the social justice committee. This committee was entrusted with presenting a proposal. After the committee made its report to the DPC, a vigorous discussion followed. Many questions were raised. Only after that discussion did the bishop speak. He had authorized the work of the committee, and the committee was eager to hear his response. He praised the committee for its work and also raised some criticisms that he felt would sharpen the report and make it more concrete. In other words, he engaged in dialogue. The committee went back and revised its work, the DPC accepted it, and the bishop ratified it. The recommended actions were taken. It is a good example of the kind of consultation that is practiced through hard work, critical listening, respectful dialogue, and profound mutual respect.

Collaboration in Parishes Today

In addition to the diminished number of priests available for parish ministry, the two biggest changes in parish life in the post–Vatican II era are the employment of lay ecclesial ministers on parish staffs and the widespread parishioner ministry of the laity. How a pastor manages this tremendous resource determines the level of evangelizing power that can be released in the parish.

The recent publication *Excellent Catholic Parishes*[33] documents conclusively that collaborative leadership is one of the single most important characteristics of successful parishes. In *Called and Gifted for the Third Millennium,* the bishops state that the "church's pastoral ministry can be more effective if we become true collaborators, mindful of our weaknesses, but grateful for our gifts. Collaboration challenges us to understand that we are, in reality, joined in Christ's body, that we are not separate but interdependent."[34] The bishops make a special point of the need to foster collaboration between clergy and laity for the sake of the mission. They state: "The new evangelization will become a reality only if ordained and lay members of Christ's faithful understand their roles and ministries as complementary, and their purposes joined to the one mission and ministry of Jesus Christ."[35]

We have already noted that the explosion of lay ministry in the church since the Second Vatican Council is a dramatic and unforeseen grace to the church. However, in order for participation to characterize the life of all the baptized, we need to bring about a greater measure of collaboration in our parishes. A collaborative leadership style enables broad participation in both the setting of parish priorities and the use of everyone's gifts for ministry. Not limited to implementation, collaboration also includes participation in decision-making.

Participation is one of the signs of our times. In our modern world, people are less and less willing to have other people decide for them in matters of importance. Democracy enshrines this principle of participation as government of the people, by the people, and for the people. Furthermore, in the United States one of the characteristics of civic life is volunteerism. We rely upon the active involvement of people at many levels in order to get things done. Many institutions simply could not function without a vast network of volunteers. The fact is that the evangelizing mission of the parish will be successfully implemented only through the widespread participation of the laity.

In 1980, when the American bishops published *Called and Gifted: The American Catholic Laity,* they highlighted one of the reasons lay ministry caught on after Vatican II: it appeals to laypeople's desire to be adult members of the church. Generally, parishioners want to be treated as adults. They want to be respected for their knowledge and experience, freedom and responsibility, and their sense of mutuality. When treated as adults, they tend to respond at an adult level. One of the clearest features of the recent sexual abuse crisis was the widespread feeling that the hierarchy was not responding to the rest of the church in a way that respected them as adults. Information was withheld; decisions were made in secret; there was a lack of forthright and honest communication and a failure to candidly admit mistakes. Furthermore, there was a general consensus that the church would be better off if it fostered lay participation in dealing with clerical sexual abuse, because it is an issue that affects the entire church.

The documents of the Second Vatican Council give us an additional theological foundation for collaborative leadership.[36] Vatican II balanced the hierarchical perspective of the church with an emphasis on our equality and unity as members of the people of God. It also stressed the hierarchy's need to consult the faithful in doctrinal and pastoral matters. Vatican II balanced the excessive clerical domination of the laity that prevailed prior to the council. By fostering collegiality, collaboration, and consultation[37] at different levels of the church, the council has opened the way for increased levels of collaboration between clergy and laity. In addition, the emphasis on full, conscious, and active participation in the liturgy as one church tends to spill over into other areas of church life (*lex orandi, lex credendi:* the experience of worship is the source for belief).

Why Is Collaborative Ministry Difficult?

What accounts for a lack of willingness or openness to collaborative ministry? It may have to do with someone's theology; it could also be fear, lack of self-esteem, a control issue, or inertia. Bernard Lonergan, in *Insight*, identifies the *bias of common sense* as a potential source of blindness as one tries to live an authentic life open to truth and love. This form of pragmatic common sense can prevent pastors from working through the challenge of developing a collaborative style of ministry, because it requires systemic change. As a pastor, I found it very difficult to look critically at how we were doing things while we needed to carry on the day-to-day tasks of ministry. We are intent on simply doing things, and too busy to step back and examine how and why we are doing them.

Collaboration is a systemic approach. It happens only if we step back from the daily tasks of ministry and make a critical inquiry into how we want to do things—and a commitment to take the necessary steps to do them. But this kind of reflection takes time away from accomplishing the many tasks that need to be done. If we are pragmatic, if we are committed to keeping our nose to the pastoral grindstone, then we may never get to the critical reflection and action that would eventually let us be much more effective at accomplishing those same ministerial tasks. But some people see such reflection and action as a waste of time and don't want to spend the time and energy necessary for this second-level task, where we don't just do something, but also critically examine the premises on which we do it.

Similarly, if we are zealous evangelizers, we may fear that if we spend any more time on internal ministerial issues we will never get around to outreach. Evangelization has to be rooted in actual outreach. Isn't it better to spend our time actually implementing the goals of *Go and Make Disciples,* rather than examining our methods for doing ministry? I do believe that it is possible to spend so much of our time on second-level reflection that we never actually get around to doing anything! However, collaboration is too important a subject not to be intentional about, because it directly affects the capacity of the parish to engage all its parishioners in carrying out the evangelizing mission of the church. My experience as a pastor is that the willingness to engage in systemic reflection on how we do things ultimately leads to more effective ministry.

Having said that, it must be admitted that collaboration is not easy. It consumes time and energy. Any community that tries to undertake something so challenging to an ego-centered way of life as collaboration will struggle. But my conviction is that collaboration is ultimately worth it, because it leads directly toward enabling all parishioners to use their gifts for the evangelizing ministry of the church.

Collaboration with the Lay Staff

The change in the role of the laity has brought about a tremendous change in the lifestyle of the priest, who is now called to provide leadership for the ministry of the entire parish. In larger parishes, one of the pastor's biggest challenges is to develop a collaborative leadership style with the parish staff. There are problems to be worked out in this area. The bishops' study on the laity points out that "fifty-eight percent of the pastors see the staff relationship as collaborative rather than independent, but only thirty-one percent of the parish ministers see it that way. Similarly, fifty percent of the pastors see the staff relationship as team rather than staff, but only thirty-five percent of the parish ministers see it that way."[38]

Official and unofficial documents continue to point to the need to improve collaboration in parishes. Relationships between pastors and staffs are often a source of pain and constant struggle. In some places, because of radically differing ecclesiologies, relationships between lay ministers and newly ordained parochial vicars have become a source of conflict and division. In all of this, we need to be reminded of the mutual responsibility of priests and lay ministers, as part of ongoing parish renewal, to find ways to collaborate with each other. Pastors must acknowledge that their ministry is fundamentally ordered to the service of the entire people of God; the lay faithful must acknowledge that the ministerial priesthood is totally necessary for their participation in the mission of the church. Oftentimes, we have the willingness but lack the know-how.

How *do* we bring about this effective collaboration between clergy and laity on parish staffs? Sofield and Juliano offer a step-by-step process of clarification, conviction, commitment, and capacity. *Clarification* is required so everyone understands what collaboration is. We need to be on the same page. *Conviction* poses the question as to whether, based on this common under-standing, the staff is willing to move ahead in that direction— quite aware of the challenges and difficulties involved, and *commitment* requires an explicit decision to do so. *Capacity* requires an ongoing assessment of the requisite skills.[39] Their work suggests that parish staffs need to start on the ongoing path to more effective collaboration.

The Parish Pastoral Council's Role in Collaboration

Many parishes today operate out of an oligarchy, centered in the parish staff and/or the parish pastoral council. They never are able to engage effectively the entire parish in collaboration. But the parish pastoral council can be an organization that facil-itates the larger parish participation.

The Second Vatican Council gave strong encouragement for the formation of various councils, including parochial councils.[40] As Mark Fischer documents in *Pastoral Councils in Today's Catholic Parish,* since Vatican II, parishes have struggled to determine exactly what the role of these councils should be. Are they consultative or decision-making bodies? Planning or coor-dinating? Around the time of the publication of the *Code of Canon Law* in 1983, things began to get clear. The code clearly states, "The pastoral council possesses a consultative vote only" (can. 536.2). The consensus seems to be emerging that councils have as their principal role assisting the pastor in the work of parish planning—investigating, pondering, and proposing prac-tical solutions about all things pastoral (can. 511).

As Fischer carefully points out, we should not let the word *consultative* be reduced to mere advice giving, or minimize the real power of the parish pastoral council to have a significant impact on the life of the parish. In fact, in many areas the skilled pastor often uses consensual decision-making in the parish pas-toral council as a way of taking consultation. A critical element of true consultation is that the leader takes seriously the input of the consultative body. He needs to dialogue with the members of the body, affirm their work, and try to equip them to create input that he can readily accept and act upon. The pastor needs to set clear parameters for the consultative process that avoid false expectations, show clear appreciation for the work of the council, and, when some element of the advisement is not followed, give sound reasons for his decision. This form of consultation empowers the council.

My own experience as a pastor of two parishes confirms the careful research of Mark Fischer and affirms his overall perspective that parish pastoral councils are a vital part of post–Vatican II parish life. A significant challenge took place in Los Angeles when we dismantled the parish council of the parish and moved to a parish pastoral council model. In the former model, elected representatives occupied themselves mostly with reporting various parish activities to each other. In the latter, members came on to the council through a discernment process so they could function as a truly consultative body to the pastor about the pastoral life of the parish. They were, in effect, a direction-setting body of consulters. Out of that experience, we were able to engage the parish in fashioning our first parish planning process.

Parish pastoral councils are not only vital to parish life in this post–Vatican II era; they are also crucial arenas in which the pastor can work to develop a collaborative leadership style. Councils can facilitate both collaboration in decision-making and widespread lay participation in the parish's missionary efforts. These are two vital characteristics of the pastoral leadership style.

I have identified the explosion of lay ministry as a powerful resource for evangelization. I have identified two essential elements of the collaboration that need to be in place in the parish: shared decision-making and parish-wide participation in the ministry. I have identified two areas where the collaborative leadership style is very important, namely, with the parish staff and parish pastoral council. Now I would like to examine what I believe is an effective strategy to help shared decision-making and parish-wide participation find their most effective expression: pastoral planning.

Pastoral Planning

Father Lyle Holman is pastor of (the fictionalized) St. Theresa's parish in Wausau, Wisconsin. He is just beginning his second six-year term there. It is a parish of about 2,000 families. Father Lyle is intent on improving the process that he undertook with the parish three years ago, when the council and the parish staff (DRE, adult formation director, liturgy director, outreach coordinator, and administrator) led the parish in its first experience of parish planning.

Though that planning process served the parish quite well and many of the objectives that the plan called for have been accomplished, there are three major problems that Father Lyle wants to correct. First of all, the planning process originated with the parish pastoral council, and the parish staff was never fully brought into it. As a result, the staff didn't fully support the process and didn't adequately integrate its own agenda into the objectives of the parish plan.

Second, while some attempt was made to involve the whole parish in the planning process, in the end it was too much a project of a select group of people, primarily council members and a small group of active parishioners already involved in the council. The result was that there was never widespread enthusiasm among the parishioners for the process, and they weren't brought into the implementation of it. Third, many of the plan's objectives were never adequately completed. Some of them went to committees and simply got lost in the shuffle. There was never an adequate mechanism for follow-up once the plan had been written.

Father Lyle wanted the collaboration of both the parish pastoral council and the parish staff in the planning process. He decided to get them engaged and involved in the process from the very beginning, so they could truly own it and get behind it. He also wanted the entire parish to participate in the process from the beginning. He wanted to make sure that all parishioners could claim the objectives and priorities of the plan as their own, which would lead to more involvement in its implementation. Finally, he wanted to create some mechanism in the planning process to ensure that the priorities the parish decided upon had a good chance of being implemented.

These, then, were the three changes that the pastor wanted to effect to improve the planning process the second time around: increased collaboration among his leadership, increased participation among the parishioners, and a more effective mechanism to ensure that the plan was implemented. Father Lyle's instincts about what was needed to improve the pastoral planning process hit the mark. For a pastoral planning process to be effective, all three of those elements are needed.

However, as our example has shown, not every planning process will bring about a collaborative experience of shared decision-making and widespread participation. Nor does every planning process lead to implementing priorities that reflect evangelization as the essential mission of the church. For this reason, in 1999 the PNCEA created a pastoral planning process that does accomplish these things. It is called *ENVISION: Planning Our Parish Future.*[41]

What makes *ENVISION* different from other pastoral planning processes? First of all, it carefully guides the parish through the process with expertly designed materials and well-trained facilitation. Second, *ENVISION* is guided by and based upon an evangelizing vision of the church's mission. The purpose of the planning process is to enable the parish to achieve its evangelizing potential. Finally, it is highly participatory, both in the decision-making processes that set parish priorities and in the careful steps to engage widespread participation to bring about results. The planning process does not end with writing the plan; it ends with accomplishing the objectives!

How Will Collaborative Leadership Release the Evangelizing Potential of the Parish?

Goal I of *Go and Make Disciples* calls all people to live their lives fully as active disciples. The operative word here is *all*. Evangelization is not the work of a committee; it is the mission of the entire parish. A collaborative leadership spirit can extend involvement in the mission of evangelization to ever-wider circles of parishioners. Every baptized person has gifts for ministry. The goal of collaboration is identification, release, and union of all the gifts of the parish for the sake of mission. When we work to make a collaborative spirit permeate all aspects of parish life, we are putting in place one of the most important operational changes that will enable us to organize the parish effectively for long-term effective evangelization.

Evangelization, as is clear from Part One of this book, is a way of being church that embraces all aspects of Catholic life. Is it any wonder that implementing it requires a complex and comprehensive pastoral strategy?

One might also argue that forming a parish in a collaborative spirit is itself an act of evangelization. We are learning more and more that if the process is faulty, so will the product be. But if we get the process right, that will go a long way to making sure that the product is right. Collaboration enshrines many of the values of the gospel: a fundamental equality before God, the experience of being gifted in baptism, and a thoroughgoing focus on the mission as the reason and purpose for ministry. Furthermore, much of the alienation in our modern society takes place around the failure of collaboration in the workplace and in society. Many people experience a great deal of hurt around these issues. Our society simply has great difficulty embodying gospel values, because of excessive rigid hierarchies, competition, greed, and pragmatism. If they can find a church community whose very way of operating enshrines those gospel values, then they will find the experience of the parish truly liberating— good news!

Too often in our society, we hear of efficiency and pragmatism exercised at the expense of the dignity and worth of persons. The Holy Spirit is the love force that binds us together. When the virtues of love and compassion are wedded to processes that enable people to accomplish effectively the mission and goals of an organization, this is a witness that is very compelling. I claim that it is the Holy Spirit at work.

It goes without saying that the transformation of a parish through a collaborative style of ministry releases an enormous variety of gifts and energy for the ministry of evangelization.

Imagine what might happen if all parishioners felt called and equipped to share their faith with inactive Catholics or unchurched people. Many of our RCIA processes, currently floundering from lack of catechumens, would be flourishing. Similarly, efforts to reach out to inactive Catholics often fail for lack of numbers; this would change if all Catholics felt called and equipped to invite inactive Catholics to return to the practice of their faith.

Goal III of *Go and Make Disciples* challenges Catholics to take their gospel values to the family, neighborhood, workplace, and society. A vital collaborative style of ministry would free parishioners not just for church-centered actions on behalf of justice in the world, but also for a widespread ministry that does not rely upon church sponsorship. The work of humanization of our world can take advantage of ecumenical and interreligious collaboration, as well as common efforts with people of good will in the secular world.

Conclusion

I began this section of the book by making the claim that parishes are where evangelization can be most fruitfully carried out. A collaborative leadership style will go a long way to enable parishes to release this evangelizing potential. The two elements of collaboration that I have singled out are shared decision-making and parish-wide participation. There is a strong correlation between these two elements: the more a pastor involves parishioners in the deciding, the more parishioners will participate in the doing.

Some might find it surprising that I have spent so much time in a book on evangelization exploring the issue of collaboration. Actually, collaboration touches on the core values of an evangelizing church. Are we going to be a servant church that takes seriously the fundamental equality of all the baptized members? Are we going to be a church that recognizes that if the process is inadequate or fundamentally flawed, so will the product be flawed? One of the most significant ways that the Catholic Church can let its light shine before all is to continue to work through the painful process of creating a community of disciples where the members truly live in service of one another, and where the body functions in such a way as to enable all to participate in the ministry by using their gifts for the sake of mission.

Since evangelization is the essential mission of the church, parishes are bound to fashion their entire parish life around this mission. This requires systemic change. Fostering a collaborative spirit in the pastoral leadership puts the chief resource for evangelization at the ready: the laity. They already feel called, they are being equipped, and collaboration releases those gifts for the mission.

CHAPTER ELEVEN

ORGANIZING THE PARISH FOR EVANGELIZATION

Insight: Pastors organize parishes for evangelization by communicating a vision, managing for results, and providing administrative support.

Reflection

Soon after I was ordained, I read a document on the spirituality of the American priesthood, published by the U.S. Catholic bishops. The message I got from it was an understanding of what spirituality is *not*. It is not twenty or thirty minutes at the beginning or end of the day, where we fill our spiritual gas tanks with spiritual energy—energy we then use to deal with people and ministries the rest of the day. Rather, the ministry itself makes us holy! We are made holy by what we do.

What a relief I found in that message—and not because I was looking for an excuse to avoid quiet prayer time! Rather, I was desperately seeking a more meaningful connection between my prayer and my life, my quiet time and my ministry. The document gave me a new image of spirituality, one that I still hold. It told me that what I did—struggling to preach a good homily week after week, counseling people, doing the dreaded parish administrative tasks, working with organizations and going to meetings, administering the sacraments and visiting the sick and needy—was spiritual. They were all part of my formation in holiness. This is the context in which I look at the daily work of the parish in this chapter.

I address the need to organize our parishes for evangelization, which is primarily an issue of leadership, management, and administration. Insofar as these tasks fall primarily on the pastor, he is the person on whom I focus. However, since leadership in the broad sense of the term is a shared reality, my remarks are also addressed to a wider circle of parish leaders.

I am presuming that many of the changes called for by Vatican II are in place: the RCIA, various lay ministries, a renewed liturgy, and adult formation opportunities. I am also presuming that, early on, the parish engaged in some kind of pastoral planning process with an evangelizing perspective, like *ENVISION*, which established the goals of *Go and Make Disciples* as real priorities.

Organizing a parish for evangelization—moving it from maintenance to mission—requires systemic change in the way the parish functions. Unless the pastoral leadership is capable of effectively producing this change, it will not succeed in carrying out the evangelizing mission of the church. Moreover, becoming a missionary parish touches all the parish's members. Everyone must change. Leadership for this change is the subject of this chapter.

Leadership for Change

Here at the PNCEA, we have learned a great deal about change. We have learned that institutions change when three elements are in place: a sufficient degree of dissatisfaction with the status quo, a compelling vision for the future, and clear first steps to move toward that future.[1] Furthermore, we have learned that resistance is one of the most significant impediments to change. In dealing with human beings and change, an immovable object will always win out over a powerful force. In order to move forward, it is not helpful to simply push harder. One must remove the resistance.

The Second Vatican Council gave us a model of church that is hierarchical but also participatory. We the people are the church. The Second Vatican Council emphasized our equality as members of the one body of the people of God, by virtue of our baptism, before it noted distinctions within the hierarchy. This important vision of complementarity, however, does not always translate into the practical day-to-day running of things in the

Catholic Church. We tend to fall back on unimaginative, non-participatory hierarchical models, rather than look for creative ways to engage the entire people in a collaborative form of church.

This chapter presumes that the pastor's leadership is not top-down, but is a form of gospel service—and based on a participatory planning process. The people have had an opportunity to create a vision and a plan for their future. I am not minimizing the pastor's role in coming to that vision or choosing desired results. But I am presuming that it has been a collaborative effort.

There is no quick fix for moving from a maintenance to a missionary model of parish. The call to become an evangelizing church is a serious piece of reform that is ongoing, slow, and sometimes very difficult. We are in this for the long haul. If evangelizing all peoples is the essential mission of the church, it is not going to be replaced by another agenda in ten or twenty years. We had best get on with it. In other words, we are promoting not the quick fix but systemic change.

When the pastor communicates a shared vision, manages for results, and provides adequate administrative support for implementing parish priorities, this systemic change comes about. The social sciences give pastors the tools to carry out these three tasks, and this chapter will look at that. However, its main thrust is that these tasks are a great spiritual challenge. They require constant conversion, prayer, and contemplation as the pastor fills his role as the chief shepherd of the parish.

The Spiritual Challenge of Leadership for Change

The New Testament tells us that the church lives in the service of Christ's kingdom. It is a pilgrim church, constantly reaching for a transcendent goal. We are meant, therefore, to get moving, to seek constantly God's will for the church, and not to have illusions about perfection. We are looking for progress, not perfection. We want to be able to look the Master in the eye and say *yes*, we are taking seriously your commandment to go and make disciples of all nations. Since evangelizing all peoples is the essential mission of the church, at the beginning of this new millennium, it would seem that there is nothing better we can be doing.

There is a great temptation in pastoral ministry to console ourselves with accomplishments that have nothing to do with our real mission. Probably the most egregious example is that of spending most of our time and energy on maintenance (contrary to Jesus' explicit example of seeking out the lost). The result is that we have failed to form Catholics for mission; rather we have been content to turn them into "consumer Catholics." Similarly, oftentimes the quality of Catholic community life has a less than adequate spiritual focus. We allow the faithful to get too comfortable. At one well-to-do parish where I worked, it seemed that the center of community life was the cocktail glass! Another example of a myopic vision of parish life is the tendency to overemphasize in-house ministries rather than equip Catholics to carry out their ministry in the world.

The lesson of the New Testament is clear: *duc in altum—put out into the deep water* (Luke 5:4). It is better, from God's perspective, to fail at the mission he has given us than to succeed at one that is not his will. The mission has a church and the mission defines who we are as church. By seeking to transform our parishes, to make them missionary parishes in the service of the kingdom, we will probably fail a lot. But whatever success we do have will be counted in our favor because it will be the very service to which Jesus calls us.

This chapter outlines a practical strategy to implement the vision of evangelization at the parish level, and it requires effective pastoral leadership, management, and administration. We want to succeed; we want to bring about results. However, results must be measured by the parameters of gospel service rather than by secular criteria. The Holy Spirit is the principal agent of evangelization (*EN*, no. 75). We are merely God's servants, doing what has been commanded us by the Master.

Pastors will find that leadership for change is challenging, frustrating, and wearying, as well as exhilarating and energizing. The spiritual challenge of leadership is particularly crucial, and it is this aspect that I will examine in detail. A number of qualities in the New Testament can help us in our leadership role. Let us begin by focusing on the personal relationship that we must have with Jesus, who is our leader and whose disciples we are.

Love

In chapter 20 of John's gospel, Jesus entrusts to Peter the leadership of the church. The task is based on, and grows out of, the loving relationship that Peter has with Jesus. "Do you love me?" Jesus asks, three times. And Peter answers three times, a reminder of his earlier denial of Jesus. Jesus then tells Peter that this leadership will involve suffering—he will have to go where he doesn't want to go, even to the point of offering his life in imitation of Jesus' own death. Leadership for change is a commitment to sharing in the paschal mystery. Pastors need to begin their journey by responding to the same question: *Do you love me?* "Yes, Lord, you know that I do." Knowing that we will be sustained by this love will take us a long way. Organizing the parish for evangelization begins with this foundation: Christ's love for us and our love for Christ.

Let's recall at this point the earlier reflection on the trinitarian character of evangelization. Evangelization is a work of love; we do it to participate in God's love, and God's very character is missionary. This is why we evangelize. Therefore, all our outreach efforts to inactive Catholics and people with no church family must be rooted in God's love for us in Christ and the Spirit. Moreover, our leadership efforts as pastors also must find their strength and inspiration in God's love (1 John 4:16). Truly, becoming leaders of evangelizing parishes is a labor of love.

Single-mindedness and Perseverance

Jesus has a clear sense of purpose (Mark 1:38: "That is what I came out to do"), and he is faithful to that purpose to the end. He clearly announces that he came to preach the kingdom of God. On the cross, he proclaims that he has completed his work (Luke 23:46: "Into your hands I commend my spirit"; John 19:30: "It is finished"). Jesus calls us to imitate this quality of single-mindedness as we serve the kingdom. Pastors in particular should realize that leadership for change depends on having this clear sense of purpose. Like Christ, we know what we are about. Additionally, we need to be aware of the effort that is required to achieve our evangelizing goals for the parish. We understand that we will face adversity; we know that we will struggle. But we persevere nonetheless. We will not abandon the effort in midcourse because we have underestimated what is needed to accomplish it (Luke 14:27–33). Jesus would have us be persistent: we anchor ourselves in our calling and live it out, come what may. We have an excellent example of a temptation against perseverance in Jesus' life when the devil tests Jesus. He promises a quick fix, tempting Jesus to resort to alien powers rather than remaining faithful to the demands of the kingdom.

Relentlessness and Ruthlessness

Many sayings in the gospels emphasize relentlessness as necessary to the service of the kingdom: "No one who puts a hand to the plow and looks back is fit for the kingdom of God" (Luke 9:62). Jesus also tells his followers, with a certain hyperbole, "Follow me and let the dead bury their own dead" (Matt 8:22). As he sends the disciples out, he commands them to shake the dust off their feet and move on if people don't receive them. Jesus' words reveal his unswerving commitment to his mission, his refusal to let himself be turned aside from it. When people mindlessly oppose him, he doesn't argue with them but simply stays on the path. To Pilate, for example, Jesus says only that those who are open to the truth will hear his voice (John 18:37). Clearly, Pilate is not open to the truth; therefore Jesus felt no great need to engage him in a serious debate. Jesus knew who he was, the reason why he came, and he was undeterred by Pilate's pretense. There is a relentless quality to the commitment Jesus requires of us.

Jesus also reveals a certain ruthlessness, if one might use the term, in the service of the kingdom. He urges would-be disciples to leave things behind in order to follow him (Matt 5:19; 9:9). Sometimes he explicitly calls people to sell what they have (Mark 10:21; Matt 19:21). When he sends his disciples on mission, he tells them to travel without anything extra (Matt 10:5–15).

Urging his disciples to avoid sin, Jesus says, "If your right eye causes you to sin, tear it out and throw it away..." (Matt

5:29). In the Sermon on the Mount, he tells us that anyone who looks on a woman with lust in his heart has already committed adultery (Matt 5:28). When he sees the barren fruit tree, he curses it and it withers (Matt 21:18–20). In Luke's version, the tree will be cut down if, after a year of cultivation, it doesn't produce anything (13:6–9). Jesus is not afraid to place demands on his disciples in the service of the kingdom. Leadership for change requires that we make demands on ourselves and on our parishioners as we respond to the challenge of becoming a missionary parish.

Relationship with the Father

Jesus' single-minded commitment to the kingdom is rooted in, and strengthened by, his intimate relationship with the Father. Luke in particular stresses the role of prayer in Jesus' ministry. Matthew and Luke, in the so-called Johannine passage, speak of Jesus' intimate relationship with the Father: "No one knows the Son except the Father, and no one knows the Father except the Son and anyone to whom the Son chooses to reveal him" (Matt 11:25–27; Luke 10:21–22). Jesus urges his disciples to have faith in God, faith at least the size of a mustard seed, and to trust in God, for whom nothing is impossible: "Fear is useless; what is needed is trust" (as the 1970 Lectionary translates Mark 5:36 and Luke 8:50). Everything is possible to one who has faith (Mark 9:24). Having faith that God will bring to completion the good work begun in us is of supreme importance in a leader seeking to bring about change.

Service

Leadership for change requires us to imitate Jesus' servant model of leadership: "For the Son of Man came not to be served but to serve, and to give his life [as] a ransom for many" (Mark 10:45). Jesus rebukes Peter, James, and John for their erroneous understanding of discipleship, for associating it with honors and taking precedence over others. He tells them that the last will be first, and the first last. The Son of Man has come to give his life in service of the many. At the Last Supper, he puts on an apron and washes the feet of the disciples and tells them, "You also should do as I have done to you" (John 13:15).

Our model for pastoral leadership is not the corporate CEO. We certainly need to utilize some of the skills of corporate leadership in order to implement effectively the goals of the pastoral plan, but the parish is not a corporation. We are seeking to empower partners in ministry, partners who are like-minded disciples of Jesus Christ. We can define ourselves as pastoral leaders to the degree that we can combine the high-level leadership skills of the corporate world with a firm commitment to imitate Jesus' model of servant leadership.

A Willingness to Suffer

Jesus speaks openly to his disciples about the need to suffer. The road of discipleship is a road that leads to Jerusalem and the cross. "Whoever does not take up the cross and follow me is not worthy of me..." (Matt 10:38). "If any want to become my followers, let them deny themselves and take up their cross and follow me" (Matt 16:24; Mark 8:34; Luke 9:23). Jesus gives his disciples an example, challenging them to follow him physically to Gethsemane—a test of discipleship that they fail. Jesus tells them that they will share his cup of suffering whether they like it or not (Mark 10:39). The New Testament, especially the Pauline letters, are filled with a paschal spirituality that calls us to suffer with Jesus in order to rise with him. Any pastor seeking to bring about systemic change in his parish has to be ready to drink of the cup of suffering.

Pastors who take seriously the spiritual demands of leadership will want to examine their consciences about these gospel virtues, which Jesus requires of those of us who are called to be leaders. Vatican II has helped all of us—laity as well as clergy—see that our spirituality has to be rooted in our vocation. Pastors can integrate their spirituality with their ministry by centering their prayer life, their spiritual direction, and their sacramental life in the challenges of priestly ministry that are part of leading for change.

A Pauline Model

Paul's letters are an excellent resource for reflecting on a spirituality of leadership. Although he was not a pastor, he not only founded communities but also continued to nurture them and guide them to carry out their mission. His relationship with the Corinthian community in particular yields a rich source of material for meditating on leadership. It was no doubt his most troubled yet most intimate relationship, and Paul models real pastoral leadership for us in the Corinthian correspondence. He dealt with a number of thorny issues relevant to today: authority, liturgy, money, sexual morality, unity and diversity in community, faith in a powerful secular environment, and the call to be evangelizers in the world. Perhaps more than in any other letters, Paul reveals himself, shares his burdens, opens a window on his own spirituality, and provides a model and inspiration to all leaders.

What can we learn about a spirituality of leadership from the writings of Paul to the Corinthians? What comes through above all is his care for the community, or what Paul calls his "daily pressure" (2 Cor 11:28). We also see this quality in 1 Thessalonians, where Paul says that he shared not only the gospel with that community, but his very self (1:8). This is doubly true with the Corinthians. At times, in responding to childish baiting and hurtful questioning, Paul rises above recrimination to speak tenderly of what God has accomplished in the Corinthians, as if they were a letter written in his heart by the Holy Spirit.

When we invest ourselves in our pastoral ministry, it is a great gift of love. In fact, the experience of mutual giving and receiving in love that constitutes pastoral ministry is one of the greatest blessings of the priestly celibate life. When I left Greensboro, North Carolina, to assume a new pastorate at St. Paul the Apostle in Los Angeles, the overwhelming feeling I had about those seven years, as I looked out into the faces of the people in the closing Eucharist, was that we had had a love affair. There was an investment and an exchange of self in true mutuality. I gave much and received much.

When I began the pastoral ministry in Los Angeles, in the first homily I gave I expressed the desire that I could have a similar love affair with the people of that parish that I had had with the people of Greensboro. I was committed to give myself to them in all aspects of the parish ministry, in what would prove to be a very difficult experience of leadership for change. The dominant experience, once again, however, was one of mutual love. When I left the parish in 1994 after eight years as the pastor to come to the PNCEA, I felt again this overwhelming sense that we had experienced a love affair. Paul tells us that our pastoral leadership must be rooted in love.

Love does not mean lack of trouble or the absence of difficulties. One of the characteristics of a good leader is the need to stay connected and yet achieve emotional differentiation (see below), so we don't get caught up in an emotional feeding frenzy. Paul accomplishes this in an exemplary way in Corinthians by not responding to their accusations and criticisms in kind. He knows it is folly to enter into a competition with the so-called false apostles, as if he has to prove his credibility. Though he does engage them on their terms, what he ultimately boasts of is his suffering, not his prowess (2 Cor 11:21–31). Paul continually reminds the Corinthians that he finds his own security in Christ (2 Cor 3:4) and that whatever has been accomplished in them has come from the Holy Spirit. He didn't succeed by the power of smooth talk or showy tactics. He came to them in human weakness by the power of the Holy Spirit.

Another noteworthy dimension of the love-based ministry that Paul exercised is the tremendous energy that was released in him. Paul tells us in 2 Corinthians 5:14 that the "love of Christ urges us on" and in Philippians he says, "Christ Jesus has made me his own." At the end of 2 Corinthians, Paul boasts of his labors in a litany of hardships that qualify him for "hazardous duty" status with the Lord. Paul is indefatigable in his commitment to bring the gospel to the known world, and no hardship or obstacle detains him. Truly God's love has been poured out in him and has taken hold of him and made of him a formidable instrument of God's service.

What comes through over and over again in Paul's relationship with the Corinthians is not only his care but also his humanity. It is true that his investment in the well-being of the Corinthians is total. He exemplifies the freedom of celibacy to give itself completely in undivided service. But this is not without pain and suffering. Paul goes through all the ups and downs that come with loving someone who is still growing. In many ways, the Corinthians are contentious children, frequently given to tantrums, manipulations, and game playing. The issues are not one-sided. Paul makes mistakes in his dealings with this difficult community, which produce misunderstanding, hurt, and resentment. All this takes a toll. Paul's leadership brings him suffering and plenty of sleepless nights. Any pastor who commits himself to building an authentic evangelizing community will come to understand and identify with many of these experiences.

Every pastor knows that competition abounds. People are all too ready to go not only to the neighboring Catholic parish but to the newest nondenominational megachurch, because the preaching is better or their needs are being met more fully. Paul faced constant criticism and unfavorable comparison to those who knew how to sell themselves and pander to the less mature instincts of the community. Paul is not a "peddler of God's word" (2 Cor 2:17), nor did he come to them with hidden and shameful practices (2 Cor 4:2). His spirituality is perfectly expressed in 2 Corinthians 3:4: "Such is the confidence that we have through Christ toward God." Paul is not competing with human beings here. He is trying to be an instrument of God for the people. It is good for spiritual leaders to know who they are, whose they are, and from whence comes their strength.

Paul establishes sound spiritual principles in response to the clever-sounding slogans that are thrown at him. He often recalls his own bold teaching about the freedom that we have in Christ. Knowledge puffs up, Paul says; only love builds (1 Cor 8:1). We can't justify scandalizing or weakening the faith of others, simply because we have achieved a certain degree of knowledge and freedom. The ultimate test of our faith is love (1 Cor 13), which expresses itself in self-sacrificing concern for others and a willingness to forgo one's own rights. Paul gives plenty of practical applications to the formulation in Galatians: "For the whole law is summed up in a single commandment, 'You shall love your neighbor as yourself'"(5:14).

Another characteristic that pervades the entire Corinthian correspondence is an authentic wisdom that is modeled on the cross. Paul continually offers solutions to difficult issues, solutions based on sound principles and common sense. We see this in the way he responds to issues of sexual morality in chapters 6 and 7 of 1 Corinthians. There is no room for ideology, no abstract legislating that fails to take into account people's humanity and their concrete circumstances. Furthermore, Paul never goes beyond the limits of his authority ("I have no command of the Lord...."). He tells people when he offers his own opinion. He seeks to persuade rather than order people by fiat. Paul's concern for unity and diversity, and the way he encourages the community to use their gifts to build up the body of Christ in love, is a model of collaborative ministry.

Paul is keenly aware of the difficulties of maintaining strong community life in the midst of a contrasting culture. He emphasizes the importance of giving authentic witness without isolating people from the world in which they live. He wants to protect the authentic quality of community life by eliminating divisions and sexual immorality, and promoting a genuine loving concern for others that expresses itself in a variety of ways. Presumably, all these efforts to keep the body of Christ whole and holy were noticed by the people who encountered Christians. Paul is also concerned about the adequacy of the Corinthians' beliefs in the resurrection of the body, because it threatened to undermine their faith in the risen Christ. All of these considerations were part of the daily anxieties Paul felt for the community.

We know from the letters of Clement to the Corinthians that Paul never managed to resolve completely all the problems he faced in his relationship with this troublesome community. Yet what God asks of us is not success, but fidelity to the task. Perhaps the most powerful aspect of Paul's spiritual leadership—which enabled him not only to survive but to thrive in the midst of all the contention—was that he knew who he was and why he was sent. The energy that enabled him to keep on going was God's love in Christ. The "love of Christ urges us on" (2 Cor 5:14) and gives us a foundation for bearing all things, believing all things, hoping all things, and enduring all things (1 Cor 13). As we take on the challenges of providing leadership for evangelizing communities, Paul offers much to inspire and encourage us in our efforts.

Michael Wilson, a parish leader at St. Clement's in Plant City, Florida, has done a lot of work on leadership in government service. He was charged with the task of reducing budgets and eliminating waste in the military—something he was certainly competent to do. Yet he found that without a strong spirituality, he could not carry on this work. The wisdom of the ages could not supplant the wisdom of the cross. At one point, he devised a creed for himself, based on a spirituality of suffering that was adapted from Ann Clark's *The Stairway of Faith*. It is worth quoting in full.

When I told God that I wanted to be a leader, he put his arm around me and told me that I must carry some crosses to learn leadership. Why, this does not look that hard, I thought.

But after carrying the first cross for a while, it started to feel heavy. I fell to my knees and called out to God for help!

You can do it because you know that I am with you each step of the way. If there are tears of struggle for the hard ones or tears of joy for the easy ones, it's okay. Some crosses you will carry longer than others and that's okay too. Just remember to carry all of them and when you get tired, tell me; I'll help you, for leadership is a lifelong learning process and I don't expect you to do it quickly or alone. I know that you will learn because you are willing to

Care more than others think is wise.
Risk more than others think is safe.
Endure more than others think is reasonable.
Expect more than others think is possible.
Dream more than others think is practical.

Leadership, Management, and Administration

At the outset, it will be important to clearly distinguish among these three areas.

Leadership

Leadership focuses on long-term pastoral strategies that will move us toward our goal. The task of leadership is to share vision, motivate and inspire, align people and resources, and empower by inspiring commitment and making it possible for people to use their gifts in service of the mission. Our vision of leadership focuses on dynamic presence. The leader accomplishes his task by knowing who he is, where he is going, and by his resolve to exercise leadership by doing the things listed above.

Management

Management focuses on shorter time frames and carrying out chosen priorities by helping to get the right people to use their gifts to carry out these various priorities. Management faces organizational challenges, budget considerations, and people problems—all of which can either undermine or facilitate progress toward our missionary goals. Many pastors are excellent leaders but poor managers. We sometimes lack the personality profile, skills, or training necessary to be good managers. Therefore, the pastor may need to put someone else in place to assist him in carrying out this management role.

Administration

Administration is the arena of adequate support: facilities, resources, and technology. Many people will have the kind of organizational skills to do this. Pastors will need to make sure that such persons are in place in the parish organization as needed, whether they are volunteers or employees. Parish administration is an area where very fruitful evangelization can be carried out simply by the way we present ourselves to the public. Are we a welcoming community that is accessible, friendly, effectively organized, and hospitable? There is much room for initiative in putting on an evangelizing lens through which we examine our facilities, our personnel, and our operational systems to make sure that they don't alienate people but invite them.

The Myers Briggs Type Indicator

We have found the Myers Briggs Type Indicator to be an excellent tool to help parish staffs, parish pastoral councils, and volunteers to discern the kind of people best suited to carry out leadership, management, and administrative roles in parishes. Based on C. G. Jung's personality theories, the Myers Briggs inventory is the most widely utilized personality preference instrument in the world. It helps people work out of their strengths and upgrade some of their weaknesses. It is also very helpful in team building, because it enables individuals to understand themselves and how others are different, thus letting them build on that understanding to create more effective teams.

The Myers Briggs identifies four different areas of life that are helpful in determining personality types. Introversion/Extroversion defines the direction of our energy flow—from within or without. Sensing/Intuitive are mental functions that define how we receive information about the world around us—more down-to-earth and practical versus more theoretical and conceptual. Thinking/Feeling tells us something about our preferred way of making decisions—do we make decisions based on impersonal principles or on emotions and relationships? The Judging/Perceiving function determines our behavior style and influences the way we function in the outer world.

We can learn a lot about ourselves, and how we can function most effectively, through the Myers Briggs Type Indicator. We can also learn a lot about others, especially those who are different from us. This can help us find ways to create teams of people with complementary personalities that can work together effectively to get things done. Pastors have the task of calling forth people's gifts and managing the way those gifts are applied, using collaboration to implement the mission. The Myers Briggs Type Indicator can be a very helpful tool in creating effective teams.

Get a Clear Vision

Once upon a time, a young monk was pondering many of life's questions. He found himself perplexed by a key one: "Why are some people faithful, and others not?" Eager to discover the answer, he raced to his master-teacher, a wise elder monk. The elder monk responded to the question with a story:

One day, a dog chased a rabbit. The rabbit ran fast and the dog, chasing after it, barked and barked. Soon the barking caught the attention of other dogs. So they, too, joined in the chase. What a noise they made!

Eventually, as the other dogs began to get tired, they fell off from the chase and went home. Finally, the only dog left was the first dog, still in pursuit of the rabbit. Up and down the roadway they ran, until the rabbit eluded the chasing dog. Once the dog realized he could not catch the rabbit, he returned home, ever watchful, for the next time and the next chase.

The young monk remained silent for a respectful period and then said to the elder monk, "I don't get it. What does that mean?"

The elder monk smiled and simply said, "The first dog was the only dog actually to see the rabbit. Those who remain faithful must see the vision."

With that, the younger monk went off to ponder his new learning.[2]

A good planning process articulates a vision for an evangelizing parish, and ought to generate excitement, enthusiasm, and commitment to implement that vision. It is the pastor's job to keep that vision in front of people. He needs to articulate the vision in a compelling fashion and keep reminding people of its significance and vitality through various leadership activities, especially preaching.

What does an evangelizing parish look like? How does it function in practice? A pastor will need to develop a clear and concrete vision of what such an evangelizing parish looks like if he is to help bring it about. Father Bob Duggan, pastor of St.

Rose of Lima Parish in Gaithersburg, Maryland, imagines an evangelizing parish that is inspired by, and modeled on, the RCIA process, which calls for the entire community to carry out its apostolic vocation:

> In light of what is said in *Christian Initiation,* General Introduction (no. 7), the people of God, as represented by the local church, should understand and show by their concern that the initiation of adults is the responsibility of all the baptized. Therefore the community must always be fully prepared in the pursuit of its apostolic vocation to give help to those who are searching for Christ. In the various circumstances of daily life, even as in the apostolate, all the followers of Christ have the obligation of spreading the faith according to their abilities.... During the period of evangelization and the pre-catechumenate, the faithful should remember that for the church and its members the supreme purpose of the apostolate is that Christ's message is made known to the world by word and deed and that his grace is communicated...[3]

An evangelizing parish, according to Duggan, is one that focuses on intentional faith. All baptized disciples, at some point, need to ratify their commitment to live their faith fully as disciples of Jesus Christ. Cultural Catholicism won't do. There is not enough exposure to Catholic thinking, worship, teaching, and spirituality to sustain us without an intentional commitment to live our lives fully as disciples. Thomas Morris, in his book *The RCIA: Transforming the Church,* makes the point that the sacramental life of the church, especially the sacraments of initiation, has as its purpose to prepare and sustain Christ's disciples on their journey.[4]

An evangelizing community itself gives witness to God's missionary presence. Therefore, in an evangelizing parish, the way that people relate to each other in love and care is paramount. The leader sets the tone, calling everyone to this love and stressing the need to avoid cliques, manipulation, and self-centered behavior, all of which undermine community life. Hospitality is understood as acceptance—the action of welcoming each person, regardless of his or her color, language, culture, or social class. Every effort is made to help people feel as if they belong and have a place. One could say, without any hesitation, that authentic community life is our greatest evangelizing tool, since authentic community is one of the hungers of the human heart.

Duggan also envisions a parish in which the word of God is richly proclaimed to the people in various ways to enable them to wrestle with it and live it out in their lives. Paul VI states that the church evangelizes when it seeks to convert. This is especially true of the preaching in a parish that strives to be evangelizing. The homily is a call to conversion of heart. That proclamation has its most important venue in the preaching at Sunday liturgy. In addition, small faith-sharing groups, Bible study, and lectionary catechesis complement the Sunday liturgy experience.

Evangelizing liturgical celebrations stress the richness of Catholic symbol and eschew tokenism. *Lex orandi, lex credendi* means that worship forms faith. The sacraments, rightly celebrated, build faith; badly celebrated, they weaken and destroy faith.[5] The sacraments are always opportunities for ongoing conversion. The sacramental celebrations of baptism, confirmation, and First Eucharist, as well as weddings and funerals, offer wonderful evangelizing opportunities. The experience of mentoring and sponsoring (characteristic of the RCIA) is fostered in parish life, not only as the doorway to faith, but as a way of ongoing conversion. Thus, these sacramental experiences can be wonderful opportunities of growth for both sponsors and candidates.

Living one's faith fully can never be real unless it is accompanied by service. Social justice is not peripheral to an evangelizing parish, but is its hallmark. Goal III calls all disciples to carry their gospel values into the family, neighborhood, workplace, and society. The parish, by the way it forms individuals as disciples and fosters habits of justice in them, calling them to serve the kingdom in the world, equips its parishioners for evangelization. In addition, by the way it strives to implement the social justice agenda of the church at all levels of parish life, it also carries out the evangelizing mission of the church. In addition to having strong social justice activities, St. Rose of Lima tithes and gives 10 percent of its collection to support various social agencies that are struggling to help people help themselves.

Evangelization is never complete without a vigorous effort to reach out to the inactive and unchurched among us. The hospitality of the community must be accompanied by invitation. Perhaps this is the area that needs encouragement and development, at St. Rose and at most parishes. Ecumenism and interfaith dialogue, as well as outreach to those without any church family, are part of the overall evangelizing vision of the church. St. Rose has had an active evangelization committee for some years. The committee had an ongoing outreach to inactive Catholics; however, it faltered for lack of newcomers. This often happens when a single parish attempts to make a continuous outreach to inactive Catholics. For this reason, some parishes (like St. Augustine's in Pleasanton, California) have undertaken their outreach to inactive Catholics as part of a cluster with other parishes.

This is a picture of how one pastor envisions an evangelizing parish—built around the values and structures of the RCIA. Father Duggan tries to place that vision before the parish in various written communications (bulletins, parish newsletters, stewardship reports, and so on) and in homilies, catechesis, and through the entire parish's active participation in the process of Christian initiation.

Father Duggan's vision of an evangelizing parish built around the values of the RCIA is clear and concrete. There are certainly other ways of envisioning an evangelizing parish; however, his vision has the merit of integrating evangelization into familiar and important components of the RCIA, which is already in place in many parishes.

Edwin Friedman's Leadership Model

There are many different approaches to parish leadership that can help a pastor implement a vision. We are going to suggest an approach that comes from Edwin Friedman's two publications, *A Failure of Nerve* (posthumously edited) and *Generation to Generation*. A number of helpful techniques in managing for change emerge from Friedman's vision. His approach to leadership has been vigorously implemented at St. Rose of Lima.

Friedman thinks of the parish as a family system and emphasizes the importance of dealing with the integrated whole, rather than focusing on problem individuals. One can needlessly spend an inordinate amount of time and energy on these people who, for their own reasons, are committed to resisting, sabotaging, and rejecting the implementation of the vision. Leaders must be able to move beyond all forms of resistance by focusing on the people who are willing to move forward and minimizing the time spent on the chronic resisters. To apply this concept to the parish, once a pastor has clarified (presumably in some kind of planning process with the people) a vision for the parish, he needs to move ahead with the people who are willing to work on furthering that vision. Friedman believes that the most important task of the leader is to negotiate those emotional entanglements. If a leader cannot do this, the result is inaction; people just keep doing things in the old way and never move beyond them. They get stuck, and the community does not succeed.

Friedman sees leadership as an emotional rather than an intellectual transaction. Leaders will be successful to the degree that they understand their own role and the role of their communities along emotional lines. Accordingly, Friedman emphasizes two important qualities of leaders. On the one hand, they need to be able to remain emotionally connected with the community; on the other hand, they need to be able to function without getting caught up in the emotional entanglements that tend to paralyze leadership (in other words, not focusing on the problem individuals). He calls this *differentiated leadership*.

In looking at leadership, Friedman also emphasizes the importance of risk-taking and the need for imaginative, courageous action. Risk-taking is characteristic of all great leaders. They are not afraid to set out and break new ground. I see parish actions that focus on mission over maintenance as an example of this kind of imaginative risk-taking activity.

Friedman also analyzes resistance to leadership, which sometimes takes the form of sabotage; other times, of rejection. He uses biological models for understanding how resistance functions (as a virus or a bacteria, for example). The solution to all forms of resistance, he adds, is a connected but well-differentiated leader who is persistent and full of staying power.

Two images help us deal with tangled emotional situations. Friedman cautions against various forms of emotional entanglements that tend to *triangle,* or insinuate a third element in unhelpful ways.[6] He encourages leaders to be aware of this third element in understanding conflict and to avoid triangling themselves into already existing conflicts.

Consider the following example. You are pastor of a large urban parish in an area where the public school system is highly dysfunctional. If people want their children to get a good education, they send them to private or parochial schools. But private schools are expensive, so many people establish nominal membership in the local church in order to enroll their children in the excellent Catholic school.

On the one hand, you sympathize with parents' desire to provide a good education for their children; on the other hand, you want the families' involvement in parish life. The challenge is considerable. Many school families resist participating in church life because their fundamental commitment is not to the church but to the school. Many parishioners resent subsidizing families who send their children to the Catholic school and don't participate in parish life or contribute to the support of the parish. Moreover, many of your finest parishioners also have children in the parish school. You as a pastor are seeking to unite school and church into a unified parish family.

Unless you as a pastor address this third element, namely, the fact that some parishioners are more committed to their children's education than to the family's involvement in parish life, you will not be able to resolve successfully the issue of uniting school and parish. Furthermore, the principal and the pastor must be of one mind on this. A noncooperating principal becomes an example of a further triangle. In that case, the families can align themselves with the principal in circumventing the pastor's efforts.

Another helpful image Friedman offers is for the leader to function like a step-down transformer, to reduce rather than heighten emotional intensity in conflict situations. Transformers are electrical devices that can increase or decrease the flow of current. When pastors function as step-down transformers in situations of intense emotional conflict, they reduce the level of the emotion by their self-differentiated presence and make it more likely that solutions can be reached.

An example of how effective pastoral leadership can reduce the feeding frenzy in an emotionally heightened situation can be seen in the all-too-common experience these days of parish closings and mergers. I am thinking of a situation in south Texas, in which a poor Hispanic parish was merged with a wealthier Anglo parish. The new entity was given a new name and an entirely new church was built on the site of the wealthier parish. As one can imagine, there were strong feelings on both sides.

Fortunately, the pastor had responsibility for both parishes prior to the merger. There was a high measure of confidence and trust. Differentiated leadership enabled the pastor to avoid feeding the emotional frenzy. He stayed connected, but distanced himself enough from some of the unsavory aspects. In the midst of this trying experience, the pastor held up a vision of what kind of parish they were seeking to become and how they were going to work confidently and patiently toward that vision. The pastor performed an excellent leadership function in reducing rather than heightening the emotional intensity in this situation, and in so doing provided the foundation for the two communities to work together to build a new parish family.

Management

In a parish, how does management differ from leadership? Management focuses on utilizing the resources and personnel to accomplish the parish's priorities. It involves budgeting, overseeing personnel, organizing resources in order to achieve results, problem-solving, and monitoring progress among the various priority groups in charge of implementing the parish plan.

The most important function of management is to empower the parishioners to carry out the evangelizing priorities of the parish. Too many parish plans are merely written documents that have no operational reality. Parish management makes sure that the personnel, the budgetary resources, and the teams of parishioners charged with implementing the plan are given the support and encouragement they need to carry out their specific tasks. Good managers align their resources to get results.

Obviously, in a parish this is partly the responsibility of the pastor, but more likely it would need to be the major responsibility of various people whom the pastor empowers to help him. Parish staff, volunteers, and parish pastoral council members could be of great service by providing the necessary skills to empower people to carry out the chosen parish priorities.

Management works best when it helps people focus on short time frames within which to achieve larger tasks. The larger tasks are broken down into manageable segments, such as ninety-day objectives. The good manager holds people accountable and helps them stay on target. Good managers also are able to support, encourage, and offer problem-solving counsel to the people entrusted with implementation. They make sure to thank people when milestones are reached.

There are two problems specific to church management that ought to be mentioned. The first is that most of the work in parishes is done by volunteers.[7] The challenge of management is not restricted to paid professional personnel, but also includes recruiting, training, supporting, and affirming all the people who freely give of themselves in their role as parishioner disciples. They are using their gifts and talents as an expression of their baptismal call to share in the mission of the church. Church management must be adapted to the specific situation of these "volunteer" parishioner disciples.

A second problem is endemic to the priesthood. Most priests were not trained to be managers. The church has no effective system of management, with clear accountability lines, support structures, and ways of fostering levels of responsibility. Recently, a friend commented on the stark contrast between his work in the church and his experience in business, where he found a strong system of management in place that included clear responsibilities and regular meetings with his superior. In those meetings the superior was generous in pointing out strengths, quick to praise and encourage, and persistent in helping him work on his weaker performance areas. Priests rarely get that kind of supervision from anyone, and it is thus difficult for them to foster such a system in a parish. This area of management presents a particular challenge to the competent pastor to find a way to manage human resources (himself included) effectively.

Administration

What is the role of administration in the overall life of the parish? Administrators have the responsibility of making sure that the facilities, technical resources, and support personnel are available to the parish in order to accomplish its priorities. Paul speaks of helpful service or administration as one of the charisms of the community (Rom 12:7; 1 Cor 12:28).

We know how important is the gift of being able to organize, to be resourceful, and to get things done. People with the gift of administration are attentive to operations, manage details well, and are conscientious in providing necessary preparation and follow-up for parish activities. According to the Myers-Briggs, certain personality profiles make good administrators and managers. When pastoral leadership takes advantage of people with a charism for administration, the necessary preparation and follow-up for meetings is evident.

In addition, those in charge of administration must put on an evangelizing lens to ensure that the facilities, staff, and technical resources serve the evangelizing purposes of the parish, especially hospitality and invitation. Administrators in parishes should look carefully at how inviting and welcoming the parish facilities are. Do various parish operations (parish office functions; newcomer registration; liturgical ministries; volunteer recruitment, training and deployment; use of facilities; and so on) tend to function smoothly to serve parishioners, newcomers, and strangers? Do volunteers and paid staff people in the office recognize how vital they are in communicating a welcoming message to the many and varied people they serve? How well do parish publications like the bulletin, the newsletter, and annual reports carry the message of evangelization?

Obviously, parishes will carry out leadership, management, and administration in different ways, depending upon various factors, such as the size of the parish. Regardless of the size, however, a well-run parish needs to carry out all three of these functions effectively in order to empower parishioners to implement the evangelizing mission of the church.

Conclusion: A Pastor's Essential Behaviors

This chapter has been dedicated to the subject of parish-based management for change. I have suggested that the communication of a shared vision, effective management for results, and provision of adequate administrative support are the three essential elements of a change management initiative. The underlying concept for this work is collaboration. I have looked at the spiritual challenge for the pastor and have examined the leadership, management, and administration work to be done. Let me end this section with a few thoughts on what the pastor must do, week in and week out, to be successful in this work. These essential behaviors have been distilled from my experience of working with pastors in the PNCEA's pastoral planning efforts.[8]

1. **The pastor must know the people and the parish, in depth.** While this may seem obvious, pastors often do not know a wide range of parishioners at the depth necessary to understand how to use the full range of talents present in the parish community. What is needed here is in-depth knowledge of the interests, strengths, and weaknesses of the people in the community. The scope, too, must be broad enough that quality resources can be applied to issues and opportunities that come up in the parish. It is critical that the pastor constantly challenge himself to invite new parishioners with *fresh* thinking into leadership roles in the parish. This requires effort, because it is easier to rely on trusted veteran parishioners than to go through the effort to integrate a new parishioner into the ongoing work of the parish.

Pastors must also involve themselves deeply in the challenges and opportunities of their parish community. They need to focus on a few key points consistently to ensure that progress toward the vision is being accomplished. However, there is a big difference between a consistent focus on key priorities and micro-management. Here are two examples that illustrate my point.

At one parish I know, the pastor is constantly attentive to the issue of including Hispanic parishioners in the community. The three-year plan at this church has a focus on ensuring that "all are welcome," and the parish community has decided to begin its effort to reach out by starting with the Hispanic community. Other ethnic groups will follow. The pastor of this church maintains a focus for himself and for his parish by consistently asking questions of others about how the various programs and ministries of the parish are embracing the focus on the Hispanic community. The key here is that this pastor is asking the right questions at the right time to cause others to reflect on the issue in their work. In so doing, he creates key turning points for the parish community. Slowly and consistently, this parish culture is transforming.

Conversely, I know another parish where the pastor chooses to take issue with the color and design of the cover of the three-year-plan booklet. During the final meeting of a nine-month effort to create and develop their plan, the pastor spent nearly half an hour explaining his rationale for changing both the color and graphic on the cover. The change was last minute and, while the argument for a different cover had a solid theological basis, the pastor really damaged his leadership position. It was the wrong time and the wrong topic. In the end, the cover of the plan really made no difference to anyone but him. His micromanagement of such a small issue was seen as almost "silly."

2. **The pastor must insist on realism.** Pastors need to ask parishioners what is going well in the parish and what needs to be improved. Collecting this information helps him get a real sense of the community. Sometimes the feedback will be complaining; people often have gripes and will take issue with the pastor personally or with the local or institutional church. But often, people have good insights and can offer a perspective that enables the priest to have a clear view of what is really going on in the parish. Learning takes place for all when this dialogue is open and fluid. This collection of viewpoints can be done formally with surveys, but most often occurs in one-on-one or small-group dialogue with parishioners.

3. **The pastor must make sure that clear goals and priorities are set.** Not only should the goals be very clear, but there should be only a handful of them. These goals should be expressed simply, with targets to specify what is to be achieved. A goal statement—like "We will establish a new regional, ecumenical outreach center to feed the hungry, assist the homeless, and provide other necessary social services by 2006"—provides the clarity and simplicity needed to provide direction. Beyond simplicity in goals and priorities, pastors should strive to make their communications clear and direct, so that people can understand what is being communicated, evaluate their response, and act.

4. **Pastors need to follow through.** Pastors need to take action to be sure that goals and priorities are carried out. The pastor can do this follow-up effort himself or delegate the task. Establishing accountability for results starts with a well-constructed plan, which includes specific assignments for who will accomplish what task by a given date. In the goal statement above, for example, if the plan to establish a new outreach center falls behind schedule, the pastor should check with the group in the parish implementing the plan. He asks why they are behind schedule and then works with the team members to ensure that progress resumes and things get back on track.

5. **Pastors need to acknowledge and reward success.** There are people in this world who get things done. They are action-oriented and achieve goals. These people work at bringing in projects on time, and their work energizes others. In the parish setting, they have a commitment to their faith, enthusiasm, and the time to work at building up the parish community. The pastor needs to find ways to reward and acknowledge people who achieve goals. This can be done through special public acknowledgments, parishwide thank-you parties, special notes from the pastor, and so on. These forms of recognition should be focused on the good works of the parishioner. Acknowledgments of this type should be frequent, yet limited to truly significant accomplishments.

6. **Pastors can nurture the growth of parishioners' spirituality and effectiveness through coaching.** Pastors have the oppor-

tunity and responsibility to help parishioners grow and can be most effective at this by asking well-considered and well-timed questions. The right question at the right time forces people to think, search, and ultimately discover their own answer. A well-placed question can be posed in a number of different situations, but one of the best places, when the entire congregation can be reached, is in the homily. Probably the finest example we have of this from Jesus is his question to his disciples at Caesarea Philippi. After asking the disciples, "Who do people say that I am?" he follows up with the daunting question: "But who do you say that I am?" (Mark 8:27–30).

7. **Great pastors have come to know themselves.** It takes emotional fortitude for pastors to share the leadership of the parish with others in the open manner that has been explored in this chapter. The model is that of a servant leader, which calls for the pastor to be self-aware, authentic, to work at self-mastery, and to have humility.

Self-awareness and self-mastery are the two key elements that provide the foundation on which a truly authentic character is built. Pastors who are aware of their strengths and their limitations, and comfortable with both, are able to contribute to and draw from the talents of others. Being self-aware gives people the ability to learn from their mistakes and successes. Pastors who have a high degree of self-awareness can act as "step-down" transformers, as Friedman suggests. Self-awareness leads to self-mastery, which is the essential ingredient of personal growth. We are aware of the people around us who have strongly developed capabilities in both self-awareness and self-mastery. They contribute to and learn from their experiences with equal intensity.

Pastors with genuine authenticity are simply who they say they are. Their actions match their words. Nothing attracts us more than a person who is authentic, and nothing builds greater levels of distrust than people who are duplicitous in their words and behaviors.

Every day, pastors find themselves in positions where they make decisions and guide others. The pastor who learns to control his ego, who is able to provide the leadership necessary to guide his parish, and does so from a position of humility and service to others, will be revered. Conversely, even the best "technical" leader or most gifted homilist will be scorned if his ego grows unchecked. The old adage, "Your actions speak so loudly, I can't hear what you are saying," applies to all positions of leadership.

CHAPTER TWELVE

FORMATION OF THE PARISH FOR EVANGELIZATION

Insight: Viewing the goals of Go and Make Disciples through the priestly-prophetic-royal lens offers a rich spirituality for the formation of disciple-makers.

Reflection

The baptismal ritual ascribes the priestly, prophetic, and royal character of Jesus to all the baptized. I have not, however, met many individuals who have manifested all three of those qualities in equal measure. One person stands out, though. Her name is Sister Maureen O'Keefe, SSND. She was a very special person, a guardian angel who came into my life before my ordination in 1968, and later became a friend and mentor for thirty years. She exhibited in exemplary fashion what it means to be a priestly, prophetic, and royal person in Christ.

Sister Maureen was a pioneer in the field of religious psychology. As a counselor, she helped people come to a holiness of life through integration and wholeness—an achievement that she exhibited in a powerful way in her own life. She showed all those who knew her that at the center of every human person God dwells, and that our lives are meant to reflect back to God that holiness of life by giving ourselves in love. She captured for me the essence of the priestly character, which is sacrifice. Because she had to embrace much suffering in her own life, she had a keen sense of the sacrificial character of Christian love.

She was also a prophet, witnessing relentlessly to the truth to individuals, to the local communities where she served, and to the national and international levels as well. Love was her quest, but truth was the path. Always gentle, but unmistakably fierce, were her words. When people dealt with her, they knew they were dealing with a force to be reckoned with. This meant that, at one point, it became necessary for her to leave her Mankato Province and relocate in Dallas. She was a prophet who was not acceptable in her own country.

If, as we shall see, the royal character of our baptism is manifested in love's power to reorder the world according to the values of justice, Maureen exhibited this quality as well. She worked in many wonderful ways with people to make the world a better place. I remember in particular her labors in the Big Brother–Big Sister Program that she ran so effectively at the Mankato Newman Center under the sponsorship of the YMCA. Thousands of children with single parents and children from broken homes came to know the love of a big brother or a big sister because of her effective leadership. Justice was never an abstract idea for Maureen. It was a way of being, to be lived out in all spheres of life. She had an Irish temperament and nothing made her angrier than instances of injustice to God's defenseless poor.

Maureen was a priestly person, who heard many confessions without the power of the keys. She exercised a prophetic ministry in everything she did, right up to her last days. She held no office, yet she was a woman of transforming power. Ironically, even though she was a psychologist, she stands out as a testimony to what David Brooks in a recent *New York Times* editorial, calls the "fire and brimstone universe," symbolized by Mel Gibson's *The Passion of the Christ*, rather than a psychobabble nation symbolized by Mitch Albom's *The Five People You Meet in Heaven*.[1]

Our religion claims allegiance to the terrifying, awesome God who is at once the Holy and the Incarnate One, who died a violent death on the cross, and who also wondrously rose from the dead. Because Christianity is rooted in these irreducible transcendent realities, we must constantly seek rituals, language, and a spirituality that strive to symbolize them adequately. The language of Christ as priest, prophet, and king points us awkwardly but instinctively toward the awesome holy God, and it also evokes the transcendent dimension of the human person. These awesome and essential dimensions may not be adequately captured by categories of priest, prophet, and king, nor are they at first blush the most attractive choice for a twenty-first century Catholic Christian. They do, however, point us in the right direction in signaling the transcendent aspects of the human person in a postmodern world that wants to flatten our universe, dilute our religious claims, and empty our language of all weight-bearing, symbol-laden words. Our world does not want anything to point to the presence of the transcendent within, beneath, and beyond the here and now. To speak about the human person as priest, prophet, and king is, it seems to me, an example of language that is sturdy enough in its traditional biblical and liturgical heritage, contemporary enough through its revival in the Vatican II documents, and just jarring enough to our ears to serve us well in our postmodern context. In this chapter, I try to make the case that the trilogy can form the basis of a solid spirituality for today and can also be a theological underpinning for the three goals of *Go and Make Disciples*.

Relevance of the Trilogy Today[2]

As already indicated, these categories—priest, prophet, and king—may seem quite alien to most people today. We hear the words, and think, "What has this got to do with me and my spiritual journey?" We may be aware that they have something to do with the person of Jesus, but we don't see them as relevant to us. We know what they mean; we have a mental image of each one. We are certainly familiar with priests; they are part of our faith tradition, an important part. Prophets are people like Isaiah and Jeremiah, extraordinary people who did extraordinary things. We read about them, but that's the extent of it. And we know what kings do; they rule—as figureheads, at least.

We accept that these words describe Jesus and what he does. Yet it is another thing entirely to comprehend that they describe us as well, those of us who are trying to follow Jesus. The fact is that these are almost the first significant words that are spoken to us and about us as Christians. They derive from our baptism. After the water ritual, we were anointed with the oil of chrism and these words were spoken to us: "The God of power and Father of our Lord Jesus Christ has freed you from sin and brought you to new life through water and the Holy Spirit. He now anoints you with the chrism of salvation, so that, united with his people, you may remain forever a member of Christ who is Priest, Prophet, and King. Amen"[3] (these words are part of the baptismal rite in its post–Vatican II form).[4]

Because of our baptism, then, we share in Christ's identity as priest, prophet, and king. The word *Christian* actually means the anointed one. When one is anointed, it is always *for* something, for some particular task. We Christians are anointed to act as priest, prophet, and king; this is what defines baptism, which brings us into a community whose head is anointed as priest, prophet, and king. We then share that anointing. Baptism and anointing are inseparable, which is a far cry from the previous notion that baptism served only to save us from original sin. Baptism does indeed do this, but it is much more than that, much richer.

What does it mean to see ourselves this way, especially in our world today? After all, these categories seem rather removed from our everyday lives. Yet they are not. Each one speaks to some major aspect, some problem, of contemporary life, and gives us a way of responding to that problem. Following Gerhard Lohfink, I will invoke the language of the church as a "contrast society" in order to capture the countercultural dimensions of the trilogy. In a thoroughgoing, secular environment, a priestly self-designation reminds me that in my deepest being, I have a religious identity. I belong to God. I share in God's holiness. As a prophet, I have a calling to proclaim God's truth wherever I go, in a world where truth has been declared relative. Furthermore, the image of a prophet invokes truth's uncompromising quality when—in the power of the Holy Spirit—we speak **knowingly** about how things are in God's world. What I have in mind here is Jesus' authority (*exousia* in the Greek), which accompanied his prophetic speech and action and aroused awe in the crowds. In a world where individuals feel helpless and powerless to bring about the kingdom, thinking of oneself in royal terms reminds us of our power in Christ to change that world. Jesus' finest and most powerful moment was his death on the cross (which, of course, by God's hand, led to the resurrection). All four gospels note that he was crucified as one who claimed to be king. He himself said that he came to bring about a kingdom. Awesome claims! It is strange language to be sure, yet well worth grappling with.

This trilogy is also—and this is where the connection with evangelization can be seen—highly missionary. Being a priestly people means living out our holiness in the world, and it is a holiness that is not monastic, not just for a few, but for everyone. Being a prophetic people means taking God's word of truth to the world. Being a royal people means reordering society according to the values of the gospel.

Viewing the goals of *Go and Make Disciples* through the priestly, prophetic, and royal lens has the added benefit of reinforcing the notion that the three goals are interactive, dynamic, and comprehensive. They must be implemented together in order to capture authentically the full vision of Catholic evangelization. Their meaning and transforming power are enhanced in their mutual interaction. The trilogy simply reinforces and gives added meaning to this mutual and interdependent perspective.

Furthermore, I believe that in addition to its theological power, the trilogy reinforces an increasingly promising strategy that is taking root in today's pastoral practice. That strategy has two dimensions: unifying and holistic. First, pastoral practice is slowly turning away from turfism to a unifying vision of the church's mission under evangelization. I have already pointed out the breakthrough that took place when the *General Directory for Catechesis* placed the catechetical ministry under the overall umbrella of evangelization, thus paving the way for uniting *all* ministries under evangelization's unifying mission.

Second, we are becoming more holistic in our approach to pastoral ministry. For example, look at the persistent, increasingly widespread conviction that catechetical ministry cannot succeed unless it is integrated into all aspects of church life. The recent movement for Whole Community Catechesis,[5] although not new, represents the persistence of a nagging ecclesial insight that all ministry must somehow be integral: catechetics, liturgy, social justice, and family life must be undertaken jointly, in an interdependent and mutual way, or they will not be done at all. Seeing the goals of *Go and Make Disciples* through the priestly-prophetic-royal lens reinforces the notion that the goals are interdependent and interactive, that the unifying ministry of evangelization must be undertaken integrally, and holistically: what is needed is whole community evangelization.

I will explore each category of the trilogy in turn. Following the example of Donald Goergen, I will speak of Jesus not only as priest but priest-healer, not only as prophet but prophet-liberator, and not only as king but servant-king. Then I will examine what these interpretations of the trilogy say about our identity as Christians in the world today. Because it is directly related, I will also outline how the trilogy gives us a new lens through which to view the three goals of *Go and Make Disciples*.

Jesus: Priest-Healer[6]

Jesus was not a priest; he was a layman. Yet he defines what it means to be a priest, the core of which is sacrifice. Unlike in the past, however, he sacrificed not animals, but himself: he gave his life for the many. Ephesians 5:2 reflects this understanding, where the author says: "Christ loved us and gave himself up for us, a fragrant offering and sacrifice to God."

In the Letter to the Hebrews, Jesus is described as the great high priest who, once and for all, entered into the heavenly sanctuary, bringing not the blood of animals but his own blood, thus achieving forgiveness and sanctification for all.[7] This framework provides an ingenious way of presenting Jesus' life, death, and resurrection as a fulfillment of the Old Testament. Christ reconciles all humanity through his atoning death on the cross.

In his reinterpretation of the category of priest, Goergen turns to African culture and shows how, in that tradition, the witch doctor or medicine man is a healer. Priest and healer are parallel.[8] Goergen suggests that this fits the picture of Jesus in the New Testament. He was a healer and an exorcist; he is a mediator of divine healing power to the world through his self-giving death on the cross. He comes to bring reconciliation and wholeness to the people. And, as Goergen emphasizes, the need for healing is immediate and universal, because we live in a broken world. It is also important to note that, in the New Testament, Jesus' healing powers are connected to his self-giving way of life. Jesus is the priest who brings healing by his wounds.[9]

Viewing Goal I through the Priestly Lens

We tend to think of sacrifice as strictly liturgical and something that only priests do. But even in the early New Testament community, there was a willingness to see the suffering of the faithful from a priestly perspective. The Christian community saw its own life of suffering as a sacrificial offering that God finds acceptable (Rom 12:1), and the first letter of Peter describes all believers as a "royal priesthood, a holy nation" (2:4–10). It was an early recognition of a fundamental reality: the life of the laity in the world is marked by sacrifice. All Christians are called to a life of sacrifice. Therefore, they share in the paschal mystery; therefore, all Christians are priestly. The documents of Vatican II emphasize the importance of sharing in the priestly dimension of Christ by the way we engage in the sacrificial activities of our day-to-day lives.

How is all this connected to Goal I of *Go and Make Disciples*? The goal says: "To bring about in all Catholics such an enthusiasm for their faith that, in living their faith in Jesus, they freely share it with others." The connection is holiness. When we follow Jesus and fully live our faith in him, offering our lives in the world as a sacrificial gift, we become holy. This is priestly work, holy work.

It can be jarring for laypeople to be told that they are a priestly people. Yet this claim leads us to realize that, in the deepest part of our being, there is a quality of holiness. Though laity live in the world, in a profound sense their lives are deeply rooted in God. (We have in recent years moved away from the idea that one needs to retreat from the world in order to be holy.) Paul called the baptized members of his congregations *saints*. Karl Rahner states that the moment of our entry into this world is the beginning of a graced existence. God is present to us and loves us with an infinite love.

This is a very different view of human beings than the one current in the world today. It has been said that we live in a therapeutic age, with psychiatrists and therapists as our secular high priests. In this secular humanist perspective, people are rooted in the world. They are important because they are at the highest level of development on the planet, the top of the evolutionary chain. In this point of view, the search for love and wholeness in relationship is a strictly human endeavor. But when we speak of ourselves as a priestly people, we proclaim that at our core we are rooted in God and experience God's grace from the moment of our birth. This is an astonishingly different perspective from the secular humanist one. It tells us that our search for human fulfillment can take place only within a religious context, because we are created in the image of God. We belong to God; we have our destiny in God.

An experience from my Paulist novitiate in 1975 to 1976 is worth recounting here. I lived a hyphenated existence as a priest-novice, because I had already been ordained for six years when I entered. We were preparing a liturgy for the feast of Christ the King, and I was in charge of the planning as well as the appointed presider. It was a time of liturgical experimentation. We decided to focus on Jesus as the Lord of the Chaos. We began the Liturgy of the Word in the lower level common room with an array of experiences of chaos. From a liturgical point of view, the entire celebration would probably be dismissed as bizarre at best. But I remember having quite a profound spiritual awakening during the liturgy. After we had gone through the Liturgy of the Word, I broke down crying. People were concerned about what was wrong with me. I tried to reassure them that I was all right. And I was. What happened to me was that I was given a glimpse of the darkness that might have existed at the center of our universe and at the center of the human person if it were not for Christ. The Lord of the Chaos, Christ, brought light into my darkness, order into a possibly infinitely chaotic world. It was at once horrifying and consoling to glimpse, in a very realistic way, what our world might be like without God. "But there is a God," as my friend Maureen would always say, and it makes all the difference in the world.

Without God, we are broken people in a broken world. Healing comes from God—and, as I noted earlier, healing is a priestly function. To say that healing is part of the priestly character of Christ and of Christian ministry is to state unequivocally that what lies radically at the core of the human person is an openness to God and an experience of grace. The human person, created in God's image, has a sacred dignity. Thus, the effort to integrate ourselves, individually and as a community, is a priestly task. It is important to note that the word *holy* is related, linguistically, to the words *hale, whole,* and *health.* To heal, to make whole, is a holy work.

This contrasts sharply with the secular humanist, therapeutic viewpoint. For one thing, the attitude toward suffering is different; it is seen as totally negative. People want to love without giving of themselves. They want to experience the good life without embracing the necessary pain that comes with growth. The secular adage "no pain, no gain" is not widely shared in our death-denying, suffering-averse society. We are addicted to feeling good and want to escape suffering at all costs.

Yet the New Testament emphasizes the sacrificial character of life. Paul speaks of his experience of preaching the gospel as a priestly task (Rom 15:16) and Christian living as a holy sacrifice. The Book of Revelation, another book that speaks of the people of God as priests, presents us with a picture of suffering Christian martyrs who are clothed in white robes for the heavenly liturgy. Thus, according to the New Testament, to be a priestly people involves suffering and sacrifice, and thus has a strong paschal character.

To summarize: we want to bring about in all Catholics an enthusiasm for their faith so that they live it and share it with others, because this is how we are healed—and healing is a priestly task. But that healing comes precisely through the wounds of the crucified one whose sacrificial life we share. It is, to be sure, a paradoxical hope: life through death, joy through suffering. The notion of ourselves as a priestly people points to these transcendent realities that underlie our faith. When we carry out the mandate of Goal I, this is what we are calling people to, a life of holiness that comes from sharing in the life-giving sacrifice of Christ the priest.

Jesus: Prophet-Liberator

Among the three titles ascribed to Jesus, *prophet* seemed to fit best Jesus' identity in the minds of the people who met him (e.g., Mark 8:27–28). Along with *Son of Man* and *Son, prophet* also could well be closest to the way he saw himself (Mark 6:4).

Jesus' role as prophet was to speak for God, to be a messenger of God's truth, not unlike the great prophets who had gone before him. It was as a prophet that Jesus denounced the things that had no future and pointed to other avenues that were filled with hope.[10]

Jesus called people to conversion in the light of the coming kingdom, but he did not do so abstractly. He condemned ways of thinking and acting that were opposed to God's plan. Thus, for example, Jesus criticized human traditions that went against God's intentions for his people.

Goergen sees Jesus' prophetic role as one of liberation. Building on liberation theology, Goergen sees Jesus' prophetic ministry as one that proclaimed right relationship of humans with God and each other. Jesus focused in particular on people at the margins of society. As Luke puts it, Jesus came to proclaim good news to the poor, liberty to captives, recovery of sight to the blind, freedom to the oppressed, and a year of favor from the Lord (4:18–19). The concern of the prophet is both with the vertical and the horizontal, with this world and beyond.

The prophet speaks with a level of certainty that arises out of being conscious of God. Because prophetic speech is grounded in God's spirit, it has an absolute quality. In this respect, it is a dangerous form of speech because it is radical, uncompromising, and sometimes alienating. This was true of Jesus the prophet. He does not mince words. He speaks of God and the things of God knowingly and sometimes harshly as well as tenderly. He sees what needs to be changed and calls people to repentance, absolutely convinced that those who are open to the truth will hear his voice (John 18:37). He knows that only the truth will set people free from enslavement. Inevitably, prophets suffer. Jesus was rejected for telling the truth, as were the authentic prophets who went before him. The prophet comes to bring true liberation from all forms of enslavement.

Viewing Goal II through the Prophetic Lens

Goal II states: "To invite all people in the United States, whatever their social or cultural background, to hear the message of salvation in Jesus Christ so they may come to join us in the fullness of the Catholic faith." We speak of this goal as the missionary goal, because it challenges Catholics in a very explicit way to become active disciple-makers, both as individuals and as a community. Viewing this goal through the prophetic lens enriches this evangelizing activity enormously by bringing to bear on it the wealth of biblical and theological reflection around the term *prophecy*.

I had a first-hand challenge in viewing Goal II through the prophetic lens several years ago. I was giving an evangelizing mission at St. Rose of Lima parish, where I frequently do weekend work when I am at home. Our evangelizing missions are based on the goals of *Go and Make Disciples*. The first three evenings focus, in turn, on the three goals, followed by a reconciliation service on Wednesday and a Eucharist on Thursday, in which we celebrate the evangelizing dimension of the parish. My partner, Sister Dominga Zapata, SH, and I had done a Hispanic mission before, but never one in English. I had known the pastor since I was in the seminary and had worked at the parish for several years, but I was nervous about doing a parish mission among my own people.

The mission got off to a good start at the weekend masses and at the first evening. But the second evening we got stuck. After having done these missions for several years with a number of different partners, I was struggling to find my voice. It seemed that recently my preaching had taken the form of a clipping essay—a story from here, a story from there; a section from that preaching experience, another from this one. But there was no coherence, no intelligibility. It turned out that our preaching that evening was flat. We found ourselves repeating over and over again the call to reach out, invite, and share the good news. My partner felt terrible. I felt worse. The pastor agreed that it was less than a successful evening.

I just couldn't get over the sense of failure, and I spent much of the night berating myself. Finally, I was able to accept what happened and surrender it. When I did, I had a real insight about how we could preach this goal, one that I will share with you now. The insight is that we can get beyond a simple repetitive injunction to share our faith by helping people come to understand why they should share their faith: **They need to share their** faith **because they have a truth to tell.** They have spiritual knowledge…about God and the way things are in God's world. We are called to invite others to embrace the faith because we have come to a deep knowledge of truth in our lives, a truth that cannot be suppressed or withheld.

Thus, I was able to understand better the prophetic character of this goal. When Jeremiah decided to stop working for the Lord, he said to himself: "If I say, 'I will not mention him, or speak any more in his name,' then within me there is something like a burning fire shut up in my bones; I am weary with holding it in, and I cannot" (20:9). Jesus, as he was entering Jerusalem, was told to rebuke his disciples, who were acclaiming him as the Messiah, the "king who comes." His response was, "I tell you, if these were silent, the stones would shout out" (Luke 19:40). God's truth is compelling. The prophet cannot keep it to himself. Those who have been anointed with the Spirit, like Jesus, are compelled to speak out and give witness to the truth.

We live in a society that is strongly relativistic—there is no absolute truth—and pluralistic—there are many roads; no one can claim to know the one true road. Anyone who claims to know something about truth is viewed with suspicion, because we don't like the idea that there are, indeed, some truths that are real and absolute. It requires too great a commitment. We human beings have a profound hunger for love but a strong resistance to truth, which is essential to love. So we keep searching for love, taking many different paths, trying out different truths. But not every path leads to love; there are many dead ends. The New Testament tells us that Jesus is the way, the truth, and the life. We must be prepared to accept the truth value of Jesus' claims and follow his path if we are going to find the answer to what we are truly seeking: love.

To say that prophetic speech speaks the truth does not for a moment exclude dialogue or suggest an arrogant presumption that one is in possession of all truth. Prophetic does not mean triumphalistic. We speak what we know, yet at the same time we open ourselves to the very real fact that we don't have a corner on all truth. So, inevitably, prophetic speech is humble speech, recognizing the limits of knowledge and open to dialogue. But we must not be afraid to make bold claims about Christianity and Catholicism.

Prophetic speech is not limited to an elite group of individuals or to those in positions of authority. In fact, from biblical times there has been an inherent tension between prophecy and institution. Prophets were often at odds with official authority. In the New Testament, prophecy is a highly regarded charism that enabled individuals to speak God's truth to the assembly. There is a great need for this charism today and it takes many forms.

For example, there is a rich tradition in the Catholic Church of recognizing the importance and centrality of the faith of the people in formulating church doctrine. The notion of universal consensus as formulated by Vincent of Lerins says that the church teaching was based on what was held "universally, always and by all."[11] We have the formulation *lex orandi, lex credendi (the law of praying is the law of believing)*. This reminds us that faith life is rooted in the prayer life of the entire faithful and that Christian worship is a norm of faith. Probably the most significant teaching on the point is the *sensus fidelium,* the sense of the faithful, the idea that the sense or opinion of the faithful, both clergy and laity, concerning church teaching and practice is important in providing insights that lead to new doctrinal formulations and in receiving doctrines promulgated by the magisterium. We have an example of the former in the way that many of the Marian teachings were formulated based on the faith of the people.

Vatican II gave renewed importance to this teaching. The documents speak about the prophetic quality of the laity in terms of this *sensus fidelium.* In the *Dogmatic Constitution on the Church,* the bishops state: "The whole body of the faithful who have received an anointing which comes from the holy one (see 1 John 2:20 and 27) cannot be mistaken in belief" (*LG* 12). In speaking of the laity, *Lumen Gentium* explicitly states that the laity are established as witnesses and have been gifted with an appreciation of the faith *(sensus fidei)* and the grace of the word. The faithful at every level have something to contribute to formulating the church's position on faith and morals.

The experience of the laity and their fidelity to the truth in their faith life enrich the entire church, but sadly have too often been ignored by the institutional church. The clericalization of the church and the excessive focus on hierarchy have often resulted in a widespread devaluation of the laity's experience of faith. By and large throughout the Catholic Church's history, the magisterium has been strong on emphasizing the teaching voice and short on listening.[12] One could make a good case that until the church begins to take seriously the experience of the laity in its teachings on sexuality and marriage, those teachings will continue to be disregarded and eventually found to be irrelevant. During the recent sexual abuse crisis, it often seemed that the laity were more astute in their understanding of what was needed than the hierarchy.

Now, let's summarize and relate all this to Goal II, which challenges Catholics to invite everyone to hear our message of salvation and join us in the fullness of the Catholic faith. We believe that God's truth abides in the church, and we feel compelled to give witness to this truth, a truth that brings freedom. Goal II embodies the newfound conviction of the post–Vatican II church that there is an ongoing experience of revelation that is rooted in the human experience of the faithful. The truth of revelation is not limited to revealed doctrine. The faith story of the ordinary Catholic is a powerful witness to the truth of the faith. In sharing that story of how God has touched them with grace and love, the laity are giving witness to the truth of what they know, a truth that desperately needs to be told today.

Furthermore, we need to find compelling and relevant language for those revealed truths that touch people's lives and move them to conversion. It is an important part of the challenge to inculturate the faith in our contemporary American experience. How do we plant the seed that is the word in a media-saturated culture? How do we till the ground to make it receptive to the truths of the faith? How do we preach in ways that again bring out the hidden energy of the good news in its transforming power? Our efforts at implementing Goal II of *Go and Make Disciples* can only be strengthened and enhanced by viewing the tasks of this goal through the prophetic lens.

Jesus: Servant-King

In the Old Testament, the function of the king was to be God's viceroy in ordering society so that those without recourse—the poor, the widows, the powerless—could be protected. All four gospels show Pilate asking Jesus: "Are you the King of the Jews?"(Matt 27:11; Mark 15:2; Luke 23:3; John 18:33). He did not deny it, and he died with a placard over his head identifying him as this king. Yet, during his lifetime, while Jesus spoke about the reign of God, at no time did he designate himself a king. The question of whether Jesus thought of himself as the Messiah, rather than king, is another, more complicated, matter. He certainly did not see himself as a political messiah.

Any attempt to understand the notion of Christ as king must reckon with Jesus' refusal to embrace political or military power. Jesus made it very clear that the power of the kingdom was not domination but service. He tells his disciples that the last will be first and the first will be last. He has come not to be served but to serve. It is a radically different kind of power and kingship. This contrast is highlighted by irony, in the fact that the only time Jesus appears with royal trappings (a crown of thorns, a royal purple robe, and a placard overhead saying "The King of the Jews") is during his suffering and death.

Priest-prophet-king must be understood dynamically and in relation to each other. Georgen's comments about Jesus as priest-healer can also be applied to Jesus as servant-king. He speaks of the African notion of kingship, which, like the European concept, is seen as a divine mandate. But in the African culture, "incumbents fulfill their sacral duties as divine agents *for the good of their subjects*"[13] (emphasis added). The servant-king, then, is one who brings justice and freedom. African nations have been "wounded by the slave trade, colonization, the postcolonial formation of the nation-states, neo-colonialism's economic dependency, intertribal violence and war, the corruption of many post-independence national leaders and so on."[14] A servant-king can speak powerfully to a tribal society that is struggling to find its way into the modern world and keep just governance structures. The healing that Jesus can bring to these nations has broad appeal to them and to the entire global community. The issue here is primarily one of leadership and the use of power to stand in solidarity with the people in order to liberate them from past slaveries and form a civilization of love based on justice. The greatest challenge that faces all leadership is the commitment to use power for the well-being of the people. Oppression can have no place in the ways of the servant-king.[15]

Viewing Goal III through the Royal Lens

Goal III reads: "To foster gospel values in our society, promoting the dignity of the human person, the importance of the family, and the common good of our society, so that our nation may continue to be transformed by the saving power of Jesus Christ." *Go and Make Disciples* states that the fruits of evangelization are changed lives and a changed world. Goal III challenges us to change the world or, to put it another way, to evangelize the culture by bringing those gospel values into every aspect of our lives. Goal III presumes that we have the power to do this. But how? Where do we get the power to change the world?

We, as Christians, receive this power from God—and we not only have it, we are meant to use it. Jesus is king, and because we share in his identity through our baptism, we share his power. As king, Jesus has the power to reorder the world according to the values of the kingdom. As a royal people, we too are given that power—the power of truth and love. By living our life in truth and love, we give witness to the reality of God's kingdom that, like a seed planted, is quietly and steadily transforming the world.

In *On Evangelization in the Modern World,* Paul VI makes the point that gospel values have to bring about change dynamically, from within. They do this by "affecting and as it were upsetting through the power of the Gospel, mankind's criteria of judgment, determining values, points of interest, lines of thought, sources of inspiration and models of life, which are in contrast with the Word of God and the plan of salvation" (no. 19). Goal III hints at the vast and complex enterprise called inculturation that takes place when the gospel dynamically roots itself in a culture. Each Christian has a role in that by the way he or she brings gospel values to the world.

Viewing this goal through the royal lens helps us remember that there is a power that is beyond us, yet works through us—the power of Christ the risen Lord, who has already come into his glory. We pray and work for Christ's kingdom to come by the way we seek to live out the gospel in our own lives and transform our world by its values. In doing this, we emulate the king in Israelite society, who was responsible for ordering society to protect the poor, the widow, and the stranger. This goal is about ordering society according to values like the worth and dignity of the individual, the common good (solidarity), and the importance of family.

The power to change the world is the servant power of love. Power corrupts when it is not imbued with a servant mindset. With his death and resurrection, Jesus unleashed into the world the transforming power of love that is the Holy Spirit. Perhaps the most powerful scene in the gospels, outside of Jesus' death, is the footwashing scene, where Jesus makes clear in deed what he spoke so clearly in word: "The Son of Man came not to be served but to serve" (Matt 20:28). The world-changing power of the gospel is the power of the servant-king who gave himself in love. As Dante put it so well, love moves the sun and other stars. When we speak about changing the world by bringing our gospel values to it, we are speaking about the power of love to change the way the world does things.

We have already discussed the importance of individuals believing that they are not helpless to change society. They can make a difference. Communities can make a difference as well. I would like to focus on the royal power of the community to impact society for good. How can the church exercise its royal power in the world for the sake of the kingdom? Let us not underestimate the importance of the church's social justice teaching. Whatever one may think of the just war theory, its place in the dialogue about modern warfare (including the most recent invasion of Iraq) is indisputable. John Paul II, insofar as he represents the universal church in his office as shepherd of the flock, has enormous power to effect change. Witness not only the important role of the Vatican in world affairs, but also his own personal role in the collapse of the Berlin wall. One of the saddest aspects of the church's sexual abuse crisis has been the weakening of the role of the bishops in national affairs. In speaking as a body for the Catholic Church on issues of pro-life (the seamless garment), war and peace, and social justice, the voice of the U.S. Conference of Catholic Bishops has been important and should continue. Catholics represent nearly 25 percent of the population of this country. We could do a lot more to effect change if all baptized Catholics, in their living of the gospel, experienced a greater conversion to justice. Our impact could be enormous, even if it were only through individuals exercising their royal character at the workplace or in society (e.g., voting). All of these are examples of using power in the service of love and justice, and thus they are examples of the royal dimensions of our baptismal anointing.

While the above examples are important, we need to emphasize another, largely untapped, aspect of the royal dimension: our community life at the local level. How can congregations exercise their royal ministry in the local community? How shall we evaluate parish efforts to bring about change in their neighborhoods and towns by influencing local power structures? Can we increase our interreligious and ecumenical collaboration on social justice issues in order to broaden our power base for good? Probably the most impressive example of a local community exercising its royal character in this country is the Church of the Savior in Washington, D.C. Our Paulist seminarians have done their pastoral work in the church's social justice ministries for many years. In Rome, we have St. Egidio, an unusual parish community whose prayer and peacemaking impact is felt worldwide. There are no limits to the possibilities if we are willing to harness the royal power of Christ at work in and through us.

To summarize: we foster gospel values in society because we want to transform the world through servant love. This reordering of society is a royal task. When we carry out the mandate of Goal III, we are living out our call as a royal people.

Conclusion

It is helpful to view the church as a contrast society, because many times what the church offers people is at least an alternative to, if not in opposition to, what society offers. I believe that by employing the trilogy as a lens through which we view the goals of *Go and Make Disciples,* we heighten the perspective of the church as a contrast society. Priest, prophet, and king are unabashedly religious categories, and, as I have pointed out, they enable us to sharpen the contrast with certain secular ways of looking at things.

By seeing Goal I through the lens of Jesus the priest-healer, we offer a contrast to society's secular, therapeutic way of looking at human beings; we restore a religious perspective by seeing every human person as a priestly person. Viewing Goal II through the prophet-liberator lens restates our claim that in a relativistic and pluralistic society, there are truth claims to be made. It is because we believe in the truth of the good news that we are compelled to share it. Finally, we look at Goal III through the servant-king lens and, in a world that often recognizes only the power of money and arms, we assert the existence of another kingdom of love, justice, and peace, to which we witness as royal servants.

By invoking the priestly-prophetic-royal lens as a theological perspective through which to view the goals of *Go and Make Disciples,* I conclude this book on both a theoretical and practical note. The theoretical note tells us that, in this interactive trilogy that plays a fairly large role in the Vatican II documents, we have a broad, comprehensive, and integral vision of Catholic evangelization that is not a program, but a way of being church. On the practical level, it suggests that the only way that evangelization will be effectively implemented is through a whole community undertaking, in which evangelization is seen as the essential unifying mission of the church and is implemented broadly by all the parts of the community working together.

NOTES

Introduction

1. Additional information on these evangelization programs developed by the PNCEA can be found in the Appendix.

Chapter One: Beyond Vatican II

1. Charles Morris, *American Catholic: The Saints and Sinners Who Built America's Most Powerful Church* (New York: Random House, 1997), 290.

2. Walter Brueggemann, *The Psalms and the Life of Faith*, ed. Patrick Miller (Minneapolis: Fortress Press, 1995), 8–32. Brueggemann bases his theory on the work of Paul Ricoeur.

3. The title of Part II of Morris's book, which tells this part of the story, is "Triumph."

4. Restorationism seeks to roll back certain aspects of the Vatican renewal and return to the pre–Vatican II paradigm as a way into future reorientation. In many ways, restorationism can be likened to the frightened response of the twelve Israelite scouts who, returning from Canaan after seeing the land of the giants, spread discouragement among the people. The people then complained to Moses and Aaron that it would be better to return to Egypt (Num 13—14). In my view, moving in faith into the future requires us to implement thoroughly the renewal agenda of the council. For similar views, see the recent article by Rembert Weakland, "The Liturgy as Battlefield," *Commonweal* 129/1 (January 11, 2002): 10–15.

5. *Integralism* is a tendency in the church that arose in the early twentieth century in response to a tendency called *Modernism*, which was an effort to reconcile Catholic faith and modern culture. It was not well received by church authorities, partly because of the uncritical embrace of modern culture and partly because of the ecclesiastical climate of the time, and the heresy was condemned by the papal encyclical *Pascendi dominici gregis* in 1907. The official response represents something of an overreaction, but it had an enduring effect until Vatican II, when the efforts of the Modernists were in some respects

vindicated. See *The HarperCollins Encyclopedia of Catholicism,* Richard P. McBrien, gen. ed. (San Francisco: HarperCollins, 1995), 887, and *The New Dictionary of Theology,* 3rd ed., ed. Joseph A. Komonchak, Mary Collins, and Dermot A. Lane (Wilmington, DE: Glazier, 1989), 668–70. Integralism insisted that nothing is "whole" unless it is brought into the orbit of the church. Everything in the world is regarded with suspicion as evil or worthless unless and until it is somehow integrated into Christianity. Integralism is the effort to "explain or master reality exclusively in the light of faith, instead of regarding faith as the key which makes the understanding or mastery of the world possible, but does not itself try to achieve it" (McBrien, 151).

6. William V. D'Antonio et al., *American Catholics* (New York: AltaMira Press, 2001), 8–16.

7. See, for example, Thomas P. Rausch, SJ, *Reconciling Faith and Reason: Apologists, Evangelists, and Theologians in a Divided Church* (Collegeville, MN: The Liturgical Press, 2000), 1–9.

8. Morris, *American Catholic,* 323.

9. Archbishop Marcel Lefebvre, a French prelate, led the only schismatic departure in the post–Vatican II period. Although he attended the council, Lefebvre refused to sign some of the conciliar documents. Disenchanted with postconciliar developments, he opened a traditionalist seminary in Switzerland in 1970. His resolute rejection of the council led to his suspension in 1976 and, after a brief period of reconciliation, a final split, which led to his excommunication in 1988 for ordaining bishops without papal authority. Lefebvre died in 1991. His movement, the Society of St. Pius X, survives as a traditionalist movement that celebrates the Latin Tridentine mass. See McBrien, *The HarperCollins Encyclopedia of Catholicism,* 762.

10. Peter Steinfels, in *A People Adrift: The Crisis of the Roman Catholic Church in America* (New York: Simon & Schuster, 2003), 10, challenges the church to move beyond this liberal-conservative paradigm in order to move into a new period of reorientation.

11. See *Gaudium et Spes (Pastoral Constitution on the Church in the Modern World),* nos. 16–17 and *Dignitatis Humanae (Declaration on Religious Liberty)* in *Vatican Council II: Constitutions, Decrees, Declarations,* gen. ed. Austin Flannery, OP (Northport, NY: Costello Publishing Co, 1996) and *Catechism of the Catholic Church* (Mahwah, NJ: Paulist Press, 1994), nos. 1776–94.

12. D'Antonio et al., *American Catholics,* 9–10.

13. Father Charles Curran, a priest of the diocese of Rochester, was a professor of moral theology at the Catholic University of America. He led the public dissent against the birth control encyclical, *Humanae Vitae,* in the late 1960s. In 1986, the Congregation for the Doctrine of the Faith determined that he could "no longer be considered suitable or eligible to exercise the function of a professor of Catholic theology." In addition to his dissent on *Humanae Vitae,* Father Curran's challenge of the Catholic Church's objective teachings on sexual morality resulted in his removal. He is a Catholic priest in good standing and currently teaches at Southern Methodist University (McBrien, *The HarperCollins Encyclopedia of Catholicism,* 386–87).

14. Proportionalist ethics is a type of analysis for determining objective moral right and wrong in conflict situations. It began in the mid-1960s as a revision of the principle of double effect, in which a good action, directly intended, has evil effects. Proportionate reason is the moral principle used to determine whether an act is right or wrong. Proportionalists argue that no judgment of moral right or wrong can be made without considering all the circumstances of the action. There continues to be a great deal of controversy about this approach. John Paul II offered some criticism of proportionalist ethics in *Veritatis Splendor (The Splendor of Truth)* (Boston: St. Paul Books & Media, 1993), nos. 74–83. See also McBrien, *The HarperCollins Encyclopedia of Catholicism,* 1058.

15. D'Antonio et al., *American Catholics,* 85–86.

16. See Chapter 2, "The Model," in Rosemary Haughton, *The Catholic Thing* (Springfield, IL: Templegate Publishers, 1979), 60–91.

17. "Attitudes Toward Vocations of Parish Involved Youth and their Parents," *CARA Compendium* (Washington, DC: CARA, 1997), 35–101.

18. Donald Cozzens, *The Changing Face of the Priesthood: A Reflection on the Priest's Crisis of Soul* (Collegeville, MN: The Liturgical Press, 2000), 19.

19. D'Antonio et al., *American Catholics,* 28.

20. This list is published as part of *Another Look,* a PNCEA outreach program, and was compiled from Gallup research and other sources in the late 1980s. See also Bishop Michael Saltarelli's summary of nine reasons why Catholics become inactive, which are based on research conducted by the U.S. Bishops' Committee on Evangelization

(Michael Saltarelli, "How to Reach Inactive Catholics," *Origins* 29/32 [January 27, 2000]: 513–18).

21. For further background on generational studies, see William Strauss and Neil Howe, *Generations: The History of America's Future, 1584–2069* (New York: Quill-William Morrow, 1991) and *Millennials Rising: The Next Great Generation* (New York: Vintage Books, 2000).

22. Data reported in D'Antonio et al., *American Catholics* and in *The Search for Common Ground: What Unites and Divides Catholic Americans,* by James D. Davidson et al. (Huntington, IN: Our Sunday Visitor, Inc., 1997), 111–39.

23. Davidson et al., *The Search for Common Ground,* 118–27.

24. D'Antonio et al., *American Catholics,* 46.

25. Dean R. Hoge et al., *Young Adult Catholics: Religion in the Culture of Choice* (Notre Dame, IN: University of Notre Dame Press, 2001), 222.

26. The three essential characteristics of evangelization correspond to the three goals of *Go and Make Disciples: A National Plan and Strategy for Catholic Evangelization in the United States* (Washington, DC: USCCB, 2002).

27. *Ad Gentes (Decree on the Church's Missionary Activity),* no. 2; *Redemptoris Missio (Mission of the Redeemer),* no. 27.

28. *Justice in the World,* no. 6. In *Proclaiming Justice & Peace,* ed. Michael Walsh and Brian Davies (Mystic, CT: Twenty-Third Publications, 1991), 268–83.

29. *General Directory for Catechesis* (Washington, DC: USCCB, 1999), no. 59.

30. Ibid.

31. Patrick Brennan, *Re-Imagining the Parish* (New York: Crossroad, 1991), 10.

32. *Code of Canon Law, Latin-English Edition* (Washington, DC: Canon Law Society of America, 1983), 201.

33. David J. Bosch, *Transforming Mission: Paradigm Shifts in the Theology of Mission* (Maryknoll, NY: Orbis Books, 1996), 52–54.

34. Stephen Ambrose, *D-Day, June 6, 1944: The Climactic Battle of WWII* (New York: Touchstone, 1994), points out that after the American soldiers hit Omaha Beach, they experienced confusion and paralysis as they reached the cliffs. It took direct orders from commanding officers to break the paralysis and get them moving. Being given a specific job to do, and taking action, helped them overcome

their fear. Similarly, clarity about the church's evangelizing mission and specific focus on ways to take action in the implementation of that mission could go a long way to address some of the malaise and low morale that prevails in some sectors of the church.

35. Ronald Rolheiser, *The Shattered Lantern: Rediscovering a Felt Presence of God* (New York: Crossroad, 2001), 28–52.

36. *Catechism of the Catholic Church,* no. 1939.

37. In his plan for preparing for the Jubilee Year 2000, John Paul II stated: "The best preparation for the new millennium, therefore, can only be expressed in a renewed commitment to apply, as faithfully as possible, the teachings of Vatican II to the life of every individual and to the whole church" *(Tertio Millennio Adveniente [On Preparation for the Jubilee of the Year 2000],* no. 20). Apparently, the Holy Father still feels this way. In *Novo Millennio Ineunte (The Apostolic Letter to the Lay Faithful at the Close of the Great Jubilee of the Year 2000),* he reminds the whole world again about the need to examine ourselves on the reception given to the council, adding, "with the passing of the years, the Council documents have lost nothing of their value or brilliance" (no. 57).

Chapter Two: Evangelization—
The Church's Essential Mission

1. An Italian word meaning *updating* or r*enewal,* which John XXIII used to indicate the nature or purpose of the council. Alberigo and Komonchak suggest that because the word *reform,* even as late as the 1950s, was suspect in Catholic circles due to its association with the Reformation, John XXIII used a "euphemistic replacement" for the word (Giuseppe Alberigo and Joseph A. Komonchak, *A History of Vatican II,* vol. 1 [Orbis: Maryknoll, NY, and Leuven, Belgium: Peeters, 1995], 72).

2. Ibid., 439.

3. Casiano Floristan, *Para Comprender Evangelización* (Estella, Navarra: Editorial Verbo Divino, 1993), 39.

4. Ibid., 41.

5. *Lumen Gentium (Dogmatic Constitution on the Church),* 1, 48.

6. *Christifideles Laici (The Lay Members of Christ's Faithful People)* (Boston: St. Paul Books and Media, 1988), no. 5.

7. *Our Hearts Were Burning Within Us: A Pastoral Plan for Adult Faith Formation in the United States* (Washington, DC: USCCB,

1999), no. 85; see also *Dialogue and Proclamation: Reflection and Orientations on Interreligious Dialogue and the Proclamation of the Gospel of Jesus Christ* (Vatican Web site, 1991), nos. 45–46.

8. *Ad Gentes,* no. 35.

9. Bosch, *Transforming Mission,* 372.

10. See the remarks on this subject in *Go and Make Disciples,* no. 44. Evangelization and ecumenism are not inherently contradictory, but they are complementary. It is interesting to note that the Missionary Society of St. Paul the Apostle may be the only Catholic religious community that has both evangelization and ecumenism as part of its charism.

11. *Nostra Aetate (Declaration on the Relation of the Church to Non-Christian Religions),* no. 2.

12. Avery Dulles, SJ, "Seven Essentials of Evangelization," *Origins,* vol. 25, no. 23 (November 23, 1995): 397.

13. *Tertio Millennio Adveniente,* nos. 21–23.

14. John Paul clearly uses the phrase "new evangelization" in *Redemptoris Missio* and other writings in the sense of reevangelization or outreach to baptized Catholics who have lost the active practice of their faith. Together with the "mission *ad gentes,*" these two constitute the entire missionary effort of the church, which he sometimes speaks of in terms of mission or evangelization. Note how John Paul explicitly connects his vision of evangelization with the foundations laid down by Paul VI in *Ecclesia in America (The Church in America),* no. 6. See also *Tertio Millennio Adveniente,* no. 21.

15. *Ecclesia in America,* no. 66.

16. Frank DeSiano, CSP, *Sowing New Seed: Directions for Evangelization Today* (Mahwah, NJ: Paulist Press, 1994), 19.

17. Ibid., 23.

18. Brennan, *Re-Imagining the Parish,* 10.

19. Ibid.

20. DeSiano, *Sowing New Seed,* 16.

21. Cardinal Francis George, "Becoming an Evangelizing People" (The First Pastoral Letter of Archbishop Francis E. George, OMI), published in *The New World* (Nov. 21, 1997): 11.

22. Francis Sullivan, SJ, "The Evangelizing Mission of the Church," in *The Gift of the Church: A Textbook on Ecclesiology,* ed. Peter C. Phan (Collegeville, MN: The Liturgical Press, 2000), 247.

Chapter Three: Disciples and Disciple-Makers

1. Excerpted from *Stories and Parables for Preachers and Teachers,* by Paul J. Wharton (Mahwah, NJ: Paulist Press, 1986).

2. *New Dictionary of Catholic Spirituality,* ed. Michael Downey (Collegeville, MN: The Liturgical Press, 1993), 281–84.

3. Avery Dulles, SJ, treated discipleship in depth in his work *Models of the Church,* in which he proposed the Community of Disciples as an ecclesiological model. He acknowledges that the discipleship model "scarcely appears in Catholic theological literature of recent centuries" but is not "alien" to it. *Models of the Church,* expanded edition (New York: Doubleday Image Books, 1987), 207.

4. Fundamentalism is a complex phenomenon that cuts across religious boundaries. For our purposes, fundamentalism, as the name suggests, is the conviction that one can find some island of clear, unshakeable, self-evident truths that one can hold onto without regard for the context and without need of human interpretation. For Protestant fundamentalists, the source of those self-evident truths is the Bible; for Catholics it might be certain dogmas. For a comprehensive study on fundamentalism in all major religions, see *Fundamentalism Observed,* vol. 1 and 2, ed. Martin E. Marty and R. Scott Appleby (Chicago and London: Chicago University Press, 1991, 1994).

5. An example of this very judgmental, fundamentalist reading of the Book of Revelation detailing the story of the earth's last days can be seen in the *Left Behind* series by Tim LaHaye and Jerry B. Jenkins (Wheaton, IL: Tyndale House Publishers, Inc., 1995).

6. Kenneth L. Woodward, "Living in the Holy Spirit," *Newsweek,* vol. 131, n. 15 (April 13, 1998): 57.

7. See, for example, Richard P. McBrien's comments on the spirit of Catholicism in *Catholicism,* New Edition (San Francisco: Harper, 1994), 8–17, 1187–1200.

8. Mary Catherine Hilkert, *Naming Grace: Preaching and the Sacramental Imagination* (New York: Continuum, 1997), 15–16.

9. I am grateful to Dr. Richard Gaillardetz for the exact source and meaning of this important Catholic dictum.

10. See, for example, *Lumen Gentium,* no. 11; *Evangelii Nuntiandi,* no. 71; John Paul II's Apostolic Exhortation *Familiaris Consortio (On the Family); The Catechism of the Catholic Church* (no. 2204); see also Dr. Joseph C. Atkinson, "My Family—A CHURCH?"

in *Share the Word,* September 26–November 27, 1999 (Washington, DC: PNCEA), 23–24.

11. John D. Zizioulas, *Being as Communion* (Crestwood: St. Vladimir's Seminary Press, 1985), 18.

12. McBrien, *Catholicism,* 166.

13. Gerhard Lohfink, *Jesus and Community* (Philadelphia: Fortress Press and Mahwah, NJ: Paulist Press, 1982), 39–50.

14. *Presbyterium Ordinis (Decree on the Ministry and Life of Priests),* no. 9.

15. Terrence L. Donaldson, "Guiding Readers—Making Disciples: Discipleship in Matthew's Strategy," in *Patterns of Discipleship in the New Testament,* ed. Richard N. Longenecker (Grand Rapids, MI: William B. Eerdmans Publishing Co., 1996), 45.

16. Jack D. Kingsbury, *Matthew as Story* (Philadelphia: Fortress Press, 1988), 129.

17. Raymond Brown, *The Gospel of John* (Garden City, NY: Doubleday, 1966), 512.

18. Fernando F. Segovia, *Discipleship in the New Testament* (Philadelphia: Fortress Press, 1985), 92–93.

19. See *Dialogue and Proclamation.*

20. Ibid., no. 68.

21. Quoted in Paul Turks, *Philip Neri: The Fire of Joy* (New York: Alba House, 1995), 109.

22. *Ecclesia in America,* no. 29.

Chapter Four:
Evangelization Is Our Deepest Identity

1. *Ad Gentes,* no. 2.

2. John Paul II has an excellent reflection on the missionary character of John's gospel in *Redemptoris Missio,* no. 23, where he states that the very purpose of mission is to enable people to share in the communion of the Father and the Son.

3. Acts 2:32, 7:55; Rom 1:3f, 5:1–11, 8:1–13, 14–17, 9:1–5; 1 Cor 12:4–6; 2 Cor 13:33; Gal 4:4–6.

4. Eph 1:3–13, 4:4–6; 1 Pet 1:2; Heb 9:14.

5. Theologians use the term *economic trinity* to emphasize the dimension of God that we come to know in salvation history through God's activity in the world, especially through the missions of the Son

and the Spirit. They use the term *immanent trinity* to refer to God's reality within himself—apart from his involvement with us in history. Recently, these same theologians have expressed grave reservations regarding what we can say about the immanent trinity apart from the economic trinity. For a discussion of the matter, see Catherine Mowry LaCugna, *God for Us: The Trinity & Christian Life* (San Francisco: Harper, 1973).

6. *Ad Gentes,* no. 2.

7. Michael Downey speaks of a "grammar" of the Trinity that enables us to speak intelligibly about this relational life of the three persons: *Altogether Gift: A Trinitarian Spirituality* (Maryknoll, NY: Orbis Books, 2000), 45.

8. Source unknown.

9. Walter Kasper, *The God of Jesus Christ* (New York: Crossroad, 1984), 308.

10. Downey, *Altogether Gift,* 38.

11. Donald Senior, gen. ed., *The Catholic Study Bible* (New York: Oxford University Press, 1990), 275.

12. Some New Testament examples are familiar. When Jesus saw the crowds, his heart was moved with pity (*splanchnizestha*—literally he was moved in his innards) because they were sheep without a shepherd (Matt 9:36, 14:14); when he saw two blind men on the roadside, his heart was moved with pity (Matt 20:34). Perhaps the most well-known example is the parable of the father, who goes out to meet his prodigal son and throws his arms around him because his heart was filled with compassion even while the son was a long way off (Luke 15:20).

13. Thomas Merton, *New Seeds of Contemplation* (New York: New Directions Books, 1961), 60.

14. Dermot Lane, *Keeping Hope Alive: Stirrings in Christian Theology* (Mahwah, NJ: Paulist Press, 1996), 137.

15. Downey, *Altogether Gift,* 45; LaCugna, *God for Us,* 332.

16. Downey, *Altogether Gift,* 83.

17. Ibid., 28.

18. Ibid., 29.

19. LaCugna, *God for Us,* 301.

20. Kasper, *The God of Jesus Christ,* 161.

21. Ibid., 190.

22. Ibid., 195.

23. LaCugna, *God for Us,* 301.

24. Ibid., 261.

25. Kasper, *The God of Jesus Christ*, 202.

26. Downey, *Altogether Gift*, 82–83.

27. See the attempt at a more missionary ecclesiology by John Fuellenbach in *Church: Community for the Kingdom* (Maryknoll, NY: Orbis Books, 2002); also appropriate essays in Peter Phan, *A Gift to the Church*.

28. Walter Kasper as quoted by Neil Ormerod, "The Structure of a Systematic Ecclesiology," in *Theological Studies* 63 (2002): 3–30.

29. Ibid. Also see Richard R. Gaillardetz, "The Ecclesiological Foundations of Ministry within an Ordered Communion," in *Ordering the Baptismal Priesthood*, ed. Susan K. Wood (Collegeville, MN: Liturgical Press, 2003), 26–51. In it, he observes that, "in addition to the vertical and horizontal relationships established by baptism, a third dimension must be conjoined, namely, the movement outward toward the world as sent in mission."

30. Dennis M. Doyle, in his book *Communion Ecclesiology* (Maryknoll, NY: Orbis Books, 2000), 16, includes a chart that lists distorted and corrective images of an adequate communion ecclesiology. One might add to his list of distortions an excessive maintenance orientation and to the corrective images an increasing mission orientation.

31. John Paul II has a curious phrase in *Redemptoris Missio* that is unexplained and spoken only in passing, about an "ecclesiology of communion in which the entire church is missionary" (no. 75).

32. John Paul II includes love as an essential part of missionary spirituality. It takes the form of "concern, tenderness, compassion, openness, availability, and interest in people's problems. Jesus' love was very deep: he who 'knew what was in man' (John 2:25) loved everyone by offering them redemption and suffered when it was rejected" (*Redemptoris Missio*, no. 89).

33. *Paradise*, canto xxxiii, trans. John Ciardi (New York: A Mentor Book, 1961).

34. Bosch, *Transforming Mission*, 390.

35. Rosemary Haughton, *The Passionate God* (Mahwah, NJ: Paulist Press, 1981), 17.

36. Edward Schillebeeckx, *Celibacy* (New York: Sheed & Ward, 1968), 21.

37. The New Testament often speaks of the word *boldness (parrhesia)* to describe this depth of freedom to proclaim the gospel. John

Paul II also makes reference to this important scriptural virtue in *Redemptoris Missio,* no. 45.

38. See *Redemptoris Missio,* no. 11.

Chapter Five: A Plan and Strategy for Catholic Evangelization

1. *Communities of Salt and Light* (Washington, DC: USCCB, 1994), 5.

2. See Appendix for a description of this PNCEA program.

3. See Appendix for a description of this PNCEA program.

4. See, for example, Lawrence L. Lippitt's *Preferred Futuring: Envision the Future You Want and Unleash the Energy to Get There* (San Francisco: Berrett-Koehler Publishers, Inc.), 1998.

5. These qualities describe the PNCEA planning process called *ENVISION: Planning Our Parish Future.* See the Appendix for more information about this and other PNCEA programs.

Chapter Six: Goal I

1. See William V. D'Antonio et al., *Laity: American & Catholic* (Kansas City: Sheed and Ward, 1996), 131–33.

2. GMD, no. 15. This is an English translation of the Latin phrase, which is somewhat of a theological slogan for Goal I: *Nemo dat quod non habet.*

3. *Ecclesia in America,* no. 30.

4. Judging from the strategies, "God's Word" in the third and sixth objective is used as a synonym for sacred scripture and is not referencing Jesus Christ as the word of God.

5. See, for example, Lawrence S. Cunningham, "Hospitality: A Theological Reflection," *Church,* vol. 15, no. 4 (Winter 1999): 15–19.

6. See *Gather Faithfully Together: Guide for Sunday Mass* from the Archdiocese of Los Angeles (Chicago: Liturgy Training Publications, 1997).

7. For more on this topic, see "Evangelization and Liturgy" in *Evangelizing America* by Thomas P. Rausch, SJ (Mahwah, NJ: Paulist Press, 2004), as well as Pope John Paul II's *Ecclesia in America,* nos. 12 and 35.

8. *Encuentro* is a Spanish word meaning encounter, meeting, or gathering. The first three *Encuentros* were specifically for U.S.

Hispanic Catholics. For the Great Jubilee 2000, however, the U.S. bishops invited the entire church—members from all cultures—to participate in the experience.

9. *Many Faces in God's House: A Catholic Vision for the Third Millennium* (Washington, D.C.: USCCB Secretariat for Hispanic Affairs, 1999), 1.

10. See "Evangelization as Conceptual Framework for the Church's Mission: The Case of U.S. Hispanics," by Allan Figueroa Deck, SJ, in *Evangelizing America*, 85–110.

Chapter Seven: Goal II

1. *Dialogue and Proclamation*, no. 19.

2. Jacques Dupuis, SJ, *Christianity and the Religions: From Confrontation to Dialogue* (Maryknoll, NY: Orbis, 2002), 99.

3. See John Borelli, "Interreligious Dialogue and Mission: Continuing Questions" in Thomas P. Rausch, SJ, *Evangelizing America*, 172–98.

4. Francis A. Sullivan, SJ, in *Salvation Outside the Church* (Mahwah, NJ: Paulist Press, 1992), narrates the long history of this doctrine and shows that, from the beginning, the church has always held some kind of flexibility in its understanding of this seemingly strict formulation. Since Pius IX, this teaching has not been strictly interpreted in the sense that there is no salvation outside actual visible membership in the Roman Catholic Church. This wider interpretation was made definite in the Vatican's response to Cardinal Cushing against the strict interpretation of Jesuit Leonard Feeney. Sullivan goes on to report on the different ways the teaching was interpreted in order to account for this wider interpretation. These efforts gave rise to unfortunate distinctions, such as belonging to the invisible church or being part of the soul of the church but not the body, or through a membership by desire (see pp. 123 ff). It was not until Vatican II that more adequate foundations for a reconsideration of the doctrine were achieved that no longer make an adequate understanding of this teaching problematic. In its place, the council speaks of a wider understanding that goes beyond the boundaries of the Roman Catholic Church, and of the real incorporation of all the baptized into the body of the church. In summary, the teaching of Vatican II on this subject makes explicit what has been implicit all along, namely, only those

who culpably exclude themselves from the church are those who cannot be saved (145–48; 151).

5. *American Religious Identification Survey*, 2001, Exhibit 1.

6. *General Directory for Catechesis*, no. 59.

7. *American Religious Identification Survey*, 2001, Exhibit 1.

8. John Paul II has moved beyond the teachings of *Evangelii Nuntiandi* in his appreciation of other religions. See Jacques Dupuis, *Toward a Theology of Religious Pluralism* (Maryknoll, NY: Orbis, 2000).

9. Recent debate on the evangelization of the Jews has been sparked by the promulgation of *Reflections on Covenant and Mission* from the Bishops' Committee for Ecumenical and Interreligious Affairs (August 12, 2002). *America* magazine followed it up with an article by Cardinal Avery Dulles and a reply from Mary C. Boys, Philip A. Cunningham, and John T. Pawlikowski (October 21, 2002). Matters are further complicated by the Congregation of the Faith's *Dominus Jesus*, promulgated in August 2000. We have tried to present a balanced presentation of the matter without presuming how these debates will ultimately be resolved.

10. *American Religious Identification Survey*, 2001, Exhibit 1.

11. U.S. Census Bureau, *Statistical Abstracts of the United States*, 2000, "Table no. 74. Religious Bodies—Selected Data," 61.

12. "For it is through Christ's Catholic Church alone, which is the universal help towards salvation, that the fullness of the means of salvation can be obtained" (*Unitatis Redintegratio*, no. 3). See Jeffrey Gross, FSC, "Toward Full Communion: Faith and Order and Catholic Ecumenism" in *Theological Studies*, vol. 64, No. 1 (March 2004): 23–43.

13. *Unitatis Redintegratio*, no. 4.

14. Komonchak, *The New Dictionary of Theology*, 318.

15. *Journey to the Fullness of Life: A Report on the Implementation of the Rite of Christian Initiation of Adults in the United States* (Washington, DC: USCCB, 2000), 6–7.

16. *Unitatis Redintegratio*, no. 4.

17. The 2001 *American Religious Identification Survey* estimates the *adult* Catholic population at 50,873,000. The survey also found that only 59 percent of those self-identifying as "Catholic" reported household membership in the Catholic Church. While it is not a perfect measure, the 41 percent of respondents (20,821,030) who *identify* but do not *affiliate* with the Catholic Church is one estimate of the size

of the inactive population. The estimate of the Southern Baptist population is taken from table "No. 74, Religious Bodies—Selected Data"
from the 2000 *Statistical Abstracts of the United States.*

18. Thomas Sweetser, for example, in *The Catholic Parish*
(Chicago: Center for Scientific Study of Religion, 1994), uses nuclear,
modal, marginal, and nominal in the following way: *nuclear* equals
mass at least once a week; *modal* equals attends Sunday mass but is not
involved in more than one parish activity; *marginal* equals mass once
a month or less; *nominal* equals mass four times a year and no involvement in the parish.

19. Gallup defines people as unchurched "if they were not members of a church or had not attended services in the previous six
months other than for special religious holidays, weddings, funerals or
the like" (The Gallup Organization, *The Unchurched American*
[Washington, DC: Paulist National Catholic Evangelization
Association, 1988], 1.) Our adaptation departs from Gallup in that we
presume membership in the Catholic Church.

20. Reevangelization applies especially to those countries having
large populations that are baptized but have never been catechized.

21. His language is similar to that of the great commissioning of
Matthew 28:19: "Go therefore and make disciples."

22. Generational sociology enables one to identity certain tenden-
cies of a given generation based on the external events of its formative
years and the response of the peer group. Thus, for example, the Great
Depression generation was defined by a common response to the defining event of its era. Life-cycle sociology suggests that as a person moves
on in life, enters into marriage and has children, that person might
become more open to an active practice of religion than during a
period of being a single adult.

23. We have witnessed a very powerful example of the media's
potential for evangelization in Mel Gibson's movie, *The Passion of the
Christ.*

24. *Thy Kingdom Come: A Manual for Diocesan Evangelization
Staff,* produced by the Committee on Evangelization of the USCCB
(Washington, DC: USCCB, 1996), 17.

25. Ibid., 23.

26. Frank DeSiano, CSP, *The Evangelizing Catholic: A Practical
Handbook for Reaching Out* (Mahwah, NJ: Paulist Press, 1998),
106–11.

27. Contrast our contemporary practice with the central function of hospitality to the stranger in the biblical world, especially in the Old Testament. Welcoming the stranger is a pillar in the social structure of primitive society. See, for example, "Hospitality" in *Anchor Bible Dictionary*, vol. 3 (New York: Doubleday, 1992), 299–301; John Koenig, *New Testament Hospitality: Partnership with Strangers as Promise and Mission* (Philadelphia: Fortress, 1985).

28. Henri Nouwen, *Reaching Out: The Three Movements of the Spiritual Life* (Garden City, NY: Doubleday & Company, Inc., 1975), 46.

29. Ibid., 49.

30. Joan Cunningham, ed., *Christian Hospitality*, rev. edition (Louisville: Office of Evangelization for the Archdiocese of Louisville, 2002), 5.

31. Ibid., 8.

32. Susan Blum Gerding, EdD, and Frank DeSiano, CSP, *Lay Ministers, Lay Disciples: Evangelizing Power in the Parish* (Mahwah, NJ: Paulist Press, 1999), 42.

33. The scriptures point to hospitality as a necessary virtue for bishops as heads of communities; see 1 Timothy 3:2 and Titus 1:8.

34. Cunningham, *Christian Hospitality*, 13.

35. DeSiano, *The Evangelizing Catholic*, 74.

36. Cunningham, *Christian Hospitality*, 26.

37. DeSiano, *The Evangelizing Catholic*, 77–78.

38. Nouwen, *Reaching Out*, 47.

39. U.S. Catholic Bishops, *Welcoming the Stranger Among Us: Unity in Diversity* (Washington, DC: USCCB, 2000), 7.

40. See also Exod 22:20, 23:9; Lev. 19:33–34; Psalm 39:13.

41. Nouwen, *Reaching Out*, 51.

42. *Welcoming the Stranger Among Us*, 33.

43. Ibid., 24.

44. Cunningham, *Christian Hospitality*, 10.

45. *Welcoming the Stranger Among Us*, 28.

46. Adapted and embellished from Virgil Elizondo's presentation, "Mutual Understanding by Engaging Piety and Culture," given at the 2002 Annual Parish Leadership Conference, sponsored by the National Pastoral Life Center, November 8, 2002, Louisville, Kentucky.

Chapter Eight: Goal III

1. These kinds of actions cross denominational lines. Two movies tell the stories of Catholics in villages in Italy (*The Assisi Underground,* 1985) and France (*Au Revoir, Les Enfants,* 1987) doing the same thing.

2. Phillip Hallie, *Lest Innocent Blood Be Shed* (San Francisco: HarperCollins, 1994), xvii.

3. John Paul II, *Centesimus Annus (On the Hundredth Anniversary of Rerum Novarum),* no. 5.

4. Henri J. M. Nouwen, *The Wounded Healer: Ministry in Contemporary Society* (Garden City, NY: Doubleday & Co., 1970), 20.

5. *Communities of Salt and Light: Reflections on the Social Mission of the Parish* (Washington, DC: USCCB, 1994), 1.

6. *Justice in the World,* no. 6, in *Proclaiming Justice and Peace: Papal Documents from Rerum Novarum through Centesimus Annus,* ed. Michael Walsh and Brian Davies (Mystic, CT: Twenty-Third Publications, 1991), 270.

7. Donal Dorr, *Option for the Poor: One Hundred Years of Catholic Social Teaching* (Maryknoll, NY: Orbis Books, 1992), 239.

8. Edward P. DeBerri, James E. Hug, with Peter J. Henriot, and Michael J. Schultheis, *Catholic Social Teaching: Our Best Kept Secret,* 4th rev. ed. (Maryknoll, NY: Orbis Books and Washington, DC: Center of Concern, 2003).

9. Ibid., 14.

10. See *Faithful Citizenship: A Catholic Call to Political Responsibility* (Washington, DC: USCCB, 2003), 13–16.

11. Quoted in Michael Paul Gallagher, SJ, *Clashing Symbols: An Introduction to Faith and Culture* (Mahwah, NJ: Paulist Press, 1998), 36.

12. See Avery Cardinal Dulles's recent treatment of this theme: "The Impact of Catholicism on American Cultures" in *Evangelizing America,* ed. Thomas P. Rausch, SJ, 11–27.

13. *Gaudium et Spes,* nos. 53–63.

14. Ibid., no. 53.

15. *Thy Kingdom Come,* 5.

16. See the comments of Michael Gallagher in *Clashing Symbols,* 46.

17. Ibid., 47.

18. Quoted in Gallagher, *Clashing Symbols,* 53.

19. *Evangelium Vitae (The Gospel of Life)* (Boston: Pauline Books and Media, 1995).

20. Quoted in Gallagher, *Clashing Symbols,* 103.

21. See *Our Hearts Were Burning Within Us,* no. 28. See also Gallagher, *Clashing Symbols,* 107.

22. Ernest Kurtz, *Not God: A History of Alcoholics Anonymous* (Center City, MN: Hazelden, 1979), 49. Elsewhere, he speaks of "self-survey, confession, restitution and the giving of oneself in service to others," 49.

23. For a fascinating account of the relationship between Father Edward Dowling and Bill W., see Robert Fitzgerald, SJ, *The Soul of Sponsorship: The Friendship of Fr. Ed Dowling, S.J. and Bill Wilson in Letters* (Center City, MN: Hazelden, 1995).

24. "Signs of the Times" in *Dictionary of Fundamental Theology,* ed. René Latourelle and Rino Fisichella (New York: Crossroad, 1994), 998.

25. Quoted in Terence L. Nichols, *That All May Be One: Hierarchy and Participation in the Church* (Collegeville, MN: Liturgical Press, 1997), 19.

26. See the fascinating observations about the relationship between self-image and behavior in John J. Evoy, SJ, and Sister Maureen O'Keefe, SSND, in *The Man and The Woman* (New York: Sheed & Ward, 1968), 11–51.

27. *Detroit News,* February 26, 2002.

28. See *Dialogue and Proclamation,* no. 28.

29. For a systematic presentation of Catholic social justice teaching in the light of the preferential option for the poor, see Dorr, *Option for the Poor.*

30. See *Faithful Citizenship,* 15.

31. *Communities of Salt and Light,* 4.

32. Ibid., 2.

33. John R. Donahue, SJ, *The Gospel in Parable* (Philadelphia: Fortress Press, 1988), 101–5.

Chapter Nine: The Parish—
An Ideal Venue for Evangelization

1. Quoted in Andrew Greeley, *The Catholic Myth: The Behavior and Beliefs of American Catholics* (New York: Collier Books, 1990), 154–55.

2. James A. Coriden, *The Parish in Catholic Tradition* (Mahwah, NJ: Paulist Press. 1997), 19.

3. William J. Bausch, *Pilgrim Church: A Popular History of Catholic Christianity* (Notre Dame, IN: Fides Publishers, Inc., 1977), 166–68.

4. Coriden, *The Parish in Catholic Tradition*, 31.

5. Quoted in Paul Lakeland, *The Liberation of the Laity: In Search of an Accountable Church* (New York: Continuum, 2003), 17.

6. Jay Dolan, *The American Catholic Parish, Vol. 1: The Northeast, Southeast and South Central States* (Mahwah, NJ: Paulist Press, 1987), 2.

7. *The Parish: A People, a Mission, a Structure* (Washington, DC: USCCB, 1980), 3.

8. James Hennesey, SJ, *American Catholics: A History of the Roman Catholic Community in the United States* (New York and Oxford: Oxford University Press, 1981), 70.

9. Jay Dolan, "To Form a More Perfect Union," *U.S. Catholic*, vol. 68, no. 10 (October 2003): 12–17.

10. Hennessy, *American Catholics*, 174.

11. Joseph Gremillion and Jim Castelli, *The Emerging Parish: The Notre Dame Study of Catholic Life Since Vatican II* (San Francisco: Harper & Row, 1987), 10.

12. "The Role of Parish in Paulist Mission," *Initiatives in Paulist Mission* (The Paulist Institute, March 1990): 12.

13. Jay Dolan, *The American Catholic Parish: Volume I*, 131.

14. Quoted in Dolan, *The American Catholic Parish: Volume II*, 83.

15. Dolan, *The American Catholic Parish: Volume II*, 83.

16. Quoted in Dolan, *The American Catholic Parish: Volume I*, 185–86.

17. Cyprian Davis, *The History of Black Catholics in the United States* (New York: Crossroads, 1998), 183.

18. For a fascinating account of urban parish life in the mid-1950s, see some of the observations of Alan Ehrenhalt in *The Lost*

City: The Forgotten Virtues of Community in America (New York: Basic Books, 1995), especially 110–35.

19. Gremillion, *The Emerging Parish*, 27.

20. An interesting historical footnote is the important effect of the Hart-Celler Immigration Act in 1965. It dropped racial and ethnic quotas in immigration, resulting in an American church that is truly a microcosm of the world. Without Hart-Celler, we would not have had the Hispanic, Asian, African, and Eastern European immigration of the last four decades.

21. *Lumen Gentium*, no. 28.

22. Ibid.

Chapter Ten: The Challenge of Collaboration

1. Andrew Greeley et al., *Parish, Priest and People: New Leadership for the Local Church* (Chicago: Thomas More Press, 1981), 137.

2. The Second Vatican Council did not speak about lay ministry, but rather made its major contribution in acknowledging the role of all the baptized faithful *(Christifideles Laici)* in carrying out the mission of the church. In many ways, as O'Meara points out, ministry practice has outstripped theology. Many theologians are now grappling with this issue of ordered ministry within the church. See also Richard R. Gaillardetz, "The Ecclesiological Foundations of Ministry within an Ordered Communion," in *Ordering the Baptismal Priesthood*, Susan Wood, ed., as an example of an attempt to provide a different perspective on lay ecclesial ministry and parishioner ministry.

3. *Lay Ecclesial Ministry: The State of the Question* (Washington, DC: USCCB, 1999), 7–9.

4. Philip Murnion and David DeLambo, *Parishes and Parish Ministers: A Study of Parish Lay Ministry* (New York: National Pastoral Life Center, 1999), 2–3.

5. *Lumen Gentium*, nos. 9–11, 31–33.

6. *Apostolicam Actuositatem (Decree on the Apostolate of Lay People)*, nos. 2–3.

7. *Christifideles Laici*, no. 56.

8. *Code of Canon Law* (Washington, DC: Canon Law Society of America, 1983).

9. *Christifideles Laici*, no. 22.

10. See "The Priest: Pastor and Leader of the Parish Community," *Origins,* vol. 32, no. 23 (November 14, 2002): nos. 22–23.

11. Thomas F. O'Meara, OP, *Theology of Ministry,* completely rev. ed. (New York/Mahwah, NJ: Paulist Press, 1999), 9.

12. Ibid., 11.

13. Murnion and DeLambo, *Parishes and Parish Ministers,* iii.

14. *Together in God's Service: Toward a Theology of Ecclesial Lay Ministry* (Washington, DC: USSCB, 1998), 3–22.

15. Greeley et al., *Parish, Priest and People,* 31–33.

16. O'Meara, *Theology of Ministry,* 9.

17. Ibid., 6.

18. David N. Power, *Gifts That Differ: Lay Ministries Established and Unestablished* (New York: Pueblo Pub. Co., 1980), 44.

19. *Christifideles Laici,* nos. 20–23; *Pastores Dabo Vobis (I Will Give You Shepherds),* no. 17.

20. *Apostolicam Actuositatem,* no. 3.

21. Eph 4:30.

22. *Presbyterium Ordinis,* no 9. See also *Lumen Gentium,* no. 30.

23. In the Latino community, *pastoral de conjunto* is sometimes translated as *collaborative ministry.* However, the term has considerably more breadth than our use of it here. In addition to the partnership between the clergy and the laity, the importance of releasing gifts for ministry, and the important strategy of pastoral planning, *pastoral de conjunto* gives strong emphasis to the analysis of the specific pastoral reality within the overall context of ministry. Thus, for example, in Medellin, the global context of ministry in the light of the global gap between rich and poor in the world becomes a key context for analyzing one's local pastoral situation and deriving specific pastoral strategies. Our use of the word *collaboration* here is much more limited, yet it shares many of the same underpinnings as *pastoral de conjunto.*

24. Loughlin Sofield, ST, and Carroll Juliano, SHCJ, *Collaboration: Uniting Our Gifts in Ministry* (Notre Dame, IN: Ave Maria Press, 2000), 17.

25. Ibid., 22.

26. Albert L. Winseman, D.Min, Donald O. Clifton, PhD, and Curt Liesveld, M. Div, *Living Your Strengths* (Washington, DC: The Gallup Organization, 2003), ix–x.

27. *Christifideles Laici,* no. 5.

28. Nichols, *That All May Be One,* 19.

29. Ibid., 18.

30. Ibid., 15.

31. Ibid., 263.

32. Mark Fischer, *Pastoral Councils in Today's Catholic Parish* (Mystic, CT: Twenty-Third Publications, 2001), 39–47.

33. Paul Wilkes, *Excellent Catholic Parishes* (Mahwah, NJ: Paulist Press, 2001), 3, 17, 23, 60.

34. *Called and Gifted for the Third Millennium*, 24.

35. Ibid., 18.

36. For further discussion of Vatican II foundations for lay-clergy collaboration, see Richard Gaillardetz, "Shifting Meanings in the Lay-Clergy Distinction," *Irish Theological Quarterly* 64/2 (1999): 115–39.

37. Collegiality, strictly speaking, deals with the relationship between the Holy Father and the bishops, the bishops and their diocese (see *Lumen Gentium*, nos. 22–23; *Christus Dominus [Decree on the Pastoral Office of Bishops in the Church]*, nos. 4, 17); collaboration and cooperation are often spoken of in the Council documents to describe ways that bishops, priests and laity need to relate (see *Presbyterium Ordinis*, nos. 7, 9; *Apostolicam Actuositatem*, nos. 10, 25–26; *Ad Gentes*, 35). The Vatican Council sees synods, provincial councils, and Episcopal conferences as important means of fostering cooperation, collaboration, and consultation at different levels of church life (*Christus Dominus*, 36–44). Canon law has developed a more technical definition of consultation and consensus affecting certain formal relationships in the church (see can. 127). All of these formal and informal processes promoted by Vatican II tend to support the need for and fostering of collaboration at the local level of the parish between the pastor and the laity.

38. *Lay Ecclesial Ministry*, 45.

39. Sofield and Juliano, *Collaboration*, 20–28.

40. See *Apostolicam Actuositatem*, no. 26; *Christus Dominus*, no. 27.

41. See Appendix for more information.

Chapter Eleven: Organizing the Parish for Evangelization

1. See Robert W. Jacobs, *Real Time Strategic Change* (San Francisco: Berrett-Koehler Publishers, 1994), 122.

2. Source unknown. Quoted in Thomas H. Morris, *The RCIA: Transforming the Church* (Mahwah, NJ: Paulist Press, 1997), 9.

3. *Rite of Christian Initiation of Adults* (Chicago: Liturgy Training Publications, 1988), 4.

4. Morris, *The RCIA*, 47.

5. *Music in Catholic Worship* (Washington, DC: USCCB, 1983), no. 6.

6. Triangling, according to Friedman, as the term suggests, requires the leader to identify the presence of a third element that is present in conflict situations and urges the leader to avoid making himself a triangle in conflicts between two parties.

7. Some parishes refuse to use the word *volunteers* to describe the work of the ordinary parish disciple. It creates a mindset that detracts from our calling to participate in the mission and ministry of Jesus through our baptism.

8. Special thanks to Jim Moyer, our planning consultant for *ENVISION*, for helping to identify these behaviors.

Chapter Twelve: Formation of the Parish for Evangelization

1. David Brooks, "Hooked on Heaven Lite," *New York Times* (March 9, 2004), A27.

2. Yves M. J. Congar, *Lay People in the Church* (Westminster, MD: Newman, 1963), is credited with the preconciliar work that eventually led to the incorporation of the trilogy into the Vatican documents. For the story of the revival of the trilogy in Vatican II, see Peter K. Drilling, "The Priest, Prophet, and King Trilogy," *èglise et theologie* vol. 19, no. 2 (1988): 179–206. For the most thorough treatment of the subject in the tradition, see Ludwig Schick, *Das Dreifache Amt Christi und der Kirche* (Frankfort am Main-Bern: Peter Lang, European University Studies, 1982). For an approving review of Schick's work, see Yves Congar, "Sur la trilogie Prophet-Roi-Prêtre," in *Revue des sciences philosophiques et theologiques* 67 (1983): 97–115. Also see Thomas Potvin, "Le Baptême comme enracinement dans la participation à la triple fonction du Christ," in *Le Laïcat: les limites d'un système,* ed. J. C. Petit and C. Breton (Montreal: Fides, 1978).

3. *Rite of Christian Initiation of Adults* (Chicago: Liturgy Training Publications, 1988), 143.

4. It is important to note that this formulation was introduced for the first time in the reformed post–Vatican II liturgy. See Schick, *Das Dreifache Amt Christi und der Kirche,* 74–75.

5. For a readable presentation of the topic, see Bill Huebsch, *Whole Community Catechesis in Plain English* (Mystic, CT: Twenty-Third Publications, 2003).

6. See Congar, *Lay People in the Church,* 55–61, for additional scriptural background.

7. See "Priest," in *The New Dictionary of Theology,* 799.

8. Donald J. Goergen, OP, "Priest, Prophet, and King: The Ministry of Jesus Christ," in *The Theology of Priesthood,* ed. Donald J. Goergen and Ann Garrido (Collegeville, MN: Liturgical Press, 2000), 194.

9. John Ford, "Ministries in the Church" in *The Gift of the Church,* ed. Peter Phan, 295.

10. Walter Brueggemann, *The Prophetic Imagination* (Philadelphia: Fortress Press, 1978), 66–70.

11. Nichols, *That All May Be One,* 126.

12. See the recommendations of the bishops' National Review Board on Sexual Abuse regarding listening, accountability, and consultation in *A Report on the Crisis in the Catholic Church in the United States* (Washington, DC: USCCB, 2004), 125–29.

13. Goergen, "Priest, Prophet, and King," 200.

14. Ibid., 194.

15. Ibid., 200–201.

APPENDIX

The following PNCEA programs were mentioned in the text.

Disciples in Mission: An Evangelizing Experience

Disciples in Mission is a parish-based formation process designed to assist parishes in implementing the evangelizing vision promulgated in the bishops' national plan and strategy for evangelization, *Go and Make Disciples*. This three-year process consists of two parts, formation and implementation. The formation takes place over three successive Lenten seasons and consists of small faith-sharing groups and family faith-sharing based on the Sunday lectionary. The program fosters eucharistic celebrations with evangelizing preaching and offers bulletin inserts for each of the six Sundays of Lent, which communicate to parishioners the evangelizing vision of the church contained in its major documents, *Evangelii Nuntiandi, Redemptoris Missio,* and *Go and Make Disciples.*

This Lenten formation experience is followed up by a modest parish discernment around the three goals of *Go and Make Disciples*. Early in the Easter season, parishioners gather on a Saturday (or some other appropriate time) to reflect upon the goals of *Go and Make Disciples* (beginning with Goal I and, in successive fashion, moving on to Goals II and III) for the purpose of growing in their understanding of evangelization, evaluating how well the parish is implementing the goals, and initiating a modest priority-setting process in order to advance the level of parish implementation. The priority choices are tabulated and formed into a profile to become an active part of the parish's plan to be implemented throughout the year.

The Lenten formation process is repeated annually with new materials appropriate to the lectionary, addressing in turn Goals II and III. Likewise, the discernment process takes place annually during the Easter season, addressing how well the parish has implemented its Goal I priorities and then moving on to define priorities for Goals II and III.

The entire season outside of Lent-Easter is devoted to implementing those priorities.

Disciples in Mission materials are in English and Spanish, but the process has been adapted for other languages as well. Special materials for teenagers have proven to be successful. Costs are based on materials purchased. For more information, visit our website at www.pncea.org or write to the PNCEA, 3131 Fourth St. NE, Washington, DC, 20017.

Parish Missions: Spirituality for an Evangelizing Parish

PNCEA Parish Missions is a program that is also designed to awaken, educate, and foster commitment to the evangelizing mission of the church, through a series of evening missions based on the goals of *Go and Make Disciples*. A team composed of a priest and a lay/religious woman preach at all the Sunday liturgies. The mission begins on Sunday evening with a worship service featuring evangelizing preaching by the team, interaction, and ritual actions, followed by an evening social. Evening I challenges the parishioners to live their faith fully as a priestly people, Evening II to share their faith fully as a prophetic people, and Evening III to transform the world in Christ as a royal people. Evening IV is a reconciliation service. The mission is concluded on Thursday evening with the Eucharist. Missions are conducted in English and Spanish. For more information, visit our website at www.pncea.org or write to the PNCEA.

ENVISION: Planning Our Parish Future

ENVISION brings the insights and experience of pastoral leaders and planning experts to parishes by providing a process for all parishioners to create their future, with a focus on evangelization. The *ENVISION* process leads parishes to

- a life-giving pastoral plan
- contagious enthusiasm for the faith
- collaboration in mission
- new energy, new skills, and new volunteers
- research-based decision-making
- short term achievements, and long term success

A centerpiece of *ENVISION* is the 350-page "how to do it" manual, *A Guide for Leaders,* that provides detailed instructions for carrying out the process. With the *ENVISION* CD, parishes have materials they may reproduce for the *ENVISION* activities that span five phases (organizing, listening, discerning, planning, and implementing). The questionnaire that the PNCEA has developed with the Center for Applied Research in the Apostolate (CARA) provides parishes with evangelization indices for the parish as a whole and for individual parishioners. The PNCEA provides training for *ENVISION* leaders, and will also arrange to serve as an on-site consultant for parishes who wish PNCEA help. Visit www.parishplanning.org or write to the PNCEA.